MW00826501

The Limits of Inference without Theory

The Limits of Inference without Theory

Kenneth I. Wolpin

The MIT Press
Cambridge, Massachusetts
London, England

© 2013 Massachusetts Institute of Technology

All rights reserved. No part of this book may be reproduced in any form by any electronic or mechanical means (including photocopying, recording, or information storage and retrieval) without permission in writing from the publisher.

MIT Press books may be purchased at special quantity discounts for business or sales promotional use. For information, please email special_sales@mitpress.mit.edu or write to Special Sales Department, The MIT Press, 55 Hayward Street, Cambridge, MA 02142.

This book was set in Palatino by Toppan Best-set Premedia Limited, Hong Kong. Printed and bound in the United States of America.

Library of Congress Cataloging-in-Publication Data

Wolpin, Kenneth I.
The limits of inference without theory / Kenneth I. Wolpin.
  p. cm. — (Tjalling C. Koopmans memorial lectures)
Includes bibliographical references and index.
ISBN 978-0-262-01908-8 (hardcover : alk. paper)
1. Inference. 2. Economics. I. Title.
BC199.I47W65   2013
001.4'2—dc23
2012036265

10 9 8 7 6 5 4 3 2 1

To Rona

Contents

Series Foreword

The Tjalling C. Koopmans Memorial Lectures were initiated by the Cowles Foundation in 1989 using a fund established by Koopmans' family, friends, and colleagues shortly after his death in 1985. These lectures offer an opportunity for preeminent scholars of economics to provide synthesis and perspective on a body of ongoing research to a broad audience of economists. The Cowles Foundation is pleased to introduce a monograph series based on these lectures, with the first volume written by Ken Wolpin, the Walter H. and Leonore C. Annenberg Professor in the Social Sciences at the University of Pennsylvania.

Tjalling Koopmans was a prominent voice in the early efforts of the Cowles Commission (later Cowles Foundation) to bring rigorous logical, mathematical, and statistical methods of analysis to the study of economics. His pathbreaking work on linear programming methods and their application to problems of optimal resource allocation led to his Nobel Prize in economics (jointly with Leonid Kantorovich) in 1975. He also made important contributions to the foundations of empirical economics, including his work on identification of structural economic relationships. Beyond his own research, Koopmans' collaborations and leadership of the Cowles Commission/Foundation influenced the paths of many important scholars in economics.

Especially relevant to the topics of the present volume was Koopmans' 1947 article "Measurement without Theory." Although written as a book review, it offered a critical assessment of an entire research program that aimed to build up knowledge through documentation of empirical regularities, unencumbered by economic theory. Koopmans' view arose not from a preference for theory per se, but from recognition of the inherent limitations of empirical analysis that is neither guided nor restricted by an economic model. He viewed theory as indispensable for revealing what quantities should be measured, how they can be measured, and how measurements can be interpreted.

In this volume, based on lectures given at Yale in November 2010, Ken Wolpin offers a modern perspective on the role of theory in empirical economics. Ken's work has followed Koopmans' vision closely, although on a range of topics Koopmans could hardly have anticipated in 1947. Ken has made major contributions to labor economics, economic demography, development economics, health economics, and empirical methodology.

Here he begins by considering what is perhaps the most common motivation for going beyond mere description of the data: *ex ante* policy evaluation. Using prominent examples from the literature, Ken illustrates the essential role theory plays in exposing which variation in the data can reveal the policy effects of interest. This is combined with a pragmatic view of the unavoidable trade-offs between the assumptions one makes in empirical work and what can be learned from the data given these assumptions. In the second part of the monograph, Ken moves to a sequence of extended examples, each drawing on a significant applied literature. These examples allow him to illustrate in detail the types of guidance empirical economists gain from theory, both in providing (or challenging) the logical foundation of an empirical strategy and in revealing the proper interpretation of results.

Ken's lectures stimulated a great deal of discussion among my colleagues. I thank him for the substantial work involved in transforming a pair of talks into a monograph that could be shared more broadly.

Philip A. Haile
Cowles Foundation Director, 2005–2011

The Koopmans Memorial Lectures

Menahem Yaari, 1989

Janos Kornai, 1991

Thomas Schelling, 1993

Alain Monfort, 1994

Peter A. Diamond, 1996

Paul R. Milgrom, 2004

James Heckman, 2006

Lars Hanson, 2008

Kenneth Wolpin, 2010

Acknowledgments

I am grateful to the many colleagues who have helped to shape my thinking about empirical methodology. In this regard, I am particularly fortunate in having had long-term collaborations with Zvi Eckstein, Michael Keane, Mark Rosenzweig, and Petra Todd. I have also benefited from interactions with the numerous graduate students with whom I have worked. Finally, I would like to thank the Cowles Foundation for giving me the opportunity to present these lectures.

1   Introduction

The two lectures that comprised my Tjalling C. Koopmans Memorial Lectures were titled "*Ex Ante* Policy Evaluation" and "The Limits of Inference without Theory." I have chosen the second as the title of this book because it encompasses a broad theme that is also illustrated by the content of the first lecture. The title obviously borrows from the famous Koopmans (1947) essay "Measurement without Theory" published in 1947. That essay was a direct response to the book by Burns and Mitchell (1946), *Measuring Business Cycles*, and, more generally, to the extensive data collection effort being conducted at the National Bureau of Economic Research on business cycle fluctuations. Koopmans supported the enterprise of collecting data to better understand business cycle fluctuations but argued that the productivity of that enterprise would be significantly enhanced if it were guided by theory. In his concluding remarks, he stated: "But, the decision not to use theories of man's economic behavior, even hypothetically, *limits* the value to economic science and to the maker of policies, of the results obtained or obtainable by the methods developed."[1]

The purpose of these lectures was not to reopen the debate about the proper use of theory in developing facts (see, for example, Christ, 1994; Kydland and Prescott, 1990) but to consider instead the role of theory in drawing inference from data and the limits that eschewing the use of theory places on inference. My intention is to illustrate the applicability of Koopman's concluding remark to inferential empirical work in economics and in the social sciences more generally. The discussion focuses on microlevel research, that is, where heterogeneity at the individual level is explicitly recognized. It is important to be clear about what empirical work is to be characterized as inferential. By that, I mean generally any research that uses data to draw conclusions that go beyond the mere statement of fact, that is, the tabulation of statistics.

There are (at least) two views about why theory and inference need not be connected. In one view, theory is seen as unnecessary or even detrimental to inferential data analysis. This view is exemplified in the expression that researchers should "let the data speak for themselves." This approach is often called "reduced form," although that terminology is a distortion of its original meaning, which stemmed from the work by Koopmans and other members of the Cowles Commission. The second view is more nuanced and arguably more sound. In this view, in a first stage of analysis, inference can be made without the use of theory. However, the ability to draw inferences without the use of theory requires what is called a "quasi-experimentalist" approach that involves implicit random assignment or an actual experiment, a randomized controlled trial (RCT).[2] Theory's role is then to provide an explanation for the inference that is derived from the experiment and as an aid toward generalization.[3] The absence of theory in inferential empirical work is pervasive. For example, of all the papers in the January 2009 maiden issue of the new American Economic Association journal *Applied Economics*, all of which were inferential, none contained an explicit model of "man's economic behavior."[4]

The reduced form and experimentalist approaches are often contrasted to what is popularly called the structural approach. In keeping with that nomenclature, I will refer to reduced form and experimental approaches as nonstructural. The structural approach is one in which the relationships that are estimated are explicitly intended to be invariant to policy, where policy is interpreted broadly to include counterfactual experiments. Under this definition, whether the relationship that is estimated is structural cannot be decided outside of a policy (or counterfactual) context. A variant of the structural approach is characterized as estimating "deep" parameters. In economics, deep parameters are usually associated with preference functions, technology, and constraints. In the first characterization, the parameters of interest may be combinations of deep parameters; deep parameters are by definition invariant to policy. The structural estimation approach requires that a researcher explicitly specify a model of economic behavior, that is, a theory. As Marschak (1953) describes it: "In economics, the conditions that constitute a structure are (1) a set of relations describing human behavior and institutions as well as technological laws and involving, in general, nonobservable random disturbances and nonobservable random errors in measurement; (2) the joint probability distribution of these random quantities."[5]

There is also a third approach to empirical work in economics that, although sometimes referred to as reduced form, is better termed quasi-structural. In that approach a formal model satisfying Marschak's first criterion is postulated, and in some cases comparative static (dynamic) results are derived. The relationships that are estimated are viewed as approximations to those that are, or could be, derived from the theory (for example, as based on the comparative statics). The parameters are functions of the underlying deep (policy-invariant) structural parameters in an unspecified way. The stochastic elements are also unspecified combinations of the "random quantities" in Marschak's second criterion. In contrast to this approach, the "reduced form" approach that eschews formal theory starts from a relationship that is to be estimated rather than derived. To be clear, what I mean by theory is not necessarily a mathematical model but rather a coherently expressed connection between assumptions and inference. Mathematics facilitates an assessment of coherency and also provides a connection between a model and its statistical specification, but mathematics is per se not necessary (nor, obviously, sufficient).

The structural/nonstructural taxonomy is not, in my view, the critical distinction in terms of empirical methodology. As was the theme of these lectures, the critical distinction is not the estimation approach but whether or not inference is theory based. Experimental work, whether based on an RCT, a natural experiment, or some other estimation approach, can in some instances be interpreted as seeking to recover a structural relationship, that is, one that is invariant to policy. However, the lack of an explicit theoretical framework, a common feature in nonstructural work, leaves the validity of any such interpretation to the reader.

In terms of organization, I begin with the first lecture on *ex ante* policy evaluation, highlighting the role of theory in that enterprise. I restrict attention to the case where there is no direct policy variation from which to extrapolate to new policies. Two structural approaches to *ex ante* evaluation are presented, nonparametric and parametric. In both approaches, the Marschak criteria are satisfied. The advantage of the nonparametric approach is that assumptions auxiliary to the behavioral model are unnecessary. The disadvantage of that approach is that it can be applied only for a restricted set of behavioral models. The parametric approach allows for richer models and thus for the consideration of a wider set of counterfactual policies but requires auxiliary functional form and distributional assumptions. The two approaches are illustrated with two examples, a wage tax and a school attendance subsidy. The results from applications are summarized.

The second lecture presents a number of examples illustrating the limits of inference without theory. The first two examples in the chapter illustrate the importance of theory in econometric specification within the context of a (seemingly) quasi-structural estimation approach. They show more generally how the quasi-structural approach, lacking the discipline of the structural approach necessitated by having to specify the exact mapping between the theory and estimation and often appealing only casually to received theory, can lead to inferential ambiguity. The first example is relevant to dozens of papers spanning over 30 years of empirical research on unemployment duration, and the second to the even larger literature on the impact of public welfare on labor and demographic outcomes of women. The third example, that of estimating the effect of school attainment on earnings, illustrates the connection between theory and the recent econometrics literature on instrumental variables (IV) estimation with heterogeneous response. The motivating example in this case is based on the natural experiment approach to estimation. The fourth example illustrates the importance of theory in addressing questions of external validity in the context of a prominent field experiment in education. Each of these illustrations is placed within the context of the broader literature, and the examples are contrasted to recent contributions to their literatures that rely on theory for inference.

2   *Ex Ante* Policy Evaluation—The Role of Theory

The goal of policy evaluation falls into two categories: *ex post* evaluation and *ex ante* evaluation. The goal of *ex post* policy evaluation is to determine the impact of policies that have been implemented. This type of evaluation is ubiquitous in economics and in the social sciences more generally. The goal of *ex ante* policy evaluation is to determine the impact of prospective or "new" policies. New policies can extend existing policies either in the dimension of a particular policy parameter beyond its current domain or introduce new parameters to an existing policy. An example of the former would be an increase in the existing minimum wage and of the latter the introduction of a time limit on public welfare eligibility or the incorporation of a drug benefit into Medicare. A new policy may alternatively be entirely outside of the historical experience, for example, the initial introduction of the income tax or the provision of subsidies for school attendance as is now prevalent in many developing countries. *Ex ante* evaluation allows the policy maker to compare the impact of alternative policies prior to choosing one of the policies to implement, for example, raising the minimum wage by 50 cents, $1, or $10, imposing a 2-year or 5-year time limit on welfare eligibility, or choosing a particular proportional or progressive income tax schedule. Effective policy decision making is clearly enhanced by the ability to perform credible *ex ante* policy evaluation.

Evaluations of existing policies make use of actual policy variation. Evaluations of new policies that are extensions of existing policy parameters, for example, increasing the minimum wage, also make use of actual policy variation, although they require an extrapolation outside of the historical experience. Evaluations of new policies that cannot be based on actual policy variation, for example, introducing a time limit on welfare eligibility or a new program that subsidizes school attendance, raise additional challenges and form the central focus of this chapter. Variation useful for *ex ante* evaluation must, in some way, provide an analogue to policy variation; that is, it must be policy relevant. The role of theory is to identify such policy-relevant variations.

The evaluation literature distinguishes between two types of evaluation methodologies: experimental and nonexperimental. The experimental methodology is based on an evaluation of a demonstration or pilot project in which participants and controls are randomly chosen. The nonexperimental methodology analyzes observational data using a combination of behavioral and statistical modeling. Each of these methodologies has been applied to *ex post* and *ex ante* evaluation.

The aim of the experimental methodology applied to a prospective policy is to determine whether and to what extent the goals of the policy would be met if implemented. In this case, the choice of the policy's characteristics, the "treatment," is determined by the experimenter. The experimental approach has been held to be the gold standard for evaluating policy. However, there has been considerable debate about that proposition (see, for example, Heckman and Smith, 1995; Deaton, 2009; Imbens, 2009). The debate has centered not so much on problems that can arise in practical implementation, for example, the effectiveness of the randomization, selective attrition, and Hawthorne effects, but rather on the conceptual issue of what it is that can and can not be learned from a social experiment. The advantage of a social experiment is that it identifies a policy effect for the population in the experiment, which, in the best of circumstances, has high internal validity. The disadvantage is that the experiment identifies the policy effect only for the treatment that is chosen and may not be applicable to other populations.

The aims of the nonexperimental methodology can be broader. The role of theory, which is often eschewed in the social experiments literature, is paramount. Theory identifies mechanisms that generate policy effects, and theory-based estimation quantifies the importance of alternative mechanisms that enable extrapolation to other policies and possibly to other populations. This payoff is achieved at the cost of untestable assumptions that are not necessary with social experimentation; in that sense, the nonexperimental methodology has lower internal validity. Just as practitioners of social experimentation must take care in designing and implementing their experiments, practitioners of theory-based estimation must provide evidence on model validity.

Natural "natural experiments," a term adopted by Rosenzweig and Wolpin (2000) to distinguish random events that arise in nature from other so-called "natural" or quasi-experiments, differ from social experiments in that the interpretation of the "policy" effect is not assumption-free. As is the case with instrumental variable estimates more generally, the implicit assumption in the natural and quasi-experimental literature is that (conditional on observables) the effect of the policy (or "treatment") is the same for all people (Heckman, 1997; Heckman, Urzua, and Vytlacil, 2006). The role of theory is to elucidate the assumptions that underlie interpretations of the policy effect.[1]

The development of methodological approaches to *ex post* policy evaluation using nonexperimental methods has been and remains an active area of research (see the recent survey by Todd, 2008). There is little methodological or applied research explicitly concerned with *ex ante* policy evaluation using nonexperimental methods, which is perhaps surprising given the potential benefits.[2] The purpose of this chapter is to summarize and provide examples of structural approaches to *ex ante* evaluation.

2.1 Structural Approaches to *Ex Ante* Evaluation

In this section I discuss two structural approaches to *ex ante* policy evaluation: nonparametric and parametric. For concreteness, the ideas are illustrated with two examples: (1) the effect of a wage (or earnings) tax on labor supply and (2) the effect of a subsidy conditioned on a child's school attendance. In both cases theory identifies surrogate variation that substitutes for the lack of explicit policy variation. In the first instance the wage itself provides the policy-relevant variation, whereas in the second, it is a combination of the child's wage and parental income. The discussion first centers on a nonparametric method for solving the evaluation problem. I then turn to a parametric approach that can accommodate *ex ante* evaluation under assumptions that the nonparametric approach cannot and that provides a potentially richer set of policies amenable to *ex ante* evaluation.

In the wage tax example I begin with the simplest economic model in which an individual is deciding on hours of work in a static context. A nonparametric matching estimator of the impact of a newly imposed tax is developed and illustrated for the case in which wages are observed for both participants and nonparticipants. The case in which wages are observed only for participants is shown to require a distributional assumption on wage offers, although, as in the case of full observability of wage offers, it is not necessary to make an assumption about the functional form of the utility function. Several extensions of the labor supply model are considered, including introducing a fixed cost of work, child care costs (including an *ex ante* evaluation of a child care subsidy), and nonlinear taxes.

The second example, the introduction of a school attendance subsidy, begins with the consideration of a static model in which parents are deciding on whether to have their only child attend school or work in the labor market. It is shown that joint variation in the child wage and parental income can be used to obtain a matching estimator of the effect of the subsidy on school attendance without making functional form or distributional assumptions (with full observability of the child wage). It is shown how multiple children, when fertility is not a choice, can be accommodated but that the nonparametric estimator is no longer valid when fertility is a choice. The nonparametric matching estimator is shown to extend to a perfect-foresight life cycle model and, in some cases, to a dynamic imperfect-foresight model. The nonparametric matching estimator does not survive the introduction of child home production. In fact, the same matching estimator now corresponds to a different policy, one in which households are provided a subsidy if the child does not work in the market but either attends school or engages in home production. There is thus, in this example, an inherent ambiguity in the interpretation of the matching estimator that is model dependent.

The school attendance subsidy also serves to illustrate *ex ante* evaluation using a parametric approach. The analogue of the matching estimator of the subsidy effect is derived given a particular parametric specification of the utility function and a distributional assumption for the unobservable taste shifter. It is shown that with these parametric assumptions, *ex ante* evaluation can be conducted in the presence of home production, which was not possible nonparametrically. The static model is formally extended to the dynamic case, which fits into the framework of discrete choice dynamic programming (DCDP) models. A brief digression discusses the estimation methodology of DCDP models as a prelude to the presentation of parametric empirical applications of a school attendance subsidy program implemented in Mexico. Two DCDP models that differ significantly in their structures are presented and contrasted. Both use data from the Mexican PROGRESA experiment that provided a school attendance subsidy to a randomly selected set of villages.

Estimates of an out-of-sample prediction of the impact of doubling the PROGRESA subsidy are presented based on two nonparametric matching estimators and on the two DCDP models. The estimates of the DCDP models and one of the matching estimators are seen to be quite close. An interesting difference in the two DCDP approaches is that one of them uses only the control group for estimation and validates the model by predicting the subsidy effect obtained from the experiment. The other DCDP model uses both the control and treatment groups in the estimation. This difference in empirical approaches raises the question of whether the value of withholding a part of the sample from the estimation for the purpose of validation is worth the loss of estimation precision. This question is briefly explored in the final section of the chapter.

2.1.1   Structural Nonparametric Approach[3]

2.1.1.1   *Wage Tax*

Suppose that a policy maker is considering the introduction of a proportional wage tax and would like to know how labor supply and, thus, tax revenues will vary with the tax rate. As a place to start, assume that labor supply behavior can be described by a standard static model in which individuals choose the number of hours to work given their wage rate, their level of nonlabor income, and their available total time. The utility function is a twice-differentiable, quasi-concave function of consumption, c, and hours of leisure, $l = 1 - h$, where h is hours of work and total available time is normalized to one. The marginal rate of substitution between leisure and consumption depends on a set of observable preference shifters, X (a vector), and unobservable preference shifters, ε. Individuals have nonlabor income y and receive wage offers w. In the absence of a wage tax, each individual thus chooses hours of work to maximize

$$U(c, 1-h; X, \varepsilon) \tag{2.1}$$

subject to the budget constraint

$$c = wh + y, \tag{2.2}$$

where consumption is the sum of labor earnings, the wage times hours of work, and nonlabor income. Optimal hours of work can be derived as a function of w, y, X, and ε, namely

$$h^* = \phi(w, y; X, \varepsilon). \tag{2.3}$$

The hours function admits to both zero (nonparticipation) and positive hours. Zero hours occurs when the marginal rate of substitution between leisure and consumption exceeds the wage evaluated at full-time leisure ($h = 0$). Otherwise, the individual works positive hours. No additional assumptions about the form of the utility function are made.[4]

Introducing a proportional tax on wage income at rate τ ($0 < \tau < 1$) alters the budget constraint to[5]

$$c = (1 - \tau)wh + y. \tag{2.4}$$

The model with the tax is, however, isomorphic to the model without the tax in the specific sense that if $h^{**} = \eta(w, y, \tau; X, \varepsilon)$ denotes the solution for optimal hours with the tax, then

$$h^{**} = \eta(w, y, \tau; X, \varepsilon) = \phi(\tilde{w}, y; X, \varepsilon) \tag{2.5}$$

where $\tilde{w} = (1 - \tau)w$.[6] Thus, the hours of work function without the tax (ϕ) is also the relevant function in the presence of the tax.[7] The implication of this observation is that the effect of introducing a tax τ on hours of work can be studied from *ex ante* population variation in wage offers.

To see that, note that the difference between the population mean hours worked (inclusive of 0 hours) for persons with wage offer $\tilde{w} = (1 - \tau)w$, nonlabor income y, and observables X and persons with wage offer w and the same values of y and X is

$$E_\varepsilon(\phi \mid \tilde{w}, y, X) - E_\varepsilon(\phi \mid w, y, X) = \int \phi(\tilde{w}, y; X, \varepsilon) f(\varepsilon \mid \tilde{w}, y, X) d\varepsilon$$
$$- \int \phi(w, y; X, \varepsilon) f(\varepsilon \mid w, y, X) d\varepsilon. \tag{2.6}$$

Under the assumption that, conditional on y and X, the distribution of unobserved preferences does not depend on the wage, that is,

$$f(\varepsilon \mid w, y, X) = f(\varepsilon \mid y, X),$$

the difference given in equation 2.6 is exactly the effect of introducing the wage tax on expected hours worked by a person with wage offer w, nonlabor income y, and observable X. In general, the effect of the tax on expected hours will differ depending on a person's w, y, and X. Thus, persons with the same wage offer but different nonlabor income and/or observable preference shifters will respond differently to the tax in terms of their hours of work, as will individuals with the same nonlabor income but different wage offers and/or observable preference shifters.[8]

Integrating over the joint population distribution of w, y, X, that is,

$$\int [E_\varepsilon(\phi \,|\, \tilde{w} = (1-\tau)w, y, X) - E_\varepsilon(\phi \,|\, w, y, X)]dG(w, y, X) \qquad (2.7)$$

gives the effect of the tax on expected hours of work over the entire population. As seen from equation 2.7, different populations, those with a different joint distribution of ε, w, y, X, will exhibit a different mean hours of work response to the introduction of the tax.

The same analysis would govern the case of changing an existing tax, τ_1, which has not varied in the past, to a new value τ_2. In that case, the initial net wage would be $\tilde{w}_1 = (1-\tau_1)w$, and the new net wage $\tilde{w}_2 = (1-\tau_2)w$. The change in hours worked would be given by modifying equation 2.6 to $E_\varepsilon(\phi \,|\, \tilde{w}_2, y, X) - E_\varepsilon(\phi \,|\, \tilde{w}_1, y, X)$. Also, although the focus has been on hours of work as the main outcome of interest, the outcome of interest could also be the work decision, which is just a transformation of hours of work [i.e., $1(h^* > 0)$] or mean hours of work conditional on participation.

It is possible to obtain sample analogues of the population mean hours necessary for calculating the policy effect. Suppose data are available for a random sample of individuals on hours worked, nonlabor income, and the observables in X and also that wage offers are available for both nonparticipants as well as participants. The case in which wages are observed only for participants is considered below. There are several estimation approaches that can be taken.

One method would be to estimate the conditional mean hours of work function $E_\varepsilon(\phi \,|\, w, y, X)$ nonparametrically using a method such as kernel, local linear regression, or series estimation. Given an estimate of $E_\varepsilon(\phi \,|\, w, y, X)$, it is straightforward to calculate equation 2.7 given G. As with any nonparametric approach, extrapolation outside of the sample variation is not possible. Thus, one cannot compute $E_\varepsilon(\phi \,|\, \tilde{w}, y, X)$ if $\tilde{w}$ is not observed in the sample for some (or all) values of y and X. Given that responses to the tax will generally be heterogeneous, the sample estimate of equation 2.7 may deviate from the population effect.

Another approach is to use a matching estimator.[9] The key insight is the observation that a person with a wage w subject to a tax τ would, on average, choose the same hours of work as an otherwise identical person, in terms of y and X, with a wage of $\tilde{w} = (1 - \tau)w$ who was not subject to a tax. Thus, in the absence of a tax, the difference in mean hours of those with wage $\tilde{w}$ and those with wage w (given y and X) provides an estimate of the tax effect on hours for those with wage w.

Taking the average over all w, y, and X provides an estimate of the population mean hours effect of the tax. An advantage of the matching estimator for recovering the policy impact relative to the nonparametric estimation of the conditional mean function is computational. The conditional mean function is more informative, but some of what is recovered is unnecessary for the *ex ante* policy evaluation.[10] The matching estimator, on the other hand, recovers only the policy effect, that is, the appropriate finite change in the conditional mean function due to the policy.[11]

The matching estimator of the policy impact of the tax on mean hours worked takes the form,

$$\hat{\Delta} = \frac{1}{n} \sum_{\substack{j=1 \\ j,i \in S_P}}^{n} \hat{E}(h_i \mid w_i = (1-\tau)w_j, y_i = y_j, X_i = X_j) - h_j(w_j, y_j, X_j), \qquad (2.8)$$

where the matches can be performed only for the n individuals whose w values and associated $(1 - \tau)w$ values both lie in the overlapping support region, $S_P = \{\tilde{w} \text{ such that } f_w(\tilde{w}) > 0\}$.[12] The estimator can be implemented using kernel methods, such as

$$\hat{E}(h_i \mid w_i = (1-\tau)w_j, y_i = y_j, X_i = X_j)$$

$$= \frac{\displaystyle\sum_{\substack{i=1 \\ i \in S_P}}^{n} h_i K\left(\frac{w_i - (1-\tau)w_j}{\lambda_n^w}\right) K\left(\frac{y_i - y_j}{\lambda_n^y}\right) I(X_i = X_j)}{\displaystyle\sum_{\substack{i=1 \\ i \in S_P}}^{n} K\left(\frac{w_i - (1-\tau)w_j}{\lambda_n^w}\right) K\left(\frac{y_i - y_j}{\lambda_n^y}\right) I(X_i = X_j)} \qquad (2.9)$$

where $K(\cdot)$ denotes the kernel function, λ_n^w and λ_n^y are the smoothing (or bandwidth) parameters, and where, for convenience, X is assumed to take on a set of finite values. The kernel function and smoothing parameters satisfy standard assumptions that guarantee asymptotic consistency of the estimator.[13]

This example illustrates the feasibility of performing *ex ante* policy evaluation without having to introduce functional form or distributional assumptions. Although nonparametric, the method is not assumption-free. Indeed, the method requires an explicit characterization of a behavioral model and a number of key assumptions. These key assumptions ensure (1) that the hours of work function with the tax takes the same form as that without the tax, $\eta(w, y, \tau; X, \varepsilon) = \phi(\tilde{w}, y; X, \varepsilon)$, and (2) that variation in wage offers, like variation in the tax rate if such variation were available, is orthogonal to unobserved preference heterogeneity (conditional on y and X).

It is useful to consider how modifications in the theory affect non-parametric *ex ante* evaluation. One characteristic of the tax example is that the tax only entered the model through a change in the budget constraint. Suppose, instead, that the tax is also allowed to affect utility directly, that is $U = U(c, 1 - h, \tau; X, \varepsilon)$. In general, this modification would change the form of the hours of work function such that the tax rate would enter parametrically as a separate argument, that is, $\eta(w, y; \tau; X, \varepsilon) \neq \phi(\tilde{w}, y; X, \varepsilon)$. This utility specification might capture, for example, the utility value of public goods supplied through taxation or a direct "feel bad" effect from the existence of the tax. However, the condition that $\eta = \phi$ would be preserved if the utility function is additively separable in τ, $U(c, 1 - h; X, \varepsilon) + v(\tau)$, in which case the tax rate only affects hours of work through its effect on the net wage, $\tilde{w}$. Notice that the policy considered here, a wage tax, requires mandatory participation. As will be seen in a later example, additive separability is not sufficient if the policy allows for voluntary participation.

The orthogonality condition between preferences and wage offers is also restrictive. Individuals with stronger preferences for leisure over their life cycle would accumulate less work experience even in a myopic (static) model. In that case, wage offers, if affected by work experience, would be correlated with preference heterogeneity, if it was persistent, violating the conditional independence assumption. To mitigate this problem would require conditioning the estimator in equation 2.9 on work experience. More generally, X must include any variables that are correlated with both preferences for leisure and wage offers.

Partial Observability of Wages
The ability to perform nonparametric *ex ante* evaluation is also affected by the available data. Direct application of the matching estimator (or of a nonparametric estimator of the hours function, ϕ) is clearly not possible if wage offers are not observed for labor market nonpartici-pants. Absent their wage offers, a nonparticipant cannot be matched either to a participant or to another nonparticipant with the appropri-ate (after tax) wage offer.[14]

To perform an *ex ante* analysis requires that one be able to consis-tently estimate wage offers for the nonparticipants. A nonparametric approach would specify the wage function (in logs as is conventional and up to an additive error) as

$$\log w = \log w(z) + \xi, \tag{2.10}$$

where z are observable wage determinants, ξ are unobservable wage determinants, and $f(\xi \mid z) = f(\xi)$, but would make no assumptions about either the functional form of $w(z)$ or the distribution of ξ. A standard control function approach can be used without imposing parametric assumptions about the utility function if (as is discussed below) it is assumed that there is no preference heterogeneity (that is, dropping ε from equation 2.1).[15]

In that case, denoting the marginal rate of substitution function evaluated at zero hours of work as

$$M(y;X) = \frac{\partial U(y,1;X)/\partial l}{\partial U(y,1;X)/\partial c}$$

the participation rule is

$$h = 0 \text{ iff } M(y;X) \ge \log w(z) + \xi,$$

$h > 0$ otherwise.

The probability that an individual with observables y, X, and z chooses to participate is

$$\Pr(h = 1 \mid y, X, z) = 1 - F_\xi(M(y,X) - \log w(z)),$$

which implies that

$$M(y,X) - \log w(z) = 1 - F_\xi^{-1}(\Pr(h = 1 \mid y, X, z)). \tag{2.11}$$

Now, the expected (log) wage for participants (the expected "accepted" log wage) is given by

$$E(\log w \mid h > 0) = \log w(z) + E(\xi \mid \xi > M(y,X) - \log w(z))$$

or

$$E(\log w \mid h > 0) = \log w(z) + \frac{\int_{-\infty}^{\infty} \int_{M(y,X)-\log w(z)}^{\infty} \xi f(\xi) d\xi}{\int_{-\infty}^{\infty} \int_{M(y,X)-\log w(z)}^{\infty} f(\xi) d\xi}$$

$$= \log w(z) + H(\Pr(h = 1 \mid y, X, z)). \tag{2.12}$$

where the last equality follows from equation 2.11.[16] Thus,

$$\log w_{h>0} = \log w(z) + H(\Pr(h = 1 \mid y, X, z)) + u \tag{2.13}$$

where u has conditional mean zero by construction.

It is possible to identify the H function up to a constant if there is at least one continuous variable that affects the participation probability, $\Pr(h = 1 \mid y, X, z)$ that is not in z. Non-earned income, y, would satisfy that condition, as would any such variable in X (that is not in z). The identification argument proceeds as follows. Given a nonparametric estimate of $\Pr(h = 1 \mid y, X, z)$ from the data, one can identify H over its full support by fixing z and varying $\widehat{\Pr}(h = 1 \mid y, X, z)$ through variation in y and/or a continuous variable in X. Then, one can estimate $\log w(z)$ by varying z and, say, y such that H is held constant. However, the constant term in $\log w(z)$ cannot be separately identified from the constant term in H. To see this, simply redefine the H function as $H - h_0$ and add h_0 to equation 2.13. Similarly, redefine the $w(z)$ function as $w(z)/w_0$ and add $\log w_0$. Then the constant term in equation 2.13 is $\log w_0 + h_0$.

For some purposes, knowledge of the constant term is unnecessary, for example, in determining the effect of schooling or work experience on wage offers (the human capital stock). However, knowledge of the constant term is critical for the *ex ante* evaluation of the introduction of a wage tax. The matching estimator requires that one be able to compare the hours of work of an individual with wage offer w to an individual with wage offer $(1 - \tau)w$. Obviously, the wage offer of a nonparticipant cannot be identified without having an estimate of the constant term in $w(z)$.

It is thus not possible to be fully nonparametric if wage offers are not observed for nonparticipants. Suppose then that ξ is assumed to be normal but, as above, the form of $w(z)$ is left unspecified. In that case, equation 2.13 becomes

$$
\begin{aligned}
\log w_{h>0} &= \log w(z) + \sigma_\xi \frac{\varphi\!\left(\dfrac{H(\Pr(h = 1 \mid y, X, z))}{\sigma_\varepsilon}\right)}{1 - \Phi\!\left(\dfrac{H(\Pr(h = 1 \mid y, X, z))}{\sigma_\varepsilon}\right)} + u \\
&= \log w(z) + \sigma_\xi \lambda\!\left(\dfrac{H(\Pr(h = 1 \mid y, X, z))}{\sigma_\varepsilon}\right) + u
\end{aligned}
\tag{2.14}
$$

where $\lambda(\cdot)$ is the familiar Mills ratio selection correction. Once the Mills ratio is constructed, $w(z)$ can be estimated without a confounding constant term.

Given an estimate of $w(z)$ and of σ_ξ (which is identified in equation 2.14 from variation in the Mills ratio), the matching estimator can be combined with simulation to obtain a consistent estimate of the policy effect. Suppose that the n observations in the data are ordered so that the first n_1 are participants for whom wages are observed and the next $n - n_1$ observations are nonparticipants for whom wages are not observed. Consider a simulation in which $n - n_1$ values of the wage error, ξ, are drawn from $f(\xi) \sim N(0, \sigma_\xi)$, thus simulating a wage offer (using equation 2.10) for each nonparticipant given z.[17] Given that there is now a full set of wage offers, for nonparticipants from the simulation and for participants from the data, one can obtain for this simulation a matching estimator of the policy effect from equation 2.8 using equation 2.9. Performing $s = 1, \ldots, S$ such simulations and denoting the wage vector associated with the sth simulation as $w_s = (w_1, \ldots, w_{m_1}, w^s_{m_1+1}, \ldots, w^s_n)$ and the policy effect from equation 2.8 based on that wage vector as $\hat{\Delta}_s$, the estimated policy effect is

$$\hat{\hat{\Delta}} = \frac{1}{S} \sum_{s=1}^{S} \hat{\Delta}_s, \tag{2.15}$$

where the double hat indicates that, for finite S, equation 2.15 is an estimate of equation 2.8.

Measurement Error

It is often suspected that hours of work are measured with error. Under classical assumptions, with additive mean zero measurement error, the consistency property of the matching estimator is unaffected, although the precision of the estimator is reduced. Measurement error in hours often translates into measurement error in wages (for example, if wages are defined as earnings over some time period divided by hours over that same period). Following the argument in the preceding section, the existence of additive measurement error in (log) wages does not change the selection correction as given by equation 2.14. Measured wages do not affect the decision problem of the individual. Thus, as without measurement error, both $w(z)$ and σ_ξ are identified.[18] The matching estimator would be obtained by simulating wage offers for both those who work (based on their values of z) and, as above, for those who do not work. The policy effect, $\hat{\Delta}_s$, would be obtained for each set of simulation draws and used to obtain the estimator (equation 2.15).

Fixed Costs of Work

Among the earliest extensions of the labor supply model was the inclusion of fixed costs of work (see Cogan, 1981; Heckman and MaCurdy, 1982). Introducing a fixed money cost of work, v_1, implies a budget constraint when there is no tax given by

$$C = wh + y - v_1 I(h > 0) \tag{2.16}$$

and the associated optimal hours function, $h^* = \varphi(w, y; v_1, X, \varepsilon)$. The budget constraint when there is a tax, in the presence of fixed costs, is now

$$
\begin{aligned}
C &= (1 - \tau)wh + y - v_1 I(h > 0) \\
&= \tilde{w}h + y - v_1 I(h > 0).
\end{aligned} \tag{2.17}
$$

As seen from equations 2.16 and 2.17, the introduction of the fixed cost alters the budget constraint when there is a tax in the same way as when there is no fixed cost. Thus, as before, the same function, ϕ, governs the choice of hours with and without the tax. The matching estimator (equation 2.8 or 2.15) again recovers the policy effect.[19]

Child Care Costs
It is possible, also, within this framework to evaluate the effect of a child care subsidy on labor supply, say of a single female parent. If we let ς be the per-child hourly cost of child care, the budget constraint, ignoring taxes, equation 2.2, becomes

$$
\begin{aligned}
c &= wh - \varsigma nh + y \\
&= (w - \varsigma n)h + y
\end{aligned}
$$

where n is the number of children requiring child care when the mother works. Suppose the government provides a child care subsidy leading to a net per-child child care cost of ς'. Then, with the subsidy, the budget constraint is

$$c = (w - \varsigma' n)h + y.$$

By analogy to the wage tax, it is possible to evaluate the effect of the net (of subsidy) child care cost on hours by matching individuals with wage $w - \varsigma n$ to individuals with wage $\tilde{w} = w - \varsigma' n$. For any given market cost of child care, ς, the effect on hours of work of the subsidy $\varsigma - \varsigma'$ can be determined. Whether it is necessary to match also on n depends on how the utility function is specified, in particular on whether the marginal rate of substitution between leisure and consumption depends on n. One cannot be agnostic about the behavioral model. By reintroducing the wage tax, it is possible to estimate the joint effect of introducing a wage tax together with a child care subsidy on labor supply by a matching estimator with $\tilde{w} = (1 - \tau)w - \varsigma' n$.

Nonlinear Taxes

Tax schedules are generally nonlinear. For that reason, there has developed a large methodological and empirical literature on the estimation of labor supply models in the presence of nonlinear taxes (see Blundell and MaCurdy, 1999, for an extensive review). Because the tax rate depends on the level of wage earnings, that is on wh, the existence of nonlinear taxes changes the budget constraint in a nontrivial way. In particular, equation 2.4 becomes

$$C = (1 - \tau(wh; \gamma))wh + y,$$

where the tax schedule, $\tau(wh; \gamma)$, depends on a vector of parameters, γ. Thus, the hours of work function is in general a function of the parameters that determine an individual's tax liability; with the utility function in equation 2.1, optimal hours are given by

$$h^{**} = \eta(w, y; \gamma; X, \varepsilon).$$

Contrary to the case of a proportional tax, the hours of work function in the presence of nonlinear taxes cannot be written as the same hours function that applies in the absence of taxes with a change in variables, that is, as $\phi(\tilde{w}, y; X, \varepsilon)$, where $\tilde{w}$ is a transform of w. The hours function is therefore not invariant to changes in the tax schedule and is, thus, not structural with respect to the tax. The implication is that starting from a world with no wage tax, it is not possible to perform an *ex ante* evaluation of the introduction of a nonlinear tax scheme.

However, recall that in the case of a proportional tax, the same *ex ante* evaluation could be performed when there is an existing proportional tax, τ_1, which has not varied in the past, that is, proposed to be changed to a new value τ_2. That result carries over, though, as will be seen in a more limited way, to the case of a change in an existing nonlinear wage tax. In several papers, Blomquist and Newey (1997, 2002) develop and implement a nonparametric estimation method for the usual case in which the tax schedule leads to a kinked budget constraint. They apply the method to an *ex post* evaluation of Swedish tax reforms making use of variation in tax schedules over time.[20] My interest is in showing the potential of this methodology for *ex ante* evaluation in the absence of variation in the tax schedule.

Figure 2.1 illustrates the budget constraint for a three-tier progressive tax schedule. In the figure, y_1 is non-earned income and $w_1 = w(1 - \tau_1)$ is the slope of the first segment, where w is the wage and τ_1 the tax rate over the first segment. At $h = k_1$, where earnings are $(1 - \tau_1)$

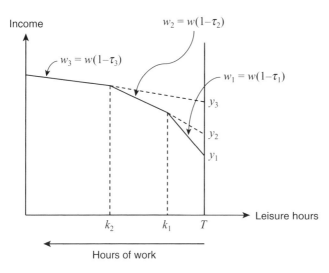

Figure 2.1
Progressive tax and labor supply.

wk_1, the marginal tax rate changes to τ_2. The second line segment thus has slope $w_2 = (1 - \tau_2)w$ with virtual income for that segment of y_2. At $h = k_2$, where earnings are $(1 - \tau_1)wk_1 + (1 - \tau_2)wk_2$, the marginal tax rate changes to τ_3. The third line segment thus has slope $w_3 = (1 - \tau_3)w$ with virtual income for that segment of y_3.

The insight of Blomquist and Newey (1997, 2002) is that under utility maximization, expected hours of work can be expressed as a function of the arguments of the budget constraint as just described. In the general case of J segments, optimal expected hours are given by the function

$$Eh^* = \phi(w_1, w_2, \dots, w_J, y_1, y_2, \dots, y_J, k_1, k_2, \dots, k_{J-1}). \tag{2.18}$$

Estimating equation 2.18 nonparametrically, the goal of their analysis, is impractical for most actual tax systems because of the high dimensionality of the function. A major simplification in terms of feasibility is achieved because, as Blomquist and Newey show, equation 2.18 can be written as the sum of lower-dimensional objects. In the case where $J = 3$, as in the figure,

$$Eh^* = \phi_1(w_1, y_1, k_1) + \phi_2(w_2, y_2, k_1) + \phi_3(w_2, y_2, k_2) + \phi_4(w_3, y_3, k_2). \tag{2.19}$$

As they also note, because the kink points are functions of the wages and virtual incomes, namely

$$k_j = \frac{y_{j+1} - y_j}{w_j - w_{j+1}}, \tag{2.20}$$

the dimensionality of equation 2.19 can be reduced further. Accounting for equation 2.20,

$$Eh^* = \phi_{12}(w_1, y_1, w_2, y_2) + \phi_{34}(w_2, y_2, w_3, y_3) \tag{2.21}$$

which is of overall dimension 6 rather than 8 as in equation 2.19. The simplification in equation 2.21 is useful if the goal is to estimate the expected hours function. However, it is not useful for the more limited goal of *ex ante* policy evaluation.

In that context, I have taken as a premise that there has been no previous variation in the tax schedule. In that case, variation in the net wages w_1, w_2, and w_3 arises only from variation in the gross wage, w, and the expected hours function (equation 2.18) simplifies to

$$Eh^* = \phi(w, \mathbf{y}; \boldsymbol{\tau}) = \phi(\mathbf{w}, \mathbf{y}) \tag{2.22}$$

where $\mathbf{y}$ is the vector of virtual incomes, $\boldsymbol{\tau}$ is the vector of tax rates, and, in the second equality, $\mathbf{w}$ is the vector of *net* wages. Recall that in the case of a proportional tax, *ex ante* evaluation was possible over the "full" range of potential tax rates given enough wage variation in the data. In the case of a nonlinear tax, the set of policies that can be evaluated is limited. In particular, if the current tax regime is characterized by a tax schedule given by the vector $\mathbf{1} - \boldsymbol{\tau}$, then *ex ante* evaluation can be performed on alternative tax schedules given by a proportionate change in each element of $\mathbf{1} - \boldsymbol{\tau}$, that is, for tax schedules in which the ratios $\dfrac{1 - \tau_i}{1 - \tau_j}$ are unchanged for all i, j. The matching estimator of the effect of such a change in the tax schedule would be based on a comparison of the hours of work of individuals with gross wage w to individuals with gross wage βw, where β is either less than 1, representing a lower tax schedule, or greater than 1, representing a tax increase.[21]

The result that only prospective tax schedules that satisfy the constant ratio requirement can be evaluated clearly severely restricts the range of policies that can be evaluated. It is not possible to evaluate a policy that changes the tax rate along only one (or multiple) segment while holding the other tax rates constant.[22] That implies that it is also not possible to evaluate new schedules that have either a smaller or larger number of segments than the existing tax schedule. Variation in the tax schedule, as used in the Blomquist and Newey (2002) application, allows for the evaluation of more types of schedules, although the set of policies is still restricted to those that satisfy the constant-ratio property of each schedule. If the variation in tax schedules is small, extrapolations outside of the constant ratio set of taxes can only be achieved through a parametric assumption.[23]

Parametric estimation of labor supply models with kinked budget constraints is considerably more complicated when the budget constraint has nonconvexities.[24] With nonconvexities there may be multiple tangencies between indifference curves and budget segments, which implies that to determine optimal hours of work requires making global comparisons of utility levels. That issue does not arise in the *ex ante* evaluation problem; implementing the matching estimator assumes only that hours observations are optimally chosen and does not require that the optimization problem be solved.

Applications
There have not been any applications, to my knowledge, of the matching estimator in the *ex ante* evaluation of tax policy, although there have been a few *ex post* evaluations using the Blomquist and Newey (2002) nonparametric approach. These include studies of Swedish tax reform in the 1980s by Blomquist, Eklof, and Newey (2001) and Blomquist and Newey (2002), the study of the U.S. Tax Reform Act of 1986 by Kumar (2008), and the study of policy changes in the U.S. EITC, AFDC, and Food Stamp programs during the 1990s by Wu (2005). All of these papers exploit policy variation. None use their estimates to perform counterfactual (*ex ante*) policy evaluation exercises. I take up applications of the matching estimator in the example that follows.

2.1.1.2 School Attendance Subsidy
Many developing countries have adopted conditional cash transfer (CCT) programs designed to increase human capital investment and reduce poverty. Such programs have been tried or currently exist in Argentina, Brazil, Chile, Colombia, Egypt, Guatemala, Honduras, Indonesia, Jamaica, Malawi, Mexico, Nicaragua, Panama, Turkey, and Zambia. CCT programs of this kind have usually included a subsidy for regular school attendance.

A policy maker contemplating the introduction of a CCT program would presumably prefer to have an estimate of the effectiveness of the policy, including how the effect of the subsidy would vary with the size and structure of the subsidy, prior to implementation. Having such an estimate would enable the policy maker to calculate the costs and benefits of alternative subsidy schedules and thus to make an informed decision about the best structure of the subsidy to implement. As in the case of the wage tax, it is possible to perform an *ex ante* evaluation without variation in the price (tuition) of schooling and without parametric assumptions. Also as with the wage tax, the feasibility of nonparametric *ex ante* evaluation is dependent on the theory that is posited about how households make school attendance choices. I again begin with the simplest optimization model and then make modifications to explore extensions and limitations of the approach.

The Basic Framework
Consider a household with one school-age child deciding between having the child attend school or having the child work in the labor market. School attendance provides direct utility to the household; work provides income, and thus consumption, to the household. Letting y denote household income net of the child's earnings, w the child's wage offer, $s \in \{0, 1\}$ school attendance, and X observable and ε unobservable taste shifters, the parents choose s to maximize

$$U(C, s; X, \varepsilon) \tag{2.23}$$

subject to the budget constraint

$$C = y + w(1 - s). \tag{2.24}$$

The optimal school attendance choice is

$$s^* = \phi(y, w; X, \varepsilon), \tag{2.25}$$

where in equation 2.25, $s^* = \phi(y, w; X, \varepsilon) = 1$ if $U(y, 1; X, \varepsilon) > U(y + w, 0; X, \varepsilon)$; that is, where the utility to the household from the child attending school exceeds that from the child working, and $s^* = \phi(y, w; X, \varepsilon) = 0$ otherwise.

Suppose that the government introduces a conditional cash transfer program that provides a subsidy of τ if the child attends school. Under this policy, the household faces a new budget constraint given by

$$C = y + w(1 - s) + \tau s. \tag{2.26}$$

Noting that one can rewrite equation 2.26 as

$$C = (y + \tau) + (w - \tau)(1 - s),$$

the optimal choice of s can be written as the same function as without the subsidy, namely

$$s^{**} = \phi(y + \tau, w - \tau; X, \varepsilon), \tag{2.27}$$

where $\phi(y + \tau, w - \tau; X, \varepsilon) = 1$ if $U(y + \tau, 1; X, \varepsilon) > U(y + w, 0; X, \varepsilon) = U((y + \tau) + (w - \tau), 0; X, \varepsilon)$ and $\phi(y + \tau, w - \tau; X, \varepsilon) = 0$ otherwise.[25] As seen in equation 2.27, the subsidy can be viewed as reducing the child wage by the amount of the subsidy, that is, reducing the opportunity cost of school attendance, and at the same time increasing household income by the amount of the subsidy. The effect of what amounts to an equal reduction in w and increase in y increases the utility from having the child attend school but leaves the utility from having the child work (not attend school) unchanged.

The implication of equation 2.27 is that a household with income y, child wage w, and preference shifters X and ε that receives the subsidy will make the same schooling decision as a household with income $\tilde{y} = y + \tau$, child wage $\tilde{w} = w - \tau$, and the same preference shifters that did not receive the subsidy. Assuming that ε is independent of w and y conditional on X, that is, $f(\varepsilon \mid w, y, X) = f(\varepsilon \mid \tilde{w}, \tilde{y}, X) = f(\varepsilon \mid X)$, and that child wage offers are observed for all households, the effect of the subsidy on school attendance can be obtained by a similar matching procedure as for the wage tax example, namely

$$\hat{\Delta} = \frac{1}{n} \sum_{\substack{j=1 \\ j,i \in S_p}}^{n} \hat{E}(s_i \mid w_i = w_j - \tau, y_i = y_j + \tau, X_i = X_j) - s_j(w_j, y_j, X_j) \tag{2.28}$$

where $s_j(w_j, y_j, X_j)$ is the school attendance decision of household j with characteristics (w_j, y_j, X_j) (that is, without the subsidy) and $\hat{E}(s_i \mid w_i = w_j - \tau, y_i = y_j + \tau, X_i = X_j)$ is an estimate of the expected school attendance that household j would choose if faced with the subsidy. As before, the average can only be taken over the region of overlapping support, S_p, that is, over the set of households j whose values $w_j - \tau$ and $y_j + \tau$ lie within the observed support of wages w_i, household income y_i, and observable characteristics X_i. The first term in equation 2.28 can be estimated from a nonparametric regression of s_i on w_i and y_i evaluated at the points $w_i = w_j - \tau$, $y_i = y_j + \tau$, $X_i = X_j$ (see the discussion below).

It is useful to consider modifications in the model to understand the robustness of the method. Throughout it is assumed that wage offers are observed for both school nonattendees (children who work) and school attendees (children who do not work). Partial observability of wages raises no new issues in this context than have already been discussed in the wage tax example.

However, that is not the case if the household's utility is directly affected by participation in the subsidy program. Unlike the wage tax, participation in the school attendance subsidy program is voluntary; indeed, the take-up rate is isomorphic to the policy impact. In that case, the school attendance decision will necessarily depend on the extent to which the policy induces a "feel good" or "feel bad" effect. Welfare programs are, for example, thought to have a stigma effect, which reduces participation. Without a strong prior, presumably based on external evidence about the existence and magnitude of such effects, it is impossible to perform a valid *ex ante* policy evaluation. It would, however, be possible to evaluate the impact of a change in an existing policy if the utility or disutility of the policy were independent of the policy change, for example, if the (dis)utility associated with a subsidy of τ were the same as that with a subsidy of a multiple or fraction of τ.[26]

Multiple Children—Exogenous Fertility
The method can be extended to households with more than one school- (and work-) age child. Consider a subsidy program in which, as has been the case in actual programs, the subsidy amount varies with grade level. Thus, the subsidy faced by a household with multiple children is a schedule that depends on the grade levels that their children are eligible to attend. Denote $n_k = 1$ if there is a child in the household who would be attending grade level $k = 1, \dots, K$ and $n_k = 0$ otherwise.[27] The household is assumed to obtain utility from the attendance of each child according to

$$U(C, s_1 n_1, s_2 n_2, \dots, s_K n_K; X, \boldsymbol{\varepsilon}), \qquad (2.29)$$

where $\boldsymbol{\varepsilon} = (\varepsilon_1 n_1, \dots, \varepsilon_K n_K)$ is a vector of child-specific school attendance preference "shocks." The household budget constraint in the presence of the subsidy schedule is

$$
\begin{aligned}
C &= y + \sum_{k=1}^{K} w_k (1 - s_k) n_k + \sum_{k=1}^{K} \tau_k s_k n_k \\
&= \left(y + \sum_{k=1}^{K} \tau_k n_k \right) + \sum_{k=1}^{K} (w_k - \tau_k)(1 - s_k) n_k
\end{aligned}
\qquad (2.30)
$$

where τ_k is the subsidy level for a child attending grade level k. Maximizing expression 2.29 subject to equation 2.30 yields the school attendance demand function for a child of grade level k

$$s_k^{**} = \phi_k(y + \sum_{k=1}^{K} \tau_k n_k, (w_1 - \tau_1)n_1, (w_2 - \tau_2)n_2, ..., (w_K - \tau_K)n_K; X; \boldsymbol{\varepsilon})$$

$$\text{for } k = 1, ..., K. \tag{2.31}$$

As seen in equation 2.31, the school attendance demand function for any child depends not only on the wage and subsidy level for that child but also on the wage and subsidy levels of all other children in the household. Thus, the matching procedure in the case of multiple children requires that the matched households have the same number of children and the same configuration of children in terms of their grade levels.[28] In that case, families with income y, wages $w_1 n_1$, ..., $w_k n_k$, and observable characteristics X would be matched with families with the same value of X, income $y + \sum_{k=1}^{K} \tau_k n_k$, and wages $(w_1 - \tau_1)n_1$, $(w_2 - \tau_2)n_2$, ..., $(w_K - \tau_K)n_K$.

Multiple Children—Endogenous Fertility

In the previous case, when fertility was taken to be exogenous, accommodating multiple children required a straightforward change in the matching procedure. When fertility is a choice, even if wages and subsidy levels are the same for all children, matching on the number of children is no longer a valid procedure. The reason is that the number of children is now itself a function of w, y, and the observable and unobservable preference shifters. Varying w or y while holding the number of children constant implies that the unobservables must also change. Thus, $f(\varepsilon | w, y, n, X) \neq f(\varepsilon | n, X)$, which violates a necessary condition for the validity of the matching procedure.

More fundamentally, when fertility is a choice, the demand functions for school attendance are no longer invariant to the subsidy. To accommodate fertility choice, assume that the utility function is augmented to include the number of children and a preference unobservable that shifts the marginal utility of the number of children.[29] In addition, to isolate the issue raised by the endogeneity of fertility, assume that neither the wage nor the school attendance subsidy varies with child characteristics (grade level). Then, denoting n as the number of children and distinguishing between the school attendance unobservable (vector) as $\boldsymbol{\varepsilon}_s$ and the fertility unobservable as ε_n, the utility function is

$$U(C, s_1, ..., s_n, n; X, \boldsymbol{\varepsilon}_s, \varepsilon_n)$$

where s_i is the school attendance of child i, and the budget constraint given the subsidy (after rearranging) is

$$C = (y + n\tau) + (w - \tau)\sum_{i=1}^{n}(1 - s_i).$$

Utility maximization leads to the demand system

$$s_i^{**} = \eta_i^s(y, w - \tau; \tau; X, \boldsymbol{\varepsilon}_s, \boldsymbol{\varepsilon}_n), \text{ for } i = 1, \dots, n^{**}, \qquad (2.32)$$

where

$$n^{**} = \eta^n(y, w - \tau; \tau; X, \boldsymbol{\varepsilon}_s, \boldsymbol{\varepsilon}_n).$$

Note that the subsidy, τ, enters as a separate parameter in the demand functions; one cannot write equation 2.32 as the same function that arises without the subsidy evaluated at different values of w and y.[30] Thus, the nonparametric approach is not applicable with endogenous fertility.[31]

Life Cycle—Perfect Foresight
It is useful to consider the extent to which nonparametric *ex ante* evaluation can be extended to a life cycle context. I take up first the case in which the household is assumed to have perfect foresight and, for expositional ease, consider a household that will have only one child (and knows it). The household makes a school attendance decision for that child in each of $t = 1, \dots, T$ periods, corresponding to the ages of the child for which work is legal. The household is assumed to have perfect foresight about household income, child wages, preference shifters, and the time sequence of school attendance subsidy levels each period. Household utility is

$$U(C_1, \dots, C_T, s_1, s_2, \dots, s_T; X, \boldsymbol{\varepsilon}), \qquad (2.33)$$

where $X = (X_1, \dots, X_T)$ and $\boldsymbol{\varepsilon} = (\varepsilon_1, \dots, \varepsilon_T)$. The household, under the subsidy policy, is assumed to satisfy the period-by-period budget constraint (no savings or borrowing)

$$\begin{aligned}C_t &= y_t + w_t(1 - s_t) + \tau_t s_t \\ &= (y_t + \tau_t) + (w_t - \tau_t)(1 - s_t).\end{aligned}$$

The optimal school attendance decision for each age, t, is determined by a global comparison of utilities at all 2^T possible combinations of s_t over all $t = 1, \dots, T$.

Defining $\widetilde{y(\tau)} = (y_1 + \tau_1, y_2 + \tau_2, \dots, y_T + \tau_T)$ and $\widetilde{w(\tau)} = (w_1 - \tau_1, w_2 - \tau_2, \dots, w_T - \tau_T)$, the school attendance demand function in each period is thus

$s_t^{**} = \phi_t(\tilde{y}, \tilde{w}; \mathbf{X}, \boldsymbol{\varepsilon})$ for $t = 1, \ldots T$.

The estimation of the subsidy effect requires matching untreated households (of given $\mathbf{X}$) with income profile $\widetilde{y(0)}$ and child wage offer profile $\widetilde{w(0)}$ to households with income profile $\widetilde{y(\tau)}$ and child wage offer profile $\widetilde{w(\tau)}$.[32]

Dynamics—Imperfect Foresight
To simplify the exposition, assume that there are only two schooling periods and, as above, that there can be no borrowing or saving. The budget constraint under the subsidy policy is

$C_t = (y_t + \tau) + (w_t - \tau)(1 - s_t)$ for $t = 1, 2,$

where the subsidy is assumed to be constant over the two periods and, in the case of period 2, independent of attendance in period 1. The school attendance decision in any period t depends on a comparison of the remaining expected lifetime utility of the household under the two alternatives, $s_t = \{0, 1\}$. Given the utility function (expression 2.33) with $T = 2$ (and dropping $\mathbf{X}$ for convenience), the schooling decision in period 2 is

$s_2^{**} = 1$ iff $U(y_2 + \tau, s_1, 1; \varepsilon_2) - U((y_2 + \tau) + (w_2 - \tau), s_1, 0; \varepsilon_2) \geq 0$
$\quad\quad = 0$ otherwise.

Note that the schooling decision in period 2 depends on whether or not the child attended school in period 1 because utility is not intertemporally separable in school attendance. If ε_2 is unknown in period 1 and the unobserved preference shifter is serially independent, $f(\varepsilon_2 \mid \varepsilon_1)$ $= f(\varepsilon_2)$, s_1 will not be correlated with ε_2.[33] In that case, conditional on s_1, the matching procedure as in the static model can be used to estimate the impact of the subsidy on period 2 school attendance. The overall impact is then the weighted sum of the conditional (on s_1) impacts, with the weights the proportion of households choosing each s_1.

The schooling decision in period 1 is based on a comparison of the sum of the expected discounted utilities over the two periods under each of the two school attendance alternatives. With these denoted as $V(s)$, they are given by

$V(s_1 = 1) = U(y_1 + \tau, 1; \varepsilon_1) +$ \hfill (2.34)

$\delta E \max(U(y_2 + \tau, 1, 1; \varepsilon_2), U((y_2 + \tau) + (w_2 - \tau), 1, 0; \varepsilon_2)),$

$V(s_1 = 0) = U(y_1 + \tau) + (w_1 - \tau), 0; \varepsilon_1) +$ \hfill (2.35)

$\delta E \max(U(y_2 + \tau, 0, 1; \varepsilon_2), U((y_2 + \tau) + (w_2 - \tau), 0, 0; \varepsilon_2)),$

where δ is the discount factor and the expectation is taken over whatever elements inside the E max function are unknown to the household and thus can be viewed as random from the perspective of the household. The school attendance decision in period 1 is thus

$$s_1^{**} = 1 \text{ iff } V(s_1 = 1) - V(s_1 = 0) \geq 0$$
$$= 0 \text{ otherwise.}$$

The feasibility of *ex ante* evaluation depends on what elements are in the household's information set. For example, and perhaps the least realistic, suppose that the household has perfect foresight about the period 2 income and child wage but not about the unobserved preference shifter, ε_2. In that case the school attendance demand function is given by

$$s_1^{**} = \phi_1(y_1 + \tau, y_2 + \tau, w_1 - \tau, w_2 - \tau; \varepsilon_1, f(\varepsilon_2)).$$

As in the perfect foresight case, the same school attendance function governs the choice of s_1 with and without the subsidy, and the same matching procedure can be adopted in estimating the policy effect. Of course, the attendance function differs from the perfect foresight case in that it depends on the density of ε_2 as opposed to the value of ε_2. Note that the evaluation of the subsidy policy does not entail estimating the ϕ_1 function (or the underlying utility function and preference distribution) and so does not discriminate a model in which all households have perfect foresight from one in which they have imperfect foresight.

Consider instead the case in which the household is uncertain about its future income, y_2, but otherwise has perfect foresight. Further assume that household income is an *iid* process. Integrating over the density of y_2 in equations 2.34 and 2.35 changes the form of the school attendance demand function. In particular, τ will in general enter parametrically, so that

$$s_1^{**} = \eta_1(y_1 + \tau, w_1 - \tau, w_2 - \tau, \tau; \varepsilon_1, \varepsilon_2, f(y_2)). \tag{2.36}$$

The matching estimator based on the household income and child wage comparisons fails in this case.[34] Given the form of equation 2.36 and the presumed population invariance of the subsidy schedule, nonparametric *ex ante* evaluation is not possible. Clearly, the same result obtains if the household is uncertain about the period 2 child wage.

Child Home Production
Children in developing countries may engage in home production as an alternative to attending school or working in the labor market. To

capture that fact, consider again the static single-child model in which the household values the child "leisure" option, that is, where the child neither attends school nor works in the market for a wage. Assuming that school attendance, work, and leisure are mutually exclusive alternatives and letting $l = \{0, 1\}$ indicate the leisure option, the household utility function[35] is now

$$U(C, s, l; \varepsilon_s, \varepsilon_l),$$

and the budget constraint under the subsidy is

$$C = y + w(1 - s - l) + \tau s. \tag{2.37}$$

With equation 2.37 rewritten as

$$C = (y + \tau) + (w - \tau)(1 - s - l) - \tau l, \tag{2.38}$$

the school attendance demand function can be seen to depend not only on $y + \tau$ and $w - \tau$, as in the model without the leisure option, but also parametrically on τ, that is,

$$s^{**} = \eta(y + \tau, w - \tau, \tau; \varepsilon_s, \varepsilon_l). \tag{2.39}$$

The school attendance demand function without the subsidy, $s^{**} = \phi(y, w; \varepsilon_s, \varepsilon_l)$, thus differs from that with the subsidy, which implies that the matching estimator cannot be used to perform an *ex ante* evaluation of the subsidy policy.[36]

Interestingly, and perhaps also surprisingly, the matching estimator based on the model with child leisure corresponds to a different policy, one that instead of subsidizing school attendance provides a subsidy to households in which the child does not work in the market, that is, in which a subsidy is provided if the child either attends school or stays home. Under that policy, the budget constraint becomes

$$C = y + w(1 - s - l) + \tau(s + l)$$
$$= (y + \tau) + (w - \tau)(1 - s - l.)$$

Thus, the school attendance and leisure demand functions,

$$s^{**} = \phi^s(y + \tau, w - \tau; \varepsilon_s, \varepsilon_l)$$

and

$$l^{**} = \phi^l(y + \tau, w - \tau; \varepsilon_s, \varepsilon_l),$$

are the same functions that would apply without the subsidy policy ($\tau = 0$).

The matching estimator of the subsidy effect on school attendance that compares households with income y and child wage w to households with income $y + \tau$ and child wage $w - \tau$ is thus consistent with either of two models and two corresponding policies. Inference about the effect of the school subsidy policy relies on there being no leisure option that the household values. There is otherwise a fundamental ambiguity in the policy interpretation of the matching estimator.

2.1.2   Structural Parametric Approach

2.1.2.1   School Attendance Subsidy

There are many models of behavior, as shown in the preceding discussion, for which a nonparametric approach to *ex ante* policy evaluation is not conceptually possible. And, although I have not explicitly discussed the computational feasibility of that approach, it is clear that empirical tractability can become an issue for models that are more complex, that is, where the matching variables are of high dimension. I now consider how parametric assumptions address these problems.

The Basic Framework
Like the nonparametric approach, the parametric approach also requires that the researcher adopt a particular behavioral model. However, the parametric approach makes additional assumptions about functional forms and error distributions. The value of these extratheoretic auxiliary assumptions is that they provide restrictions that enable the identification of the structural parameters of the model that are necessary for *ex ante* policy evaluation in cases where the nonparametric approach fails. To fix ideas, consider the single-child static school attendance decision model given by equations 2.23 and 2.24 in which the utility function (equation 2.23) takes the specific parametric form[37]

$$U(C, s; \varepsilon) = C + \alpha s + \beta C s + \varepsilon s, \tag{2.40}$$

and where ε, which shifts the marginal utility of school attendance, is assumed to be normally distributed in the population, $\varepsilon \sim N(0, \sigma_\varepsilon^2)$.[38] The school attendance decision under the subsidy policy is given by

$$s = 1 \text{ iff } \varepsilon \geq (w - \tau) - \alpha - \beta(y + \tau),$$
$$= 0 \text{ otherwise.}$$

And the probability of attendance is given by

$$\Pr(s=1) = 1 - \Phi\left(\frac{(w-\tau) - \alpha - \beta(y+\tau)}{\sigma_\varepsilon}\right),$$

where Φ is the standard cumulative normal.[39] Note that, consistent with the discussion of the model in the nonparametric case, the attendance probability is a function of $(y + \tau)$ and $(w - \tau)$. The parameters of the model can be estimated by maximum likelihood from preprogram data alone, $\tau = 0$, provided there is variation in child wage offers, assumed to be observed both for children who work and for children who attend school, and variation in household income. A normalization of σ_ε, as is usual in the case of a probit, is unnecessary because of the implicit normalization of utility in monetary units.[40] Given parameter estimates, the effect of introducing a subsidy of τ on the attendance rate can be calculated from

$$\hat{\Delta}_s = \Phi\left(\frac{(w-\tau) - \hat{\alpha} - \hat{\beta}(y+\tau)}{\hat{\sigma}_\varepsilon}\right) - \Phi\left(\frac{w - \hat{\alpha} - \hat{\beta}y}{\hat{\sigma}_\varepsilon}\right)$$

for any hypothetical subsidy level.[41] Unlike the nonparametric case, there is no condition on the support of $y + \tau$ and $w - \tau$.

As previously shown, the ability to do nonparametric *ex ante* evaluation of the subsidy policy is lost if child leisure is added to the household utility function. To see how parameterizing the model allows *ex ante* evaluation in this case, consider adding child leisure to equation 2.40 as follows:

$$U(C, s, l; \varepsilon) = C + \alpha s + \beta Cs + \gamma l + \varepsilon_s s + \varepsilon_l l, \tag{2.41}$$

where $l \in \{0, 1\}$, s and l are mutually exclusive, and ε_l is an unobservable that alters the marginal utility of child leisure. The two preference shifters are assumed to be jointly normally distributed with mean zero and variance-covariance matrix $\Lambda = \begin{pmatrix} \sigma_{\varepsilon_s}^2 & \cdot \\ \sigma_{\varepsilon_s \varepsilon_l} & \sigma_{\varepsilon_l}^2 \end{pmatrix}$. The budget constraint is given, as in equation 2.38.

It is useful to write the utilities associated with the three mutually exclusive choices, school attendance (s), leisure (l), and work (h), where $s + l + h = 1$:

$$U(s = 1) = (1 + \beta)(y + \tau) + \alpha + \varepsilon_s,$$

$$U(l = 1) = y + \gamma + \varepsilon_l,$$

$$U(h = 1) = y + w.$$

This choice model is thus in the form of a trivariate probit with the utility of one of the alternatives a nonstochastic normalized function of observables. The model parameters are identified (see Heckman and Sedlacek, 1985) and can be estimated from preprogram data ($\tau = 0$) with variation in w and y.[42] Given parameter estimates, the effect of introducing a subsidy of τ on school attendance (and on child employment) can be calculated from the cumulative bivariate normal distribution of (ε_s, $\varepsilon_s - \varepsilon_l$) for any hypothetical subsidy level. Note that $s = 1$ requires that

$$\beta(y + \tau) + \tau + \alpha - \gamma + \varepsilon_s - \varepsilon_l \geq 0$$

and

$$\beta(y + \tau) - (w - \tau) + \alpha + \varepsilon_s \geq 0,$$

which implies that the school attendance function depends, as shown in the discussion of the nonparametric matching estimator, not only on $y + \tau$ and $w - \tau$, but also separately on τ.

The structural parametric approach has been used to evaluate the PROGRESA program in two papers (Todd and Wolpin, 2006; Attanasio, Meghir, and Santiago, in press). Both of these applications adopt DCDP models, although the actual models differ greatly in their behavioral assumptions. There have been a number of recent surveys of the DCDP approach (Aguiregebaria and Mira, 2010; Todd and Wolpin, 2010; Keane, Todd, and Wolpin, 2011). Nevertheless, a brief description of the development of DCDP models will help to place these applications in context. The introduction of DCDP models is associated with independent contributions by Gotz and McCall (1984), Miller (1984), Pakes (1986), Rust (1987), and Wolpin (1984). The basic insight that enabled the estimation of DCDP models is that any DCDP model can be cast as a static discrete choice estimation problem.

To illustrate that insight, first consider the simple static model in which the only decision is school attendance of a single child. Assume that wages are observed (by the researcher) only for children who work. To focus on essentials, the utility function is specified as additively separable in consumption and school attendance (thus eliminating the income effect). Household i at time t maximizes

$$U(C_{it}, s_{it}; \varepsilon_{it}) = C_{it} + \alpha_{it} s_{it},$$

where preferences are time varying according to $\alpha_{it} = X_{it}\beta + \varepsilon_{it}$, subject to a budget constraint

$$C_{it} = y_{it} + w_{it}(1 - s_{it})$$

and a wage offer function

$$w_{it} = Z_{it}\gamma + \eta_{it}. \tag{2.42}$$

In anticipation of the dynamic setting, it is useful to distinguish the household's state space, Ω_{it}, consisting of all of the determinants of the household's decision, that is $X_{it}, \varepsilon_{it}, Z_{it}, \eta_{it}$, from the part of the state space available to the researcher, Ω_{it}^-, consisting only of the determinants X_{it}, Z_{it}. Denoting v_{it}^* (the latent) as the difference in the utility of the household under the alternatives $s_{it} = 1$ and $s_{it} = 0$,

$$\begin{aligned} v_{it}^* &= Z_{it}\gamma - X_{it}\beta + \eta_{it} - \varepsilon_{it} \\ &= \xi^*(\Omega_{it}^-) + \xi_{it}, \end{aligned} \tag{2.43}$$

where ε and η are distributed joint normal with covariance matrix Λ.[43] The sample likelihood incorporating the wage information for working children is

$$L(\theta; X_{it}, Z_{it}) = \Pi_{i=1}^{i=I} \Pr(s_{it} = 1, w_{it} \mid \Omega_{it}^-)^{s_{it}} \Pr(s_{it} = 0 \mid \Omega_{it}^-)^{1-s_{it}}$$

where

$$\Pr(s_{it} = 1, w_{it} \mid \Omega_{it}^-) = \Pr(\xi_{it} \geq -\xi_{it}^*(\Omega_{it}^-),$$
$$\eta_{it} = w_{it} - Z_{it}\gamma),$$
$$\Pr(s_{it} = 0 \mid \Omega_{it}^-) \mid = \Pr(\xi_{it} < -\xi_{it}^*(\Omega_{it}^-)).[44]$$

The parameters to be estimated include $\beta, \gamma, \sigma_\varepsilon^2, \sigma_\eta^2$, and $\sigma_{\varepsilon\eta}$. As is well known, joint normality is sufficient to identify the wage parameters (γ and σ_η^2) as well as $(\sigma_\eta^2 - \sigma_{\varepsilon\eta})/\sigma_\xi$ without exclusion restrictions (Heckman, 1979). The data on work choices identify γ/σ_ξ and β/σ_ξ. To identify σ_ξ, note that there are three possible types of variables that appear in the likelihood function, variables that appear only in Z, that is, only in the wage function, variables that appear only in X, that is, only in the utility function, and variables that appear in both X and Z. Having identified the parameters of the wage function (the γ's), the identification of σ_ξ (and thus also $\sigma_{\varepsilon\eta}$) requires the existence of at least one variable that appears only in the wage equation. For example, variables that affect the demand for child labor, and thus the child wage, must not affect the utility value the household places on the child's school attendance.

In the static model there is no connection between the decision made in the current period and future utility. Thus, even if agents are forward looking, maximizing the expected present value of discounted lifetime utility would be equivalent to maximizing current utility in each period. There are many ways in which dynamics may arise in the model. For example, suppose the child's wage increases with actual work experience, H. In that case, rewrite equation 2.42 as

$$w_{it} = Z_{it}\gamma_1 + \gamma_2 H_{it} + \eta_{it}, \tag{2.44}$$

where $H_{it} = \sum_{\tau=1}^{\tau=t-1}(1-s_{i\tau})$ is work experience at the start of period t. Given this specification, working (not attending school) in any period increases future wages, which, if the household is forward looking, will reduce the incentive for having the child attend school. Alternatively, or in addition, we could suppose that the child wage and/or parents' utility depends not only on current attendance but also on the current number of years of schooling the child has completed. In that case, attending school in any period affects future utility either indirectly through its effect on future wage offers or directly on future utility.

Continuing with the example, modified to account for the wage offer function in equation 2.44, assume that the couple maximizes the expected present discounted value of remaining lifetime utility at each period starting from an initial period, $t = 1$, and ending at period T, the assumed terminal decision period. If we let $V_t(\Omega_{it})$ be the maximum expected present discounted value of remaining lifetime utility at t given the state space and discount factor δ (the value function),

$$V_t(\Omega_{it}) = \max_{s_{it}} E\left\{ \sum_{\tau=t}^{\tau=T} \delta^{\tau-t}[U_{i\tau}^1 s_{i\tau} + U_{i\tau}^0(1-s_{i\tau})] \,|\, \Omega_{it} \right\},$$

where U^1 and U^0 are the levels of utility with $s = 1$ and $s = 0$. The state space at t consists of all factors known to the household at t that affect current utility or the probability distribution of future utilities. With the wage relationship given by equation 2.44, H_{it} becomes part of the state space and evolves according to

$$H_{it} = H_{i,t-1} + (1-s_{i,t-1}).$$

The value function can be written as the maximum over the two alternative-specific value functions, $V_t^k(\Omega_{it})$, $k \in \{0, 1\}$,

$$V_t(\Omega_{it}) = \max(V_t^0(\Omega_{it}), V_t^1(\Omega_{it})), \tag{2.45}$$

each of which obeys the Bellman equation

$$\begin{aligned} V_t^k(\Omega_{it}) &= U_{it}^k + \delta E[V_{t+1}(\Omega_{i,t+1}) \,|\, \Omega_{it}, s_{it} = k] \text{ for } t < T, \\ &= U_{iT}^k \text{ for } t = T. \end{aligned} \tag{2.46}$$

The expectation in equation 2.46 is taken over the distribution of the random components of the state space at $t + 1$ conditional on the state space elements at t, that is, over the unconditional joint distribution of the random shocks at $t + 1$, given that all shocks are mutually serially independent.

The latent variable in the dynamic case is the difference in alternative specific value functions, $V_t^1(\Omega_{it}) - V_t^0(\Omega_{it})$, namely

$$
\begin{aligned}
v_t^*(\Omega_{it}) &= Z_{it}\gamma_1 + \gamma_2 H_{it} - X_{it}\beta - \varepsilon_{it} + \eta_{it} \\
&\quad + \delta\{E[V_{t+1}(\Omega_{i,t+1}) \mid \Omega_{it}, s_{it} = 1] - E[V_{t+1}(\Omega_{i,t+1}) \mid \Omega_{it}, s_{it} = 0]\} \\
&= \xi_{it}^*(\Omega_{it}^-) + \xi_{it}.
\end{aligned}
\tag{2.47}
$$

When the latent variable function in the dynamic case (equation 2.47) is compared to that of the static case (equation 2.43), the only difference is the appearance of the difference in the future component of the expected value functions under the two alternatives in equation 2.47. A full solution of the dynamic programming problem consists of finding $E[\max(V_t^0(\Omega_{it}), V_t^1(\Omega_{it}))]$ at all values of Ω_{it}^-, denoted by $E\max(\Omega_{it}^-)$, for all $t = 1, \dots T$.

Estimation of the dynamic model requires that the researcher have data on the children's work experience, H_{it}. More generally, assume that the researcher has longitudinal data and denote t_{1i} and t_{Li} as the first and last periods of data observed for household i. In that case, the likelihood function is

$$
L(\theta; X_{it}) = \Pi_{i=1}^{i=I} \Pi_{\tau=t_{1i}}^{\tau=t_{Li}} \Pr(s_{i\tau} = 0, w_{i\tau} \mid \Omega_{it}^-)^{1 - s_{i\tau}} \Pr(s_{i\tau} = 1 \mid \Omega_{it}^-)^{s_{i\tau}},
$$

where

$$
\Pr(s_{i\tau} = 0, w_{i\tau} \mid \Omega_{it}^-) = \Pr(\xi_{i\tau} \geq -\xi_{i\tau}^*(\Omega_{i\tau}^-)),
$$
$$
\eta_{i\tau} = w_{i\tau} - Z_{i\tau}\gamma_1 - \gamma_2 H_{it}),
$$
$$
\Pr(s_{i\tau} = 1 \mid \Omega_{i\tau}^-) = 1 - \Pr(\xi_{i\tau} \geq -\xi_{i\tau}^*(\Omega_{i\tau}^-)).^{45}
$$

Identification requires the same exclusion restriction as in the static case, that is, the appearance of at least one variable in the wage equation, that is, in Z, that does not affect the utility value of school attendance, that is, does not appear in X. Work experience, H_{it}, would serve that role if it did not also enter into X_{it}. Note that the difference in the future component of the expected value functions under the two alternatives in equation 2.47 is a nonlinear function of the state variables, Z_{it}, H_{it}, and X_{it} and depends on the same set of parameters as in the static case. Equation 2.47 can be rewritten as

$$
v_t^*(\Omega_{it}) = Z_{it}\gamma_1 + \gamma_2 H_{it} - X_{it}\beta + \delta G(Z_{it}, H_{it}, X_{it}) - \varepsilon_{it} + \eta_{it},
\tag{2.48}
$$

where $G(\cdot)$ is the difference in the future component of the expected value functions; the nonlinearities in G that arise from the distributional and functional form assumptions may be sufficient to identify the discount factor. Estimation of the dynamic model is in principle no different from the estimation of the static model. The practical difference is that the dynamic programming problem must be solved at each iteration of the likelihood function, and the solution of the dynamic programming problem is often not analytic.

Analyzing the impact of the policy experiment of introducing the school attendance subsidy is not any different in the dynamic than in the static setting. If the critical value of ξ that determines the choice of working or attending school is $\xi_{i\tau}^*(\Omega_{i\tau}^-)$ without the subsidy, with the subsidy it is $\xi_{i\tau}^*(\Omega_{i\tau}^-) - \tau$. The increase in school attendance is thus $\Phi(\dfrac{-\xi_{i\tau}^*(\Omega_{i\tau}^-) + \tau}{\sigma_\xi}) - \Phi(\dfrac{-\xi_{i\tau}^*(\Omega_{i\tau}^-)}{\sigma_\xi})$, again highlighting the importance of having the necessary exclusion restrictions to identify σ_ξ.

The Multinomial Choice Problem
The dynamic analogue to the static multinomial choice problem is conceptually no different than it was for the binary choice problem. Indeed, it does not do much injustice to simply allow the number of mutually exclusive alternatives, and thus, the number of alternative-specific value functions in equation 2.45 to be greater than two. Analogously, if there are $K > 2$ mutually exclusive alternatives, there will be $K - 1$ latent variable functions (relative to one of the alternatives, arbitrarily chosen). The static multinomial choice problem raises computational issues with respect to the calculation of the likelihood function because its calculation requires multivariate integrations. Having to solve the dynamic multinomial choice problem, that is, for the E max one can use $(V^0(\Omega_{it}), V_t^1(\Omega_{it}), \dots, V_t^K(\Omega_{it}))$ function that enters the multinomial version of equation 2.45 at all values of Ω_{it}^- and at all t, adds significantly to that computational burden. A number of methods have been developed to ameliorate this burden (see Keane, Todd, and Wolpin, 2011, for a review). For example, Rust (1987) shows that in the case of additive errors that are distributed independent extreme value for each mutually exclusive alternative, the E max$_t$ functions have closed forms.

Unobserved Heterogeneity
The stochastic components of the model, preference, and wage shocks were assumed to be mutually serially uncorrelated. There is nothing that rules out general serial correlation other than computational feasibility in solving the dynamic programming problem and in estimating the model. A standard specification that allows for serial dependence,

conditional on observable state variables, assumes that agents can be distinguished, in terms of preferences and opportunities, by a fixed number of types. For example, if a household was of type j, the preference for school attendance might be specified as $\alpha_{ijt} = \alpha_{oj} + X_{it}\beta + \varepsilon_{it}$, and the child's wage offer as $w_{ijt} = \gamma_{oj} + Z_{it}\gamma_1 + \gamma_2 H_{it} + \eta_{it}$.[46] A type j household would be distinguished by the $(\alpha_{oj}, \gamma_{oj})$ pair. Thus, potentially, families who value child schooling more might also have children who are more (or less) productive in the labor market. The dynamic program, in this case, must be solved for each of the J types, and the likelihood function is a weighted average of the type-specific likelihoods. The weights are the proportions of each type in the sample and are estimated along with the other parameters.[47]

More Flexible Specifications
Estimable DCDP models are not nonparametrically identified (Rust, 1994) and usually fully parametrically specified.[48] However, any DCDP that can be numerically solved can, in principle, be estimated, and the DCDP structure does not restrict the choice of functional forms for preferences, technologies, and institutional constraints (e.g., tax rules), including the way in which unobservables enter (e.g., nonadditive errors, serial correlation), nor does it restrict the distributional assumptions of unobservables. The restrictions that are typically imposed arise from practical considerations, for example, about the size of the state space and the number of parameters that must be estimated, as well as from parameter identification.

Alternative Estimation Approaches
The main limiting factor in estimating DCDP models is the computational burden associated with the iterative process, regardless of whether estimation is by maximum likelihood or method of moments. It is therefore not surprising that there have been continuing efforts to reduce the computational burden of estimating DCDP models. Hotz and Miller (1993) developed a method for implementing DCDP models that does not involve solving the DP model, that is, calculating the $E \max(\Omega_{it}^-)$ functions. They prove that, for additive errors, the $E \max(\Omega_{it}^-)$ functions can be written solely as functions of conditional choice probabilities and state variables for any joint distribution of additive shocks. More recently, Imai, Jain, and Ching (2009) and Norets (2009) have developed computationally practical Bayesian approaches to the solution and estimation of DCDP models that rely on Markov Chain Monte Carlo (MCMC) methods.

2.2   Applications

2.2.1   Nonparametric *Ex Ante* Evaluation with the Matching Estimator

In this section, I report on two applications of the matching estimator to school attendance subsidy programs. Todd and Wolpin (2008) conducted an *ex ante* evaluation of the Mexican PROGRESA program, and Azevedo, Bouillon, and Yanez-Pagans (2009) evaluated the Mexican *Oportunidades* program (which replaced and extended PROGRESA).

The PROGRESA program, introduced in Mexico in 1998, provided transfers to households contingent on their children's regular school attendance.[49] To evaluate the impact of the program, the Mexican government conducted a randomized experiment: of 506 rural villages involved in the experiment, 320 were randomly assigned to receive the treatment and the remaining 186 to serve as controls. Eligibility of households residing in villages chosen to receive the treatment was based on a "marginality" index that depended on preprogram characteristics such as whether the home had a dirt floor, ownership of assets, household composition, and children's school attendance.

The subsidy schedule, as shown in table 2.1 for the first semester of the 1998/1999 academic year, depends on the child's grade level and gender.[50] The subsidy begins at grade 3 and extends through grade 9.

Table 2.1
Monthly School Attendance Subsidies

School Level	Grade	PROGRESA[a]		*Oportunidades*[b]	
		Girls	Boys	Girls	Boys
Primary	3	70	70	120	120
	4	80	80	140	140
	5	105	105	180	180
	6	135	135	240	240
Secondary	7	210	200	370	350
	8	235	210	410	370
	9	235	225	450	390
Upper Secondary	10	0	0	675	585
	11	0	0	715	630
	12	0	0	760	665

[a]Todd and Wolpin (2008).
[b]Azevedo, Bouillon, and Yanez-Pagans (2009).

The subsidy level increases with grade level, recognizing the higher opportunity cost of school attendance for older children (children are legally permitted to work in the formal labor market at age 12), and is slightly higher for girls at secondary school grades (grades 7–9), who traditionally have lower school enrollment rates at those grades. Overall, the transfers received by the treated households were substantial, amounting to about 20–25 percent of total annual income (Skoufias and Parker, 2000).

In addition to data on school attendance, which is necessary for the experimental evaluation, detailed information was also collected from all treatment and control village households on household demographics, school attainment of household members, household income, and employment and wages of children. Data were gathered in two baseline surveys, conducted in October 1997 and March 1998, and several follow-up surveys, in October 1998, May 1999, and November 1999. Supplemental data were also gathered at the village level, including distance to the nearest secondary school, distance to the nearest city, and a village-level minimum wage for day laborers. The experiment ran for 2 years, after which households in the control villages were incorporated into the program. Data were collected on both eligible and ineligible households in the village. There were approximately 9,000 households in the control villages and 15,000 in the treatment villages.

The PROGRESA program was renamed the *Oportunidades* program in 2002 and extended school attendance subsidies to urban areas and to upper secondary grade levels (grades 10–12). Unlike the PROGRESA program, the extension was not implemented experimentally. There were other differences as well. In the rural program, a census of the targeted villages was conducted, and all households that met the eligibility criteria for the program were informed of their eligibility status. For cost reasons this type of census was not feasible in urban areas, and an alternative system of advertised sign-up periods was adopted. Households that thought themselves potentially eligible had to apply at local offices that were placed in areas with high concentrations of poor households. Table 2.1 shows the subsidy schedule for the first semester of the 2006/2007 academic year. As seen, the schedule is similar in structure to the rural program, with the subsidy increasing with grade level and differing by gender in secondary and upper-secondary grades. The subsidy amounts differ in nominal terms, although they are similar after adjustment for changes in the national price level. A baseline survey had been conducted in the fall of 2002, just prior to the start of the program. The sample respondents consisted of eligible and ineligible households in the treatment areas and of households in nontreatment areas that would meet the eligibility criteria. Two additional rounds of data were collected in the fall of 2003 and 2004.

2.2.1.1 PROGRESA

Todd and Wolpin (2008) used a sample of children aged 12 to 15 in 1998 residing in *control* group villages who were reported to be children of the household head and for whom information was available in the 1997 and 1998 surveys. Household income was taken to be the sum of earned income of the children's parents, and the child wage was the reported village level minimum wage, which was taken as measuring the wage (offer) available to all children in the village. Both eligible and ineligible households were used in order to facilitate matching on household income. This information was available for roughly half the villages in the sample. The minimum monthly child wage ranged from 330 to 1,320 pesos, with a median of 550 pesos, and monthly household income from 8 to 13,750 pesos, with a median of 660 pesos. Todd and Wolpin (2008) estimated the impact of the PROGRESA subsidy program on school enrollment using two modeling frameworks previously discussed, one that treats each child in the household as a singleton and one that accounts for multiple children (exogenous fertility) in the household. The estimation method allows the school enrollment decision to potentially differ for girls and boys, which would accommodate, for example, differences in the utility that parents get from girls' and boys' schooling.

For the single-child model, the estimator of the predicted program effect is given by

$$\hat{\Delta}_s = \frac{1}{n} \sum_{\substack{j=1 \\ j,i \in Sp}}^{n} \{\hat{E}(s_i \mid w_i = w_j - \tau_j, y_i = y_j + \tau_j, g_i = g_j) - s_j(w_j, y_j, g_j)\},$$

where g_j denotes the child's gender and where τ_j is the subsidy level for which the child is eligible, which, as noted, varies by grade level. This estimator matches program-eligible control-group children with offered wage w_j and household income y_j to other (program-eligible and -ineligible) control group children with offered wage $w_j - \tau_j$ and

$y_i = y_j + \tau_j$, with the matches restricted to be between children of the same gender.

Expected school attendance, $\hat{E}(s_i \mid w_i = w_j - \tau_j, y_i = y_j + \tau_j, g_i = g_j)$, is estimated nonparametrically using a kernel regression estimator. With $w_0 = w_j - \tau_j$ and $y_0 = y_j + \tau$, the estimator is given by

$$\hat{E}(s_i \mid w_i = w_0, y_i = y_0, g_i = g_0) = \frac{\displaystyle\sum_{\substack{i=1 \\ i \in S_P}}^{n} s_i K\left(\frac{w_i - w_0}{\lambda_n^w}\right) K\left(\frac{y_i - y_0}{\lambda_n^y}\right) 1(g_i = g_0)}{\displaystyle\sum_{\substack{i=1 \\ i \in S_P}}^{n} K\left(\frac{w_i - w_0}{\lambda_n^w}\right) K\left(\frac{y_i - y_0}{\lambda_n^y}\right) 1(g_i = g_0)},$$

where $K(\cdot)$ denotes the kernel function and λ_n^w and λ_n^y are the smoothing (or bandwidth) parameters.[51]

The nonparametric estimator is defined only at points where the data density is positive. For this reason, estimation is restricted to points of evaluation that lie within the region S_P, where $S_P = \{(w, y) \in R^2\}$ such that $f(w, y) > 0)$ and $f(w, y)$ is the density. It was determined empirically whether a particular point of evaluation (w_0, y_0) lies in S_P by estimating the density at each point and checking whether it lies above a cutoff trimming level, q_α, that is small and positive, that is, whether $\hat{f}(w_0, y_0) > q_\alpha$, where $\hat{f}(\cdot, \cdot)$ is a nonparametric estimate of the density. The cutoff level q_α corresponds to the 2 percent quantile of the positive estimated density values.[52]

For the multiple-child case, Todd and Wolpin (2008) consider the potential earnings of all children in the household. If all the children within a household had the same subsidy levels and potential wages, the estimator for the program effect would be given by:

$$\hat{\Delta}_s = \frac{1}{n} \sum_{\substack{j=1 \\ j, i \in S_P}}^{n} \{\hat{E}(s_i \mid w_i = w_j - \tau_j, y_i = y_j + n\tau_j, n_i = n_j, g_i = g_j)$$

$$- s_j(w_j, y_j, n_j, g_j)\}, \tag{2.49}$$

where n_j denotes the number of children in child j's household and where matches are restricted to households with the same numbers of children. This estimator needs to be slightly modified to take into account that different children within the same household face different potential subsidies. To accommodate this feature, Todd and Wolpin (2008) estimate the program effect from

$$\hat{\Delta}_s = \frac{1}{n} \sum_{\substack{j=1 \\ j,i \in S_P}}^{n} \{\hat{E}(s_i \mid w_i = w_j - \bar{\tau}_j, y_i = y_j + n\bar{\tau}_j, n_i = n_j, g_i = g_j)$$
$$- s_j(w_j, y_j, n_j, g_j)\}.$$

where $\bar{\tau}_j$ is the average subsidy level of the children in the household. The child's wage offer, which is the village-level wage, does not vary for children within households.[53]

Table 2.2 reports program impacts using the matching estimator based on the single- and multiple-child models. Estimates are reported separately over three different age ranges by gender and for both girls and boys. The estimation results that combine boys and girls of different age ranges still restrict matches to be between children of the same gender and the same age bracket. That is, a girl aged 12–13 would only be matched to other girls in the same age range, even for the results that aggregate across categories.[54] The percentage of observations that lie within S_P is also shown.

As seen in table 2.2, all of the treatment effect estimates for both the single- and multiple-child models are positive, although nothing in the implementation of the matching estimator ensures that the estimated

Table 2.2
Ex Ante Impact of PROGRESA Subsidies on School Attendance by Age and Gender[a]

	Single-Child Model		Multiple-Child Model	
	Impact	% Overlapping Support	Impact	% Overlapping Support
Girls				
Age 12–13	0.01 (.03)[b]	87%	0.05 (.03)[b]	68%
Age 14–15	0.01 (.04)	83%	0.09 (.05)	61%
Age 12–15	0.06 (.03)	86%	0.06 (.03)	64%
Boys				
Age 12–13	0.06 (.03)	91%	0.04 (.04)	67%
Age 14–15	0.07 (.05)	89%	0.11 (.06)	68%
Age 12–15	0.06 (.03)	90%	0.07 (.04)	68%
Girls and Boys				
Age 12–13	0.04 (.02)	89%	0.04 (.03)	67%
Age 14–15	0.09 (.04)	86%	0.10 (.04)	64%
Age 12–15	0.06 (.02)	88%	0.07 (.02)	66%

[a]Todd and Wolpin (2008).
[b]Bootstrap standard errors in parentheses.

ex ante treatment effect will have that sign. Within-gender estimates, however, for a number of age ranges have 95 percent confidence intervals that span zero. Estimates that combine girls and boys have confidence intervals that, except in one case, do not span zero. The matching estimator implies that the PROGRESA program increased school attendance of girls aged 12–15 by 6 percentage points regardless of the model and that of boys aged 12–15 by 6 or 7 percentage points, depending on the model.

In considering the impact of any conditional cash transfer program, it is desirable to know to what extent the conditionality makes a difference and whether similar impacts might be achieved through unconditional transfers. Therefore, Todd and Wolpin (2008) used a matching estimator to determine whether giving families an unconditional income transfer in the amount of 5,000 pesos per year would significantly impact school enrollments, an amount almost half of parental income. Their estimates, based on matching households by parent income levels (households with income y and households with income $y + 5000$), indicate that the unconditional income transfer would not lead to any statistically significant impacts on school enrollment.

2.2.1.2 *Oportunidades*

Azevedo, Bouillon, and Yanez-Pagan (2009) implemented the matching estimator of the single-child model (equation 2.49) using data from a large biannual nationally representative household survey, the Mexican National Household Income and Expenditure Survey, rather than the much smaller data set collected as part of the *Oportunidades* program. The 2006 national data set contains over 9 million children aged 12–18 and identifies beneficiaries of the *Oportunidades* program. Moreover, unlike *Oportunidades* program data, which are mainly composed of poor households, the national data include a large sample of higher-income households as is useful for the matching procedure. Matching is conditioned on household size and on the number of children over age 14 but not on gender or age subbrackets. The sample consists of households that are not beneficiaries of the program; households in this sample that would be eligible for inclusion as beneficiaries are matched potentially to those that would not be eligible. The matching estimator implies that the *Oportunidades* program increased the school attendance rate of eligible 12- to 18-year-olds by 1.7 percentage points.[55]

Both Todd and Wolpin (2008) and Azevedo, Bouillon, and Yanez-Pagan (2009) performed counterfactual exercises of alternative subsidy schedules. These additional *ex ante* evaluations are discussed below. I first turn to a discussion of applications of the structural parametric approach.

2.2.2 Structural Parametric *Ex Ante* Evaluation

In this section, I report on two structural parametric evaluations of the PROGRESA school attendance subsidy program based on DCDP models, those by Todd and Wolpin (2006) and by Attanasio, Meghir, and Santiago (in press). Todd and Wolpin (2006) performed an *ex ante* evaluation using control group households, whereas Attanasio, Meghir, and Santiago (in press) conducted an *ex post* evaluation using both control and treatment group households. Both, however, performed *ex ante* evaluations of alterations in the program.

It is important to stress that although both papers adopt the DCDP approach, the models differed nontrivially in their structure. We present each of the models in some detail both to illustrate those differences and, for those not familiar with the estimation of DCDP models, to highlight implementation methods and their associated assumptions.

2.2.2.1 *The Todd and Wolpin Model*

The structure of the Todd and Wolpin (2006) model is an extended version of the models previously presented. In describing the model, I therefore forego writing the complete model equations to avoid additional notation. In the Todd and Wolpin model, in each year of their (known) finite lifetimes, a married couple decides on whether each of their children between the ages of 6 and 15 will attend school, remain at home, or, for those aged 12 to15, work in the labor market. These alternatives are assumed to be mutually exclusive. The couple also decide whether the wife will become pregnant in that period (while the woman is fecund).[56]

The couple receives flow utility in each period from consumption, from their current stock of children, from their children's current years of schooling (for example, the average years of schooling of their children, the number of children with 9 years of schooling), from the set of children at home by their ages and gender, and from the wife's pregnancy status. There are also preference interactions, for example, consumption is interacted with the number of children, the number of children at home, and their average schooling. To capture a quality-quantity tradeoff (Becker and Lewis, 1973; Rosenzweig and Wolpin, 1980), the number of children is interacted with average years of schooling completed. Additional interactions allow for complex choice dynamics. For example, the value the parents place on an older girl remaining at home may depend on the existence of pre-school-age children, and reentering school may entail a psychic cost. There is also a utility cost to attending school (grades 7–9) that depends on the distance from the village to a school. Households differ in their preferences over choice variables according to their discrete "type," and household preferences are subject to time-varying serially independent shocks.

Household income includes the income of both parents and the wage income of the children who work, both of which depend on the discrete household type and are subject to time-varying serially independent shocks. A child's wage (offer) also depends on the child's age and sex and the distance of the village to the nearest city. Attendance in school is not the same as grade completion. Grade progression is probabilistic, given attendance, and depends on the grade the child is attending, the child's age and gender, and the household type. In each period, household consumption is equal to household income.

It is useful to demonstrate the mechanisms through which the subsidy may have an effect, particularly because the estimation is conducted without recourse to data on the treatment villages. Consider the school attendance decision in the static model with household utility given by equation 2.40. As seen in that model, the introduction of a subsidy of τ increases the probability of school attendance by the same amount as would a reduction in the child wage together with an increase in household income by the same subsidy amount, τ. Absent an income effect, as in the utility specification equation 2.40 with $\beta = 0$, the subsidy effect could be identified solely from the wage effect, exactly as in the wage tax example. That is not the case in the Todd and Wolpin (2006) model, as there are several avenues through which there are income effects.[57]

First, utility is constant relative risk aversion CRRA in consumption, which in itself leads to an income effect. Second, although in the Todd and Wolpin (2006) specification consumption is separable from contemporaneous school attendance, it is not separable from past school attendance (years of schooling). A forward-looking model, as in Todd and Wolpin (2006), that implies that households that draw income from a distribution with a higher mean, for example, will also choose to send children to school more often; that is, there is a "permanent" income effect on school attendance. Given that the subsidy is multiperiod, a larger subsidy in every period will also increase school attendance through an income effect. To see this, consider a two-period perfect-foresight model, as previously discussed, in which the flow utilities in the two periods are:

$$U_2 = C_2 + \alpha s_2 + \gamma C_2 s_1 + \varepsilon_2 s_2,$$

$$U_1 = C_1 + \alpha s_1 + \varepsilon_1 s_1$$

The budget constraint in each period is $C_t = (y + \tau) + (w - \tau)s_t$, where both income and the child wage are assumed to be the same in both periods. Note that in this specification there will be no contemporaneous income effect on the choice of school attendance in either period. Thus, there is no income effect on period 2 school attendance. The period 1 choice is determined by comparing the discounted sum of utilities over the two periods under the two alternatives, which are given by

$$V_1(s_1 = 1) = (y + \tau) + \alpha + \varepsilon_1 + \delta \max\{(y + \tau)(1 + \gamma) + \alpha + \varepsilon_2, (y + w)(1 + \gamma)\},$$

$$V_1(s_1 = 0) = (y + w) + \delta \max\{(y + \tau) + \alpha + \varepsilon_2, y + w\}.$$

The difference, $V_1(s_1 = 1) - V_1(s_1 = 0)$, can take on any of four different forms depending on γ and ε_2. For example, if $\gamma < 0$, it is possible that when $s_1 = 1$ it is optimal to choose $s_2 = 1$, and when $s_1 = 0$, it is optimal to choose $s_2 = 0$. In that case, the decision rule in period 1 is

$$s_1 = 1 \text{ iff } -(w - \tau)(1 + \delta) + \delta \gamma(y + \tau) + \alpha(1 + \delta) + \varepsilon_1 + \delta \varepsilon_2 \geq 0$$
$$= 0 \text{ otherwise.}$$

Thus, with forward-looking behavior, $\delta > 0$, the effect of the subsidy on period 1 school attendance depends on household income (discounted one period). The conclusion can be shown to hold when there is imperfect foresight about future preferences, where ε_2 is not known in period 1 (see below).

In addition to income effects, the subsidy effect will not be equivalent to the wage effect alone whenever the subsidy itself also affects the school attendance decision. Recall that in the static model in which child leisure is added to household utility, the subsidy level affects the school attendance decision (see equation 2.39) differently than the child wage even if there is no income effect ($\beta = 0$). As this discussion shows, the utility specification can be quite general without requiring the use of treatment data to be able to perform the *ex ante* evaluation of introducing the attendance subsidy.[58] As already noted, and discussed in more detail below, control data alone are not sufficient if there is a direct utility effect of participating in the program.

The parameters of the Todd and Wolpin (2006) model are estimated by simulated maximum likelihood. The observed outcomes at each period are: (1) the choice (from the feasible set) made by the couple of whether or not to have a pregnancy, which children to send to school, which to work in the market, and which to remain at home; (2) the wages received by the children who work in the market; (3) the success or failure of those children who attend school to complete a grade level; and (4) parental income. The likelihood jointly incorporates the entire set of outcomes. Implementation requires additional assumptions. In particular, initial conditions at the time of marriage, the ages of marriage of both parents and the distances to the city and school, are assumed to be exogenous conditional on a household's type. For households observed in the first survey year (in 1997) that already have school-age children, the assumption of serial independence in the preference, child wage, and parent income shocks implies that the state variables at any time (for example, the stock of children, the average schooling of children) are also exogenous conditional on household type. Given that household type is unobserved, the likelihood function is a weighted average of the type-specific likelihoods. The weights, the type probabilities, are specified as derived from a multinomial logit in the state variables.[59] This procedure can be justified as an approximation to the type probability functions that would be the outcome of solving the dynamic programming problem back to the "true" initial period (say, the date of marriage) and using Bayes' rule to update the type probabilities given outcomes up to the first observation period of each household.[60] In addition, because the child wage shock is household specific, having an observation on the wage for two children in the same household working in the same period who have different wages (conditional on the relevant observable determinants of child earnings, child age, and sex) would lead to a degenerate likelihood. To avoid this degeneracy, Todd and Wolpin (2006) assume that the children's wages are measured with error.[61] As previously discussed, identification of the model parameters, in addition to functional form and distributional assumptions, requires an exclusion restriction, that there be at least one variable that affects the child wage that does not affect preferences. Todd and Wolpin (2006) assume that distance to the nearest city satisfies that restriction.

The model parameters enter the likelihood through the choice probabilities that are computed from the solution of the dynamic programming problem. Subsets of parameters enter through other structural relationships as well, such as child wage offer functions, the parents' income function, and the school failure probability function. The estimation procedure, maximizing the likelihood function, involves iterating between the solution of the dynamic program and the calculation of the likelihood.

The estimation sample consisted of landless nuclear households in which there was a woman under the age of 50 reported to be the spouse of the household head. Estimation was based on 1,316 households that were in the control villages. As of the October 1997 survey, there were 4,012 children born to these control households and 1,958 children between the ages of 6 and 15.[62] In estimating the model, to avoid a choice-based sampling problem, Todd and Wolpin (2006) used data on both program-eligible and -ineligible households as the eligibility criteria depended on the number of children attending school, a choice variable in the model.

As is standard practice in the DCDP literature, Todd and Wolpin (2006) compute goodness-of-fit statistics for a number of dimensions of the data. I report one such table because it illustrates the rationale for the seemingly complex specification of the utility function.[63] Table 2.3 compares the actual and predicted school attendance rates for children whose schooling attainment differs from their maximum potential, defined as the level they could have achieved had they enrolled at age 6 and attended school continuously without repeating grades. Note that school attendance rates fall precipitously as children aged 12 to 15

Table 2.3
Actual and Predicted School Attendance Rates by Number of Years Lagging Behind in School, Age 12–15[a]

	Boys			Girls		
Age	Actual	Predicted	χ^2	Actual	Predicted	χ^2
Not behind	88.3	82.1	8.50	83.8	78.2	6.02
Behind 1 year	79.8	76.4	1.56	75.4	74.5	0.09
Behind 2 years	65.8	62.5	0.91	52.9	51.0	0.20
Behind 3 years or more	49.1	51.7	0.62	44.7	42.7	0.39

$\chi^2(.05, 1) = 3.84$
[a]Todd and Wolpin (2006).

fall further behind in school, with the rate falling from 88.3 percent for boys who are not behind to 49.1 percent for boys 3 or more years behind. The decline predicted by the model is somewhat less steep, from 82.1 percent to 51.7 percent. The model fit is rejected for children not behind but not for children 1, 2, or 3 or more years behind. Without incorporating a utility cost of school reentry that varied with how much children deviated from their maximum potential schooling, the model would not have been able to mimic the patterns shown in table 2.3.[64]

This table illustrates another point. It is probably obvious that the utility function was not specified in its final form prior to beginning the estimation. In fact, the final specification was the outcome of a process of trial and error in which specifications were modified (many times) as the fit of the model was assessed. Thus, the final fit statistics reflect this data-mining process and cannot be taken as a pure indication of the validity of the model. My best guess is that all DCDP models mature in this way. Todd and Wolpin (2006) deal with this by using the treatment sample for out-of-sample validation. I defer discussion of this methodology, that is, of holding out a portion of the sample (in this case the entire treatment sample) for model validation, until the concluding section of this chapter.

2.2.2.2 The Attanasio, Meghir, and Santiago Model

The Attanasio, Meghir, and Santiago (2011) model differs in fundamental ways from the model in Todd and Wolpin (2006). Attanasio, Meghir, and Santiago (2011) consider the binary choice of school or work, excluding the "at home" option, and the decision about each child is considered independently of the other children in the household. Because the model differs from those considered in the previous discussion and the authors raise the issue of whether or not to hold out part of the sample, as in Todd and Wolpin (2006), I provide the details of the model specification. I maintain the variable notation previously used as much as possible.

Attanasio, Meghir, and Santiago (2011) specify the flow utility of a household associated with the school attendance of child i at age t as:

$$U_{it}^s = Y_{it}^s + \theta_s \tau_{it} D_{it} \tag{2.50}$$

$$Y_{it}^s = \mu_i^s + X_{it}\gamma^s + \psi^s S_{it} + Q_{1it}\varsigma_1 I(S_{it} \le 5) + Q_{2ij}\varsigma_2 I(6 \le S_{it} \le 8) + \varepsilon_{it}^s, \tag{2.51}$$

where Y_{it}^s, the net benefit of attending school (absent the subsidy) for child i at age t, is composed of a child-specific fixed factor μ_i^s, preference shifters (X_{it}), the current school attainment of the child (S_{it}), factors that affect the cost of attending primary school (Q_{1it}), factors that affect the cost of attending secondary school (Q_{2it}), child- and time-varying factors observable to the household but unobservable to the researcher, ε_{it}^s, and $I(\bullet)$ is the indicator function equal to one when the expression inside the parenthesis is true and equal to zero otherwise. Recall that τ_{it} is the subsidy amount, where the i subscript is included to capture the difference in the subsidy for children of different genders and where child age is implicitly treated as identical to grade level (which is what actually determines the subsidy amount). The school attendance subsidy, τ_{it}, affects the utility of school attendance for eligible households only in the treatment villages, with $D_{it} = 1$ denoting a treatment village and $D_{it} = 0$ denoting a control village

The flow utility from work is given by

$$U_{it}^w = Y_{it}^w + \theta_w w_{it} \tag{2.52}$$

$$Y_{it}^w = \mu_i^w + X_{it}\gamma^w + \psi^w S_{it} + \varepsilon_{it}^w, \tag{2.53}$$

where, in addition to the wage, w_{it}, the utility from working includes a child-specific fixed factor μ_i^w, preference factors (X_{it}), the current school attainment (S_{it}), and child- and time-varying factors observable to the household but unobservable to the researcher, ε_{it}^w. The unobservables, ε_{it}^s and ε_{it}^w, are assumed to be independently distributed extreme values. The child-specific fixed factor is modeled as discrete types.

It is instructive to consider the static version of the model. If $Y_{it}^s = \overline{Y_{it}^s} + \varepsilon_{it}^s$ and $Y_{it}^w = \overline{Y_{it}^w} + \varepsilon_{it}^w$, then the school attendance decision would be determined by

$$s_{it} = 1 \text{ iff } \varepsilon_{it}^s - \varepsilon_{it}^w \geq -(\overline{Y_{it}^s} - \overline{Y_{it}^w}) - \theta_s \tau_{it} D_{it} + \theta_w w_{it}$$
$$= 0 \text{ otherwise.} \tag{2.54}$$

Attanasio, Meghir, and Santiago (2011) stress the point that the model allows the effect of the subsidy θ_s to differ from the effect of the child wage, θ_w. They argue that θ_s cannot be identified without variation in $\tau_{it}D_{it}$, that is, without the treatment data, thus making it impossible to perform an *ex ante* evaluation of the introduction of the subsidy policy based solely on control group data.

Although the necessity of combining treatment and control data seems transparent from equation 2.54, the validity of that conclusion depends on the underlying constrained optimization problem of the household from which the attendance decision (equation 2.54) is derived. Consider the previous static model in which equation 2.40 is augmented to include a direct effect of the subsidy on household utility, that is, where utility is given by

$$U(C, s; \varepsilon) = \theta_w C + \alpha s + \beta Cs + \lambda \tau s + \varepsilon s.^{65} \tag{2.55}$$

The direct utility effect, as seen in equation 2.55, is λ per unit of subsidy. With the budget constraint under the subsidy given as $C = y + w(1 - s) + \tau s$, the school attendance decision is

$$s = 1 \text{ iff } \varepsilon \geq \theta_w w - \alpha - \beta y - (\theta_w + \beta + \lambda)\tau,$$
$$= 0 \text{ otherwise.} \tag{2.56}$$

It is easily seen that equation 2.56 is identical to equation 2.54 with $\beta y = \overline{Y_{it}^s} - \overline{Y_{it}^w}$ and $\theta_s = \theta_w + \beta + \lambda$, so the two models are observationally equivalent. The first thing to notice is that even if $\lambda = 0$, so that there is no direct utility effect of participating in the program, θ_s will not equal θ_w as long as $\beta \neq 0$, that is, as long as there is an income effect. In that case, if $\lambda = 0$, $\theta_s = \theta_w + \beta$ can in fact be identified using only control group data, for which $\tau_{it} D_{it} = 0$ given that θ_w and β are each identified.[66] Indeed, as previously shown, interpreting the Attanasio, Meghir, and Santiago (2011) model as above, *ex ante* evaluation can be conducted nonparametrically.

The second thing to notice is that the Attanasio, Meghir, and Santiago (2011) specification of the attendance decision (equation 2.54), even when using treatment group data, does not allow separate identification of β and λ. To obtain identification, the constrained optimization problem that corresponds to the specification of the alternative specific utility functions (equations 2.50–2.53) would need to be specified.[67] In that way, parameter restrictions, as in equation 2.56, can be exploited. Otherwise, the models with $\lambda = 0$ and $\lambda \neq 0$ are observationally equivalent, and estimation provides no evidence on the existence of a direct utility effect. Thus, although they are not explicit, by asserting that treatment data are necessary, Attanasio, Meghir, and Santiago (2011) are assuming that $\lambda \neq 0$. In their model, the need for treatment data would arise solely from the existence of a direct utility effect of participation.[68]

An important feature of the Attanasio, Meghir, and Santiago (2011) model, not incorporated by Todd and Wolpin (2006), is the inclusion of equilibrium effects of the subsidy program on the village-level child wage. Because eligible households are a significant proportion of the village population, the withdrawal of children from the labor market due to the subsidy program will tend to increase the equilibrium child wage in the village. This equilibrium effect on the wage will mitigate the impact of the subsidy program on school attendance. To estimate the impact of the program on the equilibrium wage, Attanasio, Meghir, and Santiago (2011) include a dummy variable in the wage function indicating whether a village was in the treatment sample. Given randomization of villages into treatment and control groups, the difference in their mean (offer) wages must be due to the equilibrium effects of the program. Evaluating the effect of the program involves including both the subsidy for school attendance and a concomitant increase in the child wage. However, the equilibrium effect that is estimated in this way is the effect only for the actual subsidy schedule implemented in the PROGRESA program.

To perform counterfactual exercises that change the subsidy schedule, one also needs to estimate how the child wage changes with the quantity of child labor; that is, one needs an estimate of the village-level demand for child labor. Attanasio, Meghir, and Santiago (2011) estimate the relative child-to-adult labor demand function using the random assignment of villages to treatment and control groups to generate exogenous variation in child labor supply.[69] A full-information estimation procedure, not pursued by Attanasio, Meghir, and Santiago (2011), would explicitly solve for the equilibrium wage in the estimation of the school attendance decision model, that is, aggregate the school attendance decisions that solve the optimization problem of each household in the village to calculate the supply of child labor and then find the wage that equates the supply and demand for child labor.[70]

The Attanasio, Meghir, and Santiago (2011) model is dynamic given that school attainment, that is, the accumulation of past school attendance decisions, directly affects alternative-specific utilities and also because the subsidy amount varies with grade level. The school/work decision is made at each age from 6 to 17, at which time there is a terminal payoff that depends on the number of years of schooling completed. Child wages are observed only for those who work. The (log) child wage offer received in each period depends on the child's education, age, the village-level minimum wage, and, as discussed above, the village's treatment status. Attanasio, Meghir, and Santiago (2011) also allow for failure; the probability of passing a grade given attendance depends on the grade level and the child's age.[71] The difference in independent extreme value preference errors is logistic; fixing the scale parameter of the logistic, the parameters represent normalized effects on utilities. The alternative specific value functions, taking into account the dynamics, are specified similarly to those already discussed.

Attanasio, Meghir, and Santiago (2011) follow a two-stage procedure in estimating the household decision model. In the first stage they estimate the wage offer function, using a Heckman two-step selectivity correction and the school failure probability function.[72] In the second stage they substitute the predicted wage obtained from the first stage into the flow utility function and take the parameters of the failure probability function as given in solving the dynamic programming problem. The implicit assumption in making this predicted wage substitution is that the stochastic component of the wage offer is observed only after the school/work decision has been made.[73] The extreme value error assumption implies that the DP problem as well as the choice probability have closed-form representations (Rust, 1987). Attanasio, Meghir, and Santiago (2011) deal with the initial conditions problem, that is, that years of schooling completed, the outcome of prior school attendance decisions, is related to the child-specific fixed factor $(\mu_i^s - \mu_i^w)$, by positing an ordered probit as governing the determination of preprogram years of schooling that also includes the child-specific fixed factors.[74] As in Todd and Wolpin (2006), this procedure can be justified as an approximation to the probability distribution of accumulated schooling that would be the outcome of solving the dynamic programming problem back to the "true" initial period (say, the date at which the firstborn child is age 6, the school entry age) and then integrating school attendance decisions up to the first observation period.

2.2.2.3 Results

Table 2.4 presents the estimated impacts of the PROGRESA subsidy on attendance rates for the two Todd and Wolpin papers and for the Attanasio, Meghir, and Santiago paper. The Todd and Wolpin (2006, 2008) papers are *ex ante* evaluations (out-of-sample predictions), whereas the Attanasio, Meghir, and Santiago (2011) paper is an *ex post* evaluation (within-sample prediction). The estimates in Todd and Wolpin (2006) are calculated as the difference in the predicted attendance rate of the control observations if they had been given the PROGRESA subsidy schedule (out-of-sample prediction) and the predicted attendance rate of the control observations with no subsidy (within-sample prediction). Attanasio, Meghir, and Santiago (2011) calculate the difference between

Table 2.4
The Predicted and Experimental Effect of the PROGRESA Subsidy Policy on School
Attendance Rates of Children Aged 12–15

	Boys		Girls	
	Predicted	Experimental	Predicted	Experimental
Todd and Wolpin (2008): S-NP[1]				
Single child	0.056	0.033	0.060	0.090
Multiple children	0.059		0.070	
Todd and Wolpin (2006): S-P	0.077	0.038	0.064	0.080
Attanasio, Meghir, and Santiago: S-P	0.065[a]	0.056	na	na

[a]This number is not reported in Attanasio, Meghir, and Santiago but is calculated by the author from a figure showing the impacts by single ages and taking a simple average.

the predicted attendance rate of the treatment observations with the subsidy (within-sample prediction) and the predicted attendance rate of the treatment observations with no subsidy (equivalent, given randomization, to the within-sample prediction of the control observations). Table 2.4 also shows the actual impacts obtained from the experiment, which differ across the papers as a result of the different samples used in estimation. For Todd and Wolpin (2006) the comparison of the predicted and experimental effect constitutes an external validation, whereas for Attanasio, Meghir, and Santiago (2011) the comparison demonstrates within-sample fit.

As seen from the table, the difference between the predicted and experimental effects for boys is somewhat smaller for Attanasio, Meghir, and Santiago (2011) than for Todd and Wolpin (2008) and Todd and Wolpin (2006), both absolutely and proportionally. Attanasio, Meghir, and Santiago (2011) do not report estimates for girls, but the difference for girls in both Todd and Wolpin (2006, 2008) papers is about the same as that for boys in the Attanasio, Meghir, and Santiago (2011) paper. One would expect Attanasio, Meghir, and Santiago (2011) to do better because the experimental treatment effect is in the data they use in estimation, whereas that is not the case for Todd and Wolpin (2008) or Todd and Wolpin (2006). Indeed, the model specification in Attanasio, Meghir, and Santiago (2011), except for functional form and distributional assumptions, provides a direct estimate of the subsidy effect from the treatment and control observations.

2.2.2.4 Alternative Policies

Designing an optimal subsidy scheme to achieve some desired increase in schooling requires knowledge of the effects of alternative subsidy schedules on take-up rates. As noted earlier, a limitation of experiments is that they do not typically provide a reliable way of extrapolating to learn about effects of counterfactual policies. Although a small change in the subsidy schedule might be well approximated by a simple extrapolation of the experimental treatment effect, it is unclear on what basis extrapolations of more radical changes would be made.

Attanasio, Meghir, and Santiago (2011) and Todd and Wolpin (2006, 2008) simulated the effect of alternative policies. Attanasio, Meghir, and Santiago (2011) and Todd and Wolpin (2008) reported results for attendance rates. Todd and Wolpin(2006) also solved the optimization problem for each household over their entire life cycle, including a fertility decision at each point in time, and calculated the completed schooling of all of the children ever born.[75] The results reported by Todd and Wolpin (2006) of implementing alternative policies are shown in table 2.5. As the first column shows, the model predicts, based on simulations of households from the time of marriage until the lastborn child reaches age 16, that the average years of completed schooling in the absence of the program would be 6.29 for girls and 6.42 for boys and that 19.8 percent of girls and 22.8 percent of boys would have completed the ninth grade. The first counterfactual (column 2), the perfect enforcement of a compulsory school attendance law, establishes a maximal potential program impact. Given predicted failure rates (which are lower for girls), average completed schooling would be at most 8.37 years for girls and 8.29 for boys. The next column shows the predicted effects of the PROGRESA subsidy schedule. The model predicts an increase in completed schooling of about one-half year for both boys and girls, or 26.0 percent of the maximal potential increase for girls and 28.9 percent for boys. The last row of the table reports the per-family government budgetary cost of the program over the lifetime of the families in the sample, that is, from the woman's age at marriage to age 59. The model predicts that cost per family to be 26,000 (1997) pesos.

As noted, the PROGRESA subsidy schedule rewards school attendance starting at grade 3. However, attendance in grades 3–5 is almost universal, making this aspect of the program essentially a pure income transfer. Todd and Wolpin (2006) calculated that the per-family cost of the program could be held roughly constant if the subsidy in grades 3–5 were eliminated and the subsidy in grades 6–9 were increased by

Table 2.5
The Effectiveness and Cost of Alternative Education Policies: SP Estimation[a]

	Baseline	Compulsory Attendance	Original Subsidy	Modified Subsidy	Bonus for Completing Grade 9	Build Schools	Income Transfer (5,000 pesos/yr)	Subsidy + 25% Increase in Child Wage
Mean Completed Schooling								
Girls	5.29	8.37	6.83	6.97	6.50	6.39	6.41	6.75
Boys	6.42	8.29	6.96	7.07	6.58	6.55	6.53	6.79
Cost per Family	0	?	26,096	25,193	36,976	?	237,000	25,250

[a]Todd and Wolpin (2006).

about 45 percent. Column 4 shows that the cost of the grade 3–5 subsidy in terms of forgone completed schooling would be 0.14 years for girls and 0.11 years for boys. Moreover, under the modified plan, the proportion of girls completing ninth grade would increase by 3.4 percentage points, and the proportion of boys by 3.8 percentage points, although there would also be a small decline in the proportion of children who complete at least the sixth grade.

An alternative subsidy scheme would reward grade completion rather than attendance. As the next column in table 2.5 shows, the impact of a ninth-grade graduation bonus of 30,000 pesos would have a relatively small impact on average schooling, 0.21 years for boys and 0.26 years for girls. In fact, the increase in average schooling is not as large as the effect of the original subsidy even though the cost of the bonus program is about 40 percent higher.[76]

Todd and Wolpin (2006) also simulate the effect of building a grade 7–9 school in each village where its absence is indicated by setting to zero the distance of such a school from the village. As seen in table 2.5, this intervention would raise mean schooling by 0.10 years for boys and 0.13 for girls. They also simulate the impact of a pure income transfer program, one that pays 5,000 pesos per year to families without any school attendance requirement.[77] Under that policy, mean schooling would increase by a little over 0.20 years for both genders. However, that increase in schooling is only about 20 percent as large as the original attendance-based subsidy. Moreover, its cost per family is an order of magnitude larger.

Attanasio, Meghir, and Santiago (2011) performed two similar counterfactuals. As in Todd and Wolpin (2006), (1) they simulated the impact of eliminating the subsidy to primary school and redistributing the savings to increase the subsidies at later grades, and (2) they simulated the impact of building schools.[78] As did Todd and Wolpin (2006), they found the effect of the first experiment to be large. The modified program would increase school attendance rates of boys from 0.065 to 0.106, an increase of about 70 percent.[79] Attanasio, Meghir, and Santiago (2011) found a modest effect of building schools relative to the first experiment, as did Todd and Wolpin (2006). The similarity of the findings between these studies in both experiments is perhaps surprising given the very significant differences between the model structures and estimation samples.

As discussed, Attanasio, Meghir, and Santiago (2011) accounted for general equilibrium effects on the child wage. They found that the child wage increased 6 percent due to the withdrawal of child labor induced by the PROGRESA school attendance subsidy. Attanasio, Meghir, and Santiago (2011) report the effect of taking into account the increased child wage as only minimally reducing the impact of the program on school attendance. Todd and Wolpin (2006), having estimated the treatment effect assuming no general equilibrium effects, performed a counterfactual experiment, as shown in the last column of table 2.5, in which the wage was increased by 25 percent, four times the increase estimated by Attanasio, Meghir, and Santiago (2011). Todd and Wolpin (2006) find the increase in completed school would be 85 percent of the partial equilibrium effect of the original subsidy for girls and 69 percent for boys.[80]

Todd and Wolpin (2006, 2008) and Attanasio, Meghir, and Santiago (2011) performed the identical counterfactual policy experiment of doubling the subsidy at all grades.[81] The first column of table 2.6 repeats the results from table 2.4 showing the predicted effect of the actual subsidy on the attendance rate of 12- to 15-year-olds (by gender). As seen in column 2 of the table, three of the predictions are remarkably close, particularly given the different behavioral models, estimation samples, and estimation methods: the single-child matching estimator in Todd and Wolpin (2008) implies that doubling the subsidy would increase the attendance rate for boys by a factor of 2.08, the estimate from the DCDP model of Todd and Wolpin (2006) implies an increase by a factor of 2.06, and the DCDP model of Attanasio, Meghir, and Santiago (2011) an increase by a factor of 1.87. The multiple-child

Table 2.6
The Predicted Effect of Doubling the PROGRESA Subsidy on School Attendance Rates of Children Aged 12–15

	Boys		Girls	
	1 × Subsidy	2 × Subsidy	1 × Subsidy	2 × Subsidy
Todd and Wolpin (2008): S-NP[1]				
Single child	0.056	0.116	0.060	0.141
Multiple children	0.059	0.078	0.070	0.089
Todd and Wolpin (2006): S-P	0.077	0.159	0.064	0.146
Attanasio, Meghir, and Santiago: S-P	0.070	0.131	na	na

matching estimate of Todd and Wolpin (2008), on the other hand, implies an increase by a factor only of 1.32. Of course, the closeness of the three estimates does not by itself imply that they provide a more accurate prediction.[82]

In assessing the value of the DCDP structural approach, it is useful to recall the finding in both papers about the effect on schooling of a budget-neutral shift in resources toward the higher grades. That such a shift would increase schooling overall must be true from the fact that the attendance up to grade 5 is essentially universal without the subsidy. However, it is not possible to determine the impact quantitatively from the experiment alone. A policy maker with limited resources could not make an informed decision about whether to continue the subsidy to the lower grades, given its redistributive function, without knowing its quantitative tradeoff with forgone schooling. The structural approach permits a quantitative cost–benefit analysis of alternative programs without having to conduct costly field experiments.

2.3   Is the Use of Holdout Samples for Validation and/or Model Selection Justified?

Should one have a stronger belief in the predictions of the counterfactual experiments from the Todd and Wolpin (2006, 2008) studies as opposed to the Attanasio, Meghir, and Santiago (2011) study because the Todd and Wolpin studies used a holdout sample for external validation? Additionally, how should a policy maker come up with an estimate of the effect of doubling the subsidy based on the four estimates? The first question can be thought of as one of model validation and the second one of model selection. Schorfheide and Wolpin (2011) present a formal framework within which these questions can be rigorously addressed.

Let me first, however, provide some background discussion.[83] One goal of empirical research is to provide evidence on the validity of decision-theoretic models that describe the behavior of economic agents. There are two approaches to this endeavor that stem from different epistemological perspectives. The first stems from a view that there exists a "true" decision-theoretic model from which observed data are generated. This leads naturally to a model validation strategy based on testing the validity of the behavioral implications (and possibly the assumptions) of the model and/or testing the fit of the model to the data. A model is not deemed invalid if it is not rejected in such tests according to some statistical criterion. Rejected models are deemed invalid and discarded, although they may serve as building blocks for more refined models.

The second approach stems from a pragmatic view in which it is assumed that all models are necessarily simplifications of actual decision-making behavior. Hypothesis testing as a means of model validation or selection is eschewed because, given enough data, all models would be rejected as true models. There is no true decision-theoretic model—only models that perform better or worse than other models in addressing particular questions. Models should be chosen that are "best" for some specific purpose, and alternative models may be valid for different purposes.

Decision-theoretic models are typically designed and estimated with the goal of predicting the impact on economic agents of changes in the economic environment. Thus, one criterion for model validation/selection that fits within the *pragmatic view* is to examine a model's predictive (out-of-sample) accuracy, that is, how successful the model is at predicting outcomes of interest within the particular context for which the model was designed. In contrast, in the *absolutist view*, a model would be considered useful for prediction only if it were not rejected, despite the fact that nonrejection does not necessarily imply that predicted effects will be close to actual effects. Nor will nonrejected models necessarily outperform rejected models in terms of their (context-specific) predictive accuracy.

A particularly challenging use of decision-theoretic models is to forecast the impact of large changes in the environment. Often, these changes are related to policy interventions that are outside of the scope of current policies, such as the PROGRESA program. A good in-sample fit or nonrejection of a model's implication is unlikely, in itself, to give us much confidence in its forecasting ability in such contexts. This problem arises because of the common practice of using the same data both for estimation and for model development, that is, the ubiquitous and unavoidable practice of data-mining.

The idea for using a holdout sample, as in Todd and Wolpin (2006, 2008), is that if a model can provide a good forecast for a holdout sample that faces a policy regime well outside the support of the data (and that is not used in model formulation), then we should gain confidence that it can provide a good forecast of impacts of other policy changes along the same dimension (such as the doubling of the PRO-

GRESA subsidy) or perhaps even other dimensions (such as a gradua-tion bonus rather than an attendance subsidy).[84]

Among the earliest uses of a randomized social experiment for the purpose of model validation and selection is that by Wise (1985). Wise exploited a housing subsidy experiment to evaluate a model of housing demand. In the experiment, families that met an income eligibility criterion were randomly assigned to control and treatment groups. The latter were offered a rent subsidy. The model was estimated using only control group data and was used to forecast the impact of the program on the treatment group. The forecast was compared to its actual impact. In addition to Todd and Wolpin (2006, 2008), recent examples of this approach to validation, within a randomized controlled experimental design, include Bourgignon, Ferreira, and Leite (2003), Lise, Seitz, and Smith (2003), and Duflo, Rema, and Ryan (2012).

McFadden et al. (1977) provides an early example in which a large regime shift in a nonexperimental setting is exploited. McFadden esti-mated a random utility model (RUM) of travel demand before the introduction of the Bay Area Rapid Transit (BART) system, obtained a forecast of usage, and then compared the forecast to actual usage after BART's introduction. McFadden's model validation treats pre-BART observations as the estimation sample and post-BART observations as the validation sample.

McFadden did not purposefully hold out the post-BART data; the point of the analysis was to forecast usage prior to BART having been built. A number of later papers have mimicked that validation design by purposefully holding out a part of the sample. Lumsdaine, Stock, and Wise (1992) estimated a model of retirement behavior of workers in a single firm who were observed before and after the introduction of a temporary 1-year pension window. They estimated several models on data before the window was introduced and compared the forecast of the impact of the pension window on retirement based on each estimated model to the actual impact as a means of model validation and selection. Keane and Moffitt (1998) estimated a model of labor supply and welfare program participation using data after federal leg-islation (Omnibus Budget Reconciliation Act , 1981) that significantly changed the program rules. They used the model to predict behavior prior to that policy change. Keane (1995) used the same model to predict the impact of planned expansions of the Earned Income Tax Credit in 1994–1996. Keane and Wolpin (2007) estimated a DCDP model of welfare take-up (along with choices about schooling, fertility, marriage, and work) using a set of five states, with medium to high welfare generosity, and validated the model based on the forecasts of those choices in a low-welfare state. Cohen-Goldner and Eckstein (2010) estimate a model of the assimilation of female immigrants to Israel from the former Soviet Union using data from the first 5 years of Israeli residence and validate the model using 10 years of data from samples not used in estimation. Kaboski and Townsend (2011) structurally estimated a model of credit-constrained households deciding on consumption, indivisible investment, and savings. They estimated the model using data collected prior to the introduction of a large-scale government microfinance program, the Thai Million Baht Village Fund Program, and then validated the model using postprogram data.

The common and essential element in all of these validation exercises, regardless of whether they are based on randomized experiments or whether the researcher has chosen a nonrandom holdout sample, is the existence of some form of regime change radical enough to provide a degree of distance between the estimation and validation samples.[85] The more different the regimes, the less likely are forecasted and actual behavior in the validation sample to be close purely by chance. Although this latter statement is true, it does not in itself justify the loss of observations in the estimation sample.

Because the work reported by Schorfheide and Wolpin (2011) is a work in progress, I provide only a very brief discussion. Schorfheide and Wolpin (2011) consider the following problem of a policy maker who has run an experiment, like PROGRESA. The policy maker recognizes that the experiment provides an estimate only of the impact of the specific experimental policy, for example, the impact of the original PROGRESA subsidy schedule. But, the policy maker would like to know what would have happened had a different subsidy level been chosen, for example, had it been doubled, or if the gradient of the subsidy with grade level had been different. The policy maker also realizes that there are researchers who have different models that can be used to extrapolate effects to these alternative policies. For concreteness, the policy maker is going to decide whether or not to double the size of the subsidy when the program is implemented.

The policy maker would like to be able to assess the relative validity of different models in deciding which estimate to use or how to combine the estimates. From a Bayesian perspective, the best the policy maker can do is to give researchers all of the data from the experiment, from both the treatment and controls, and evaluate the models on the basis of the marginal likelihood of attendance. The policy maker can then model average to calculate the effect of doubling the subsidy. The policy maker, however, recognizes that the researchers may data mine and not truthfully report their marginal likelihoods.

The policy maker has the option of holding out part of the data, for example, giving researchers only the control group data, as opposed to giving the researcher all of the data from both groups. If the policy maker holds out part of the sample, then the policy maker would request from researchers the predicted likelihood for the holdout sample and the predicted density for the treatment effect. Note that the policy maker knows the actual distribution of attendance in the holdout sample and the average treatment effect based on all of the data. Schorfheide and Wolpin (2011) represent data mining by the researcher who is given data from both groups as data-based modification of the researcher's prior distribution of the subsidy effect. In this way, the researcher is able to increase the marginal likelihood that is reported to the policy maker. If the policy maker gives the researcher only the control data, then the researcher cannot data mine. Schorfheide and Wolpin (2011) show by simulation that there are circumstances in which the policy maker with a quadratic loss function would be better off by providing only data from the control sample.

3   The Limits of Inference without Theory

3.1   The Role of Theory in Econometric Specification

3.1.1   The Effect of Unemployment Compensation on the Duration of Unemployment

3.1.1.1   Background

In 1977, the *Industrial and Labor Relations Review* (*ILRR*) published a conference volume, "The Economics of Unemployment Insurance: A Symposium." The purpose of the volume was to gather together papers that would evaluate the extent to which the unemployment insurance (UI) system affects labor market behavior. Four of the papers were original empirical studies attempting to provide quantitative estimates of the effect of UI benefit generosity on the search behavior of the unemployed (Classen, 1977; Ehrenberg and Oaxaca, 1977; Holen, 1977; Burgess and Kingston, 1976), one of the papers surveyed the empirical literature on that question (Welch, 1977), and one provided a theoretical model for interpreting the estimates from the empirical literature (Mortensen, 1977).[1] According to the editor's introduction to the volume, the empirical contributions were founded on "recent job search theories," that is, on the (then new) sequential job search model of McCall (1970) and Mortensen (1970).

In the classification scheme I have adopted, these empirical papers would be considered quasi-structural in the sense that the parameters of the estimating equations, which are (approximations of) decision outcomes, are functions of the underlying parameters of the optimization problem. Since that symposium, there have been dozens of quasi-structural papers addressing the same question, either implicitly or explicitly based on the sequential search model (or its extensions). Over time the statistical procedures used in estimation have been improved. However, the basic specification of the relationship between search outcomes, the duration of unemployment in particular, and their determinants has not been altered. That commonality, of course, would be appropriate had the connection between the theory and the empirical specification been unassailable from the beginning. However, that was not the case then, and, unfortunately, it is not the case now.

Given the development of estimation methods for discrete choice dynamic programming (DCDP) models, it was natural that the sequential job search model would be structurally implemented. Structural estimation of the standard nonstationary partial equilibrium job search model was first considered by Wolpin (1987) and van den Berg (1990) and later extended beyond the standard model.[2] Examples include Stern (1989), who allowed for simultaneous search, that is, for the submission of multiple job applications in a period; Blau (1991), who dropped the assumption of wealth maximization, allowing for job offers to include not only a wage offer but also an hours offer; Ferrall (1997), who modeled search accounting for all of the rules of the Canadian UI system; Gemici (2007), who considered the joint husband and wife search-migration decision in an intra-household bargaining framework; and Paserman (2008), who adopted a behavioral approach and allowed for hyperbolic discounting. The standard search model has also been extended beyond the consideration of the single transition from unemployment to employment. Wolpin (1992) incorporated job-to-job transitions and both involuntary and voluntary transitions into unemployment.[3] Rendon (2006) allowed for a savings decision in a setting where agents can also transit, both through quits and layoffs, from employment to unemployment.[4] Both of these latter papers also allowed for wage growth with the accumulation of work experience, employer-specific (tenure) in the case of Rendon (2006) and both general and employer-specific in the case of Wolpin (1992).

The standard job search model assumes that *ex ante* identical workers may receive different wage offers or, analogously, that the same unemployed worker may receive different offers over time. Diamond (1971) showed that with the assumptions of the standard job search model, in a game in which firms are aware of worker search strategies, the wage offer distribution will be degenerate at the worker's reservation wage or outside option. This result led to the development of models in which wage dispersion could be rationalized as an equilibrium outcome, which in turn led to a structural empirical literature. The empirical literature has focused on two kinds of models, those based on a search-matching-bargaining approach to wage determination (Diamond and Maskin, 1979; Mortensen, 1982; Wolinsky, 1987) and those based on wage posting by firms that gain monopsony power through search frictions (Albrecht and Axell, 1984; Burdett and Mortensen, 1998). These models not only rationalized wage dispersion but also allowed for quantification and policy analyses in an equilibrium setting, for example, for changes in UI benefits or changes in the level of the minimum wage.

The empirical implementation of equilibrium search models has become a major strand of the structural job search literature. Embedded within those models are different variants of the standard partial equilibrium search model, and, in that sense, the development of the DCDP estimation approach was an important precursor. That literature is instructive in terms of empirical methods. The empirical literature on estimating equilibrium search models began with the implementation of the wage-posting model; Eckstein and Wolpin (1990) implemented the Albrecht and Axell (1984) model, followed by a number of papers based on the Burdett and Mortensen (1998) model. Without going into details about them individually, the hallmark of those papers was the development of theoretical extensions of the Burdett and Mortensen (1998) model, incorporating more realistic features of the labor market that went hand in hand with the empirical implementation. These papers include contributions by Kiefer and Neumann (1993), van den Berg and Ridder (1998), Bontemps, Robin, and van den Berg (1999, 2000), Bowlus, Kiefer, and Neumann (2001), and Postel-Vinay and Robin (2002). Papers based on search-matching-bargaining models include, among others, Eckstein and Wolpin (1995), Cahuc, Postel-Vinay, and Robin (2006), and Flinn (2006). The papers that have resulted from the equilibrium search enterprise in structural estimation demonstrate the best examples of combining theory, econometrics, and data to produce empirical results that are policy relevant and that have the potential to fundamentally alter our view of the working of the labor market.[5]

As I have noted, the conventional empirical specification in the quasi-structural literature, although putatively based on the standard search model, has not been faithful to the theory. To demonstrate the possible consequences of that failure, and to make the discussion self-contained, I begin with a brief review of the standard search model.[6]

3.1.1.2   The Standard Discrete-Time Job Search Model

In the discrete-time formulation, an unemployed individual receives a job offer in each period with probability q. Wage offers are drawn from the known cumulative distribution function, $F(w)$. An accepted job offer and its associated wage are permanent. While unemployed, an individual receives unemployment benefits, which, net of the cost of search, is denoted by b. The individual is assumed to maximize the present discounted value of net income. We consider both infinite and finite horizon models, which have somewhat different empirical implications, and implications for the identification of model parameters.

Infinite Horizon Model

The value of a wage offer of w, given a discount factor of $\delta(=\dfrac{1}{1+r})$, is

$$W(w) = w + \delta w + \delta^2 w + \ldots = \frac{w}{1-\delta}.$$

In any period, the value of continuing to search, V, either because an offer was rejected or because an offer was not received, consists of the current period payoff (unemployment benefits net of the cost of search), b, plus the discounted expected value of waiting another period. In that case, if an offer is received, with probability q, the individual chooses between the maximum of the value of working at a wage w, $W(w)$, and the value of continuing to search, V. If no offer is received, which occurs with probability $1 - q$, the individual must continue to search. Thus, the alternative-specific value function, the Bellman equation, for the search decision is

$$V = b + \delta[qE\max(W(w), V) + (1-q)V].$$

Rearranging yields

$$V(1-\delta) = b + \delta qE\max(W(w) - V, 0),$$

which has a unique solution for $V > 0$ as long as the cost of search is not so large as to make the right-hand side negative.[7] Defining w^*, the reservation wage, to be the wage offer that equates the value of search and the value of accepting the job, that is, $w^* = (1 - \delta)V$, a little further algebra yields the following implicit equation for the reservation wage (which must have a unique solution given that V does):

$$w^* = b + \frac{q}{r}\int_{w^*}^{\infty}(w - w^*)dF(w).[8] \tag{3.1}$$

Thus, the reservation wage is a function of b, $\frac{q}{r}$, and $F(w)$:

$$w^* = w^*(b, \tfrac{q}{r}, F). \tag{3.2}$$

The individual accepts any wage offer that exceeds the reservation wage and declines offers otherwise.

Although the reservation wage is a deterministic function, the length of an unemployment spell is stochastic because the timing and level of wage offers are probabilistic. Thus, measures of the outcomes of search, such as the duration of unemployment spells and the level of accepted wages, are probabilistic. In particular, the survivor function, the probability that the duration of unemployment is at least as large as some given length, is

$$\Pr(T_u \geq t_u) = [qF(w^*) + (1-q)]^{t_u} = [1 - q(1 - F(w^*))]^{t_u}. \tag{3.3}$$

The term inside the brackets in equation 3.3 is the probability of receiving an offer in a period and rejecting it (because it is below the reservation wage) plus the probability of not receiving an offer. The *cdf, pdf,* and hazard function are:

$$cdf : \Pr(T_u < t_u) = 1 - [1 - q(1 - F(w^*))]^{t_u},$$

$$pdf : \Pr(T_u = t_u) = [1 - q(1 - F(w^*))]^{t_u} q(1 - F(w^*))$$

$$Hazard Function : \Pr(T_u = t_u \mid T_u \geq t_u) = \frac{\Pr(T_u = t_u)}{\Pr(T_u \geq t_u)} = q(1 - F(w^*)) = h.$$

The survivor function, the *cdf*, and the *pdf* can all be written as functions of the hazard rate, the exit rate from unemployment conditional on not having previously exited. As seen, the hazard rate is constant. Thus, in a homogeneous population, the infinite horizon search model implies the absence of duration dependence.

Given parameter values, mean duration is given by

$$E(t_u) = \sum_0^{\infty} t_u \Pr(T_u = t_u)$$

$$= q(1 - F(w^*))^{-1} = \frac{1}{h}.$$

Notice that mean duration is simply the reciprocal of the hazard rate.[9] Likewise, the mean of the accepted wage is

$$E(w \mid w \geq w^*) = \int_{w^*}^{\infty} \frac{w}{1 - F(w^*)} \, dF(w),$$

which clearly is larger than the mean of the wage offer distribution.[10]

In addition to implying a constant hazard rate, the infinite horizon model has predictions about the impact of changes in $b, \frac{q}{r}$, and $F(w)$ on the reservation wage, on the hazard rate, and on the moments of the accepted wage distribution. It thus is, in principle, possible to test the theory. Comparative static effects of the hazard rate (and thus mean duration) with respect to its arguments are given by (see Mortensen, 1986):

$$\frac{dh}{db} = -\lambda f(w^*) \left(\frac{1}{1+h/r} \right) < 0,$$

$$\frac{dh}{dq} = -f(w^*) \left(\frac{w^* - b}{1+h/r} \right) + \left(1 - F(w^*)\right) \gtrless 0,$$

$$\frac{dh}{d\mu} = -qf(w^*) \left(\frac{h/r}{1+h/r} \right) > 0,$$

$$\frac{dh}{ds} = -qf(w^*) \left(\frac{(\lambda/r)\int_0^{w^*} F_s(w,s)dw}{1+h/r} \right) < 0.$$

An increase in the level of unemployment compensation benefits increases the reservation wage and reduces the unemployment hazard rate. An increase in the offer probability has an ambiguous effect: it increases the reservation wage, which reduces the hazard rate, but also directly increases the hazard rate through the higher offer probability.[11] Increasing the mean of the wage offer distribution, μ, increases the hazard rate; although an increase in μ increases the reservation wage, the increase is less than one for one. Finally, increasing the mean preserving spread of the distribution, s, reduces the hazard because an increase in the mass of the right tail of the wage offer distribution increases the payoff to search, thus increasing the reservation wage. An additional set of implications follow about the mean of the accepted wage; anything that increases the reservation wage also increases the mean accepted wage.

Quasi-Structural Approach to Estimation
As exemplified by the papers in the *ILRR* symposium, the early quasi-structural approach to estimating the job search model was regression based. The primary concern of that literature, as well as the later litera-

ture based on hazard modeling, was the estimation of the impact of unemployment benefits on the duration of unemployment and postunemployment wages.[12] As noted, the regression specification was motivated by the standard job search model. Classen (1977) provides a clear statement of the connection between the two. Classen (1977) writes equations representing the outcomes of the search process as

$$D = \alpha_0 + \alpha_1 WBA + \sum \alpha_i X_i + u_D,$$

$$Y = \beta_0 + \beta_1 WBA + \sum \beta_i X_i + u_Y,$$

where D is spell duration, Y is a measure of the postunemployment wage, WBA is the weekly UI benefit amount, and the X's are "proxies" for a worker's skill level, the cost of search, and the job offer rate. As Classen notes, the determinants of both spell duration and the postunemployment wage should be exactly the same, as they are joint outcomes derived from optimal search behavior. Among the proxy variables used in Classen's analysis are demographics, such as age, race, and sex, and a measure of the wage on the job held prior to beginning the unemployment spell. Although not included in the Classen study, other variables often included in this type of specification are education, marital status, number of dependents, and a measure of aggregate unemployment in the relevant labor market.

A test of the theory amounts to a test that benefits increase both expected duration and the mean accepted wage, that is, that α_1 and β_1 are both positive. Any further test of the theory would involve specifying how proxy variables are related to the structural parameters, q, the offer probability, and $F(w)$, the wage offer distribution.

Classen is clear as to the purpose of including the preunemployment wage, namely as a proxy, most directly perhaps for the mean of the wage offer distribution. However, although the inclusion of that variable or, as is also common, of the replacement rate, the ratio of the benefit level to the preunemployment wage, was and continues to be standard in the quasi- structural literature, the need for stating a rationale has been lost. Without an explicit rationale, the point that the inclusion of the preunemployment wage (or the replacement rate) cannot be justified by the standard search model (it does not appear in equation 3.2) and thus should not have any impact on search outcomes given q and $F(w)$, has also been lost.

Regardless of whether it is stated, the original rationale for its inclusion remains, namely to avoid omitted variable bias. For example, suppose that the preunemployment wage is meant to proxy the mean of the wage offer distribution, μ, which is assumed to vary in the sample. Now, UI benefits are usually tied to the preunemployment wage, at least up to some limit. Thus, if some determinants of μ are omitted, variation in the benefit level will reflect, in part, the fact that those with higher preunemployment wages have higher μ's. In that case, a positive correlation between UI benefit levels and the preunemployment wage will lead to a negative bias in the effect of UI benefits on the duration of unemployment (recall that the higher μ is, the greater will be the hazard rate).

Although omitted variable bias is well understood, the potential for bias introduced by using proxy variables is less well appreciated. The source of the problem is that, in the context of a search model, the preunemployment wage must have been the outcome of a search during a prior unemployment spell. To isolate the effect of using this proxy, assume that the duration of the prior unemployment spell was governed by the same behavioral process and fundamentals as the current spell. Such an assumption is consistent with a model in which there are exogenous layoffs and resulting unemployment spells are renewal processes (the stochastic properties of all unemployment spells are the same).[13] To simplify, suppose that only the benefit level and the mean of the wage offer distribution vary in the sample. Then, taking deviations from means (without renaming the variables, to conserve on notation), the duration equation for any individual i is

$$D_i = \pi_{11}b_i + \pi_{21}\mu_i + v_{1i}. \tag{3.4}$$

Assuming μ_i is unobserved and thus omitted from the regression, the bias in the ordinary least squares (OLS) estimator of π_1 is given by

$$E(\hat{\pi}_{11} - \pi_{11}) = \pi_{21}\frac{\sigma_\mu^2}{\sigma_b^2}\beta_{b,\mu},$$

where $\beta_{b,\mu}$ is the regression coefficient of b on μ. Thus, if b and μ are positively correlated, and $\pi_{21} < 0$ as theory suggests, the bias in the estimated effect of UI benefits on duration will be negative.

Now, because the preunemployment wage, Y_{-1}, is the result of a prior search, it will have the same arguments as equation 3.4, namely

$$Y_{i,-1} = \pi_{12}b_i + \pi_{22}\mu_i + v_{2i}$$
$$= \pi_{22}\mu_i + \omega_i, \tag{3.5}$$

where $\omega_i = \pi_{12}b_i + v_{2i}$ and where $E(\omega b_i) \neq 0$ given the definition of ω_i. To derive a regression equation that includes b_i and $Y_{i,-1}$, solve for μ_i in equation 3.5 and substitute into equation 3.4, yielding

$$D_i = \pi_{11}b_i + \pi_{21}\frac{(Y_{i,-1} - \omega_i)}{\pi_{22}} + v_{1i}$$

$$= \pi_{11}b_i + \frac{\pi_{21}}{\pi_{22}}Y_{i,-1} + v'_{1i},$$

where $v'_{1i} = -\frac{\pi_{21}}{\pi_{22}}\omega_i + v_{1i}$. We are interested in whether the OLS estimator for π_{11} is biased, that is, whether $E(b_i v'_{1i} \mid Y_{i,-1}) = E(-\frac{\pi_{21}\pi_{12}}{\pi_{22}}b_i^2 \mid \pi_{12}b_i + \pi_{22}\mu_i + v_{2i}) = 0$. It is easiest to see whether this holds by explicitly deriving the bias expression. The bias is given by

$$E(\hat{\hat{\pi}}_{11} - \pi_{11}) = \pi_{21}^2 \frac{\sigma_\omega^2 \sigma_\mu^2}{\sigma_b^2 \sigma_{Y_{-1}}^2 - (\sigma_{bY_{-1}})^2}(\pi_{21}^{-1}\beta_{b,\mu} - \pi_{22}\beta_{b,\omega}).$$

The bias is zero if either $\sigma_\omega^2 = \pi_{12}^2\sigma_b^2 + \sigma_{v_2}^2 = 0$ or if $\pi_{21}^{-1}\beta_{b,\mu} - \pi_{22}\beta_{b,\omega} = 0$, either of which would be a fortuitous property of the sample.

What is the relationship between the biases that arise from omitting μ_i (omitted variable bias) and those from including $Y_{i,-1}$ (proxy variable bias)? It turns out that a sufficient condition for the bias from omitting the preunemployment wage to be smaller than from including it is that $\beta_{b,\omega} = \pi_{12}\sigma_b^2 = 0$, which only will hold if $\pi_{12} = 0$, a violation of the theory. In general, the biases cannot be ordered, and it is unclear which is the better strategy to follow to minimize the bias. The implicit (that is, without justification) assumption made by almost all researchers is that omitted variable bias is greater than proxy variable bias in this context. Moreover, if the benefit level varies with the preunemployment wage and we have good measures of the mean of the wage offer distribution, variation in the benefit level from this source is helpful in identifying the UI benefit effect. The variation in the preunemployment wage around the mean of the offer distribution that induces benefit variation is purely due to random draws from the wage offer distribution.

Researchers adopting the quasi-structural approach have universally included the preunemployment wage and thus assumed that omitted variable bias is greater than proxy variable bias. There is a larger point reflected by this choice. Structural work requires that all variables be explicitly accounted for in the model. A similar standard for quasi-structural work might have revealed the existence of the choice between omitted variable and proxy variable bias, a choice not explicitly acknowledged in the empirical literature.

As we noted, it is also usual to include some aggregate labor market statistic such as the local unemployment rate. The idea is that the aggregate statistic reflects labor market demand and so will affect the offer rate or the wage offer distribution. However, because the aggregate statistic is simply the aggregation of the search decisions over the unemployed population, it does not solely reflect demand conditions, and estimates of UI benefit effects suffer from proxy variable bias.

Finite Horizon Model
Spells of unemployment tend to be short (weeks or months) in relation to an individual's life span. A finite lifetime would not seem, therefore, to be a reason to explore the implications of a finite horizon search model. On the other hand, it is reasonable to assume that individuals generally will not be able to self-finance extended periods of unemployment and that external borrowing is limited. One can think, then, of the finite (search) horizon as corresponding to the maximal unemployment period that can be financed through internal and external funds. Once a job is accepted, however, it lasts forever; that is, the horizon is infinite subsequent to accepting a job. In addition to the previous notation, denote by T the end of the search horizon. To close the model, it is assumed that if the terminal period is reached without having accepted a job, the individual receives b forever.[14]

Without going into the details, the reservation wage path can be shown to satisfy the following difference equation:

$$\frac{w_t^*}{1-\delta} = b + \frac{\delta}{1-\delta} w_{t+1}^* + \frac{\delta}{1-\delta} q \int_{w_{t+1}^*}^{\infty} (w - w_{t+1}^*) dF(w) \text{ for } t < T, \tag{3.6}$$

$$w_T^* = b. \tag{3.7}$$

Notice that equation 3.6 reduces to the implicit reservation wage equation for the infinite horizon problem if $w_t^* = w_{t+1}^*$. Given a distributional assumption for wage offers, $F(w)$, the solution of the finite horizon reservation wage path can be obtained numerically by starting from period T and working backward.[15]

In the finite horizon case, the reservation wage is decreasing in the duration of the spell, $\frac{dw_t^*}{dt} < 0$, rather than being constant as in the infinite horizon case. In addition, the reservation wage is bounded from below by b (at T), and from above by the infinite horizon reservation wage (w^*). The hazard rate is thus increasing in t, $\dfrac{dh_t}{dt} = -\lambda f(w^*)\dfrac{dw_t^*}{dt} > 0$. As a result, the longer the spell duration, the greater the exit rate. The important property of the finite horizon reservation wage is that it depends on the time left until the horizon is reached. The reservation wages are equal under two different horizons not when they have the same amount of time elapsed since beginning the spell of unemployment (t) but when they have the same amount of time left until the horizon is reached ($T - t$).

The finite horizon model can be used to incorporate the fact that UI eligibility is exhausted after a fixed number of weeks (typically 26 weeks). Mortensen (1977) incorporates benefit exhaustion into a more general search model that also allows for endogenous search intensity as well as multiple spells resulting from layoffs. Benefit exhaustion, in a single spell search model, can be easily accommodated by combining the infinite and finite horizon models. The period subsequent to exhaustion can be treated as an infinite horizon search problem with zero UI benefits, and the preexhaustion period as a finite horizon problem with positive benefits (Engberg, 1990). The infinite horizon value function serves as the value function at the time of benefit exhaustion. Specifically, the solution to the model is given by replacing equation 3.7 with the infinite horizon reservation wage obtained from solving equation 3.1 for the case that UI benefits are zero, together with equation 3.6, where T is the period at which benefits are exhausted. The reservation wage declines until T and is constant thereafter.

Meyer (1990) incorporated benefit exhaustion into his quasi-structural specification of the duration hazard. A complication is that the length of eligibility changed for some individuals in the sample during their unemployment spell. Although Meyer loosely appeals to a search model with a fixed eligibility period, the relevant search model would be one that took into account the probability of a change in the eligibility period occurring at any future time.[16] Suppose, for example, that the normal eligibility period is T_1, but may be changed to $T_2 > T_1$ with probability $\omega(Z)$, where Z are variables that reflect the state of the economy that would trigger a change in the eligibility period.[17] Assume that once the eligibility period is changed for an individual who had already started an unemployment spell, the eligibility horizon cannot revert back to T_1 for that individual. Given the assumption that the agents solve the infinite horizon model on reaching the end of eligibility, the value function is the same at both T_1 and T_2, given by $\dfrac{w^*}{r}$ where w^* is the solution to equation 3.1.

The reservation wage at any unemployment duration depends on which of the eligibility horizons prevails at the time. Any individual who has been unemployed longer than the current eligibility period has a reservation wage w^*. If the individual currently faces an eligibility horizon of T_2 and has been unemployed less than T_2, then the reservation wage is given by solving equation 3.6 recursively back from T_2 to the current period. If an individual currently has been unemployed less than T_1 and the eligibility horizon is T_1, then, with the value function of search at period t under the horizon T_i denoted as $V_t^{T_i}$, the value of search is

$$V_t^{T_1} = b + \delta\{(1-\omega(Z_t))[qE\max(W(w),V_{t+1}^{T_1}) + (1-q)V_{t+1}^{T_1}]$$
$$+ \omega(Z_t)[qE\max(W(w),V_{t+1}^{T_2}) + (1-q)V_{t+1}^{T_2}]\} \tag{3.8}$$

for $t < T_1$.[18] Rewritten in terms of reservation wages, this becomes

$$\frac{w_t^{*T_1}}{1-\delta} = b + \delta(1-\omega(Z_t))\frac{w_{t+1}^{*T_1}}{1-\delta} + \delta\omega(Z_t)\frac{w_{t+1}^{*T_2}}{1-\delta} \tag{3.9}$$
$$+ \frac{\delta}{1-\delta}q(1-\omega(Z_t))\int_{w_{t+1}^{*T_1}}^{\infty}(w-w_{t+1}^{*T_1})dF(w) + \frac{\delta}{1-\delta}q\omega(Z_t)\int_{w_{t+1}^{*T_2}}^{\infty}(w-w_{t+1}^{*T_2})dF(w)$$

for $t < T_1$. The reservation wage path for any t when the eligibility horizon is T_2 is

$$\frac{w_t^{*T_2}}{1-\delta} = b + \frac{\delta}{1-\delta}w_{t+1}^{*T_2} + \frac{\delta}{1-\delta}q\int_{w_{t+1}^{*T_2}}^{\infty}(w-w_{t+1}^{*T_2})dF(w) \text{ for } t < T_2. \tag{3.10}$$

Notice that the reservation wage under the T_1 horizon (equation 3.9) is bounded between the reservation wage that would apply if $\omega(Z_t) = 0$ for all t, that is, $T = T_1$, and the reservation wage that applies with the horizon $T = T_2$.

The reservation wage can follow two possible paths. If the eligibility period never changes, then the reservation path is declining from $t = 1$ to T_1 (according to equation 3.9) and then is constant from T_1 on. If the eligibility horizon changes from T_1 to T_2 at some $t = t_c < T_1$, then the reservation wage declines until $t_c - 1$ according to equation 3.9 and then jumps up at t_c to the reservation wage $w_{t_c}^{*T_2}$. From that point, the reservation wage declines according to equation 3.10 until T_2 and is then constant from T_2 on. The hazard rate then also can follow two paths.

Hazard

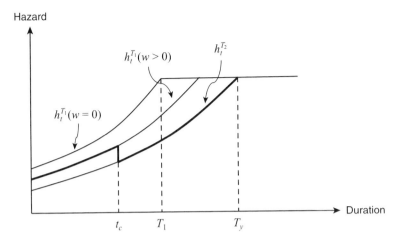

Figure 3.1
Hazard function.

In the first case, where the eligibility horizon does not change, the hazard rate is increasing until $t = T_1$ and then is constant. In the second case, the hazard rate increases until the change in the eligibility horizon, jumps down at the point at which the horizon changes, and then rises until the end of the (new) horizon, after which it is constant. The hazard rate thus has a spike at the point at which the change in the eligibility horizon occurs. Figure 3.1 illustrates the hazard rate when there is an extension of benefits.

The reservation wage at any t is thus a function of the following arguments:

$$w_t^* = w^*((T_1 - t)I(T_t = T_1, t \le T_1), (T_2 - t)I(T_t = T_2, t \le T_2), b, q, \delta, Z_t, F(w)),$$
$$(3.11)$$

where $I(T_t = T_k, t \le T_k)$ is 1 if the terminal period is T_k and the duration of the unemployment spell is less than T_k and 0 otherwise. The hazard function, $h_t = q(1 - F(w_t^*))$, has the same arguments.

Why is it important to pay attention to theory in analyzing Meyer's data? Theory is informative as to the selection of the arguments in the hazard function, both in terms of what should and what should not be included.[19] As in the case of the standard search model, as seen in equation 3.11, the preunemployment wage is not an argument of the hazard function. It is included by Meyer. Analyzing the consequence of including it as a proxy for an omitted variable can only be done in the context of a theory. Similarly, the above theory provides a direct rationale for and interpretation of aggregate variables (Z_t), such as the state unemployment rate in Meyer's specification, that are known to affect whether benefits are extended. As already discussed, the interpretation of aggregate variables as a demand-side factor is problematic.

Theory also provides guidance as to the form of the specification. As seen in equation 3.11, the reservation wage rate depends on the time left until benefit exhaustion $(T_k - t)$. Uncertainty about the eligibility horizon implies that the reservation wage is not the same for horizon T_1 and T_2 given the same amount of time left before benefit exhaustion; the possibility of an extension exists when the horizon is T_1 but not when it is T_2.[20] The reservation wages are the same if changes in the horizon are completely unanticipated $(\omega = 0)$, which is the implicit assumption made by Meyer. Notice that if the change in the horizon occurs at $t = t_c$, then the downward jump in the reservation wage is given by $w^*((T_2 - T_c)I(T_t = T_2, t_c \leq T_1), 0, \cdot) - w^*(0, (T_2 - t_c)I(T_t = T_2), t_c \leq T_1 < T_2), \cdot)$. In general, the downward jump will be greater the closer the period in which the change occurs is to the original horizon, that is, the closer that t_c is to T_1. Thus, the specification of the hazard function should capture this nonlinearity if the empirical model is to have a chance at generating the larger spikes observed in the data around typical values of T_1.[21]

It would be possible to structurally implement the search model described above. The structure would need to be modified in order to capture the fact that the hazard rate is U-shaped, for example, by adding unobserved heterogeneity and/or period effects in some of the structural parameters. One of Meyer's goals was to see whether the spikes in the hazard could be explained by covariates. Structural estimation of the search model parameters explicitly captures the inherent nonlinearities and spikes in the hazard function. Whether they would match the data is an open question.

Identification in the Standard Search Model
Identification is an important issue in structural empirical work. Constructive identification results are available in the search context. To simplify, I consider identification of the standard search model parameters assuming data on durations of unemployment and on accepted wages come from a homogeneous population.[22] To establish identification, it is useful to rewrite the reservation wage implicit equation (equation 3.1) as

$$w^* = b + \frac{q}{r}\int_{w^*}^{\infty}(w - w^*)dF(x)$$

$$= b + \frac{q}{r}[E(w \mid w \geq w^*)(1 - F(w^*)) - w^*(1 - F(w^*))$$

$$= b + \frac{h}{r}[E(w \mid w \geq w^*) - w^*]. \tag{3.12}$$

From the accepted wage data, note that a consistent estimator of the reservation wage is the lowest observed wage: $\lim_{n\to\infty}\Pr(\mid w_{\min} - w^*\mid) = 0$.[23] Then, given an estimate of h from the duration data, and recognizing that from the accepted wage data, we can also obtain an estimate of $E(w \mid w \geq w^*)$, b can be identified if we take r as given. This result does not require a distributional assumption for wage offers.

One cannot, however, separate q and F without a distributional assumption. Although $F(w \mid w \geq w^*)$ is known, given an estimate of w^*, one can recover the wage offer distribution, $F(w)$, only if it is possible to recover the untruncated distribution from the truncated distribution. Obviously, that cannot be done without making a distributional assumption. Assuming that $F(w)$ is recoverable from the accepted wage distribution, then from $h = q(1 - F(w^*))$, one can recover the offer probability, q. Recoverability of the wage offer distribution is not always possible (Flinn and Heckman, 1982). Fortunately, most of the commonly used distributions for wage offer functions, for example, the lognormal distribution, are recoverable from the distribution of accepted wages. However, there is an important lesson to draw, namely that parametric assumptions do not always assure identification.

The analysis of identification in the finite horizon case is similar. The reservation wage at each period can be consistently estimated from the period-specific minimum observed wages. By analogy to equation 3.12, we can write the implicit reservation wage equation as

$$w_t^* = b(1 - \delta) + \delta w_{t+1}^* + \delta h_{t+1}[E(w \mid w \geq w_{t+1}^*) - w_{t+1}^*].^{24}$$

This equation must hold exactly at each time t. As long as there are durations of unemployment that extend through more than two periods, that is, given $w_t^*, w_{t+1}^*, w_{t+2}^*, h_{t+1}, h_{t+2}, E(w \mid w \geq w_{t+1}^*)$ and $E(w \mid w \geq w_{t+2}^*)$, δ (or r) and b can be separately identified by solving the two difference equations for the two unknowns, δ and b. Recall that this separation was impossible in the infinite horizon case. Moreover, if we have more than three periods of data, the model is rejectable.

Identifiability of q and F, however, still requires recoverability of the wage offer distribution.

Likelihood Function

Consider the likelihood contribution of an individual solving an infinite horizon search model who has a completed unemployment spell of length d_i and accepted wage w_i^a :

$$L_i = \left[q \Pr(w < w^*) + (1-q) \right]^{d_i - 1} \times q \Pr(w_i^a > w^*, w_i^a)$$

$$= \left[q \Pr(w < w^*) + (1-q) \right]^{d_i - 1} \times q \Pr(w_i^a > w^* \mid w_i^a) f(w_i^a). \tag{3.13}$$

Recall that the reservation wage is a function of the model parameters b, δ, q, and $F(w)$. The first (bracketed) term in the likelihood is the probability that in each of the periods up to $d_i - 1$ the individual received an offer and rejected it or did not receive an offer. The second term is the probability that the individual received an offer of w_i^a in period d_i and accepted it. Individuals who have incomplete unemployment spells would contribute only the first term to the likelihood.

Observe that for any given value of the reservation wage (or the parameters that determine it), whether or not an individual works conditional on a wage draw is deterministic, that is, its probability, $\Pr(w_i^a > w^* \mid w_i^a)$ in equation 3.13, is either 1 or 0. In order that the likelihood not be degenerate, the reservation wage must be less than the lowest accepted wage in the sample; for this reason, the minimum observed wage in the sample is the maximum likelihood estimate of the reservation wage. That would not create an issue if observed wages were all reasonable. However, in most survey data sets the lowest reported wage is often quite small, less than $1 or even only a few cents. Such outliers would potentially have an extreme effect on the estimates of the structural parameters. One remedy would be to trim the wage data, say by whatever percentage led to a "reasonable" lowest wage. However, that would be essentially choosing the reservation wage by fiat. A second alternative would be to add another error to the model, for example, by allowing the cost of the search to be stochastic, in which case the reservation wage would be stochastic.[25] A very low accepted wage would be consistent with the individual having drawn a very high search cost.

Of course, adding another source of error does not deal with what is the likely root cause of the problem, which is that wages are not accurately reported.[26] That "fact" has led researchers to directly allow for measurement error in the reported wage. Introducing measurement error not only accounts for a real feature of the data, it is also convenient in that it does not require any change in the solution of the search problem. The reservation wage is itself unaffected by the existence of measurement error. If we take into account the existence of measurement error and let w_i^{aR} be the reported accepted wage and w_i^{aT} the true accepted wage, the likelihood function becomes

$$L_i = \left[q\Pr(w_i^{aT} < w^*) + (1-q)\right]^{d_i-1} \times q \int\limits_{w_i^{aT}} \Pr(w_i^{aT} > w^*, w_i^{aR})$$

$$= \left[q\Pr(w_i^{aT} < w^*) + (1-q)\right]^{d_i-1}$$
$$\times q \int\limits_{w_i^{aT}} \Pr(w_i^{aT} > w^* \mid w_i^{aR}, w_i^{aT}) g(w_i^{aR} \mid w_i^{aT}) dF(w)$$

$$= \left[q\Pr(w_i^{aT} < w^*) + (1-q)\right]^{d_i-1} \times q \int\limits_{w_i^{aT}} \Pr(w_i^{aT} > w^* \mid w_i^{aT}) g(w_i^{aR} \mid w_i^{aT}) dF(w),$$

where $g(w_i^{aR} \mid w_i^{aT})$ is the distribution of the measurement error and where the third equality emphasizes the fact that it is the true wage only and not the reported wage that affects the acceptance probability. The most common assumption in the literature is that the measurement error is multiplicative, that is, proportional to the true wage.

The estimation of the finite horizon search problem when there are extreme low-wage outliers is particularly problematic. Recall that the reservation wage is declining with duration. Thus, if an outlier observation occurs at an early duration, the entire subsequent path of reservation wages must lie below the reservation wage at that early duration. The incorporation of measurement error is, therefore, critical for estimation. The analogous likelihood contribution for an individual for the finite horizon model, which takes into account that the reservation wage is duration dependent, is

$$L_i = \prod_{j=1}^{d_i-1} \left[q\Pr(w_j^{aT} < w_j^*) + (1-q_j)\right] \times q\Pr(w_{d_i}^{aT} > w_d^*, w_d^{aR}).$$

The estimation of the partial equilibrium search model involves an iterative process as in any DCDP model, namely numerically solving a dynamic programming problem at trial parameters and maximizing the likelihood function. The generality of the DCDP approach has allowed researchers considerable flexibility in modeling choices. Thus, researchers have adopted different distributional assumptions and have extended the standard search model in a number of directions, some of which have already been mentioned.

As has been generally true in the DCDP literature, the theoretical models that serve as their foundation cannot directly be taken to the data. In the case of the standard search model, neither the infinite horizon nor the finite horizon model can fit the generally observed fact that the hazard rate out of unemployment declines with duration. Recall that the hazard rate is constant in the infinite horizon case and increasing in the finite horizon case. There are several ways to deal with this mismatch between the data and the models. In the infinite horizon model, introducing unobserved heterogeneity in model fundamentals, such as the cost of search, the offer probability, and/or the wage offer distribution, can produce negative duration dependence in the population hazard while maintaining constancy at the individual level. In the finite horizon case, allowing for time dependencies in model fundamentals, such as allowing offer probabilities to decline with duration, can create negative duration dependence, in this case at the individual level as well as at the population level.

A DCDP Example

One great advantage of the structural approach is that it enables the researcher to incorporate into estimation an exact representation of program rules. This advantage is particularly valuable in policy evaluation. It is reasonable to suppose that the closer a model mimics existing program rules, the better the model will fit the actual behavior, and the more accurately the model will be able to evaluate prospective policy changes.

3.1.1.3   A Structural Application

Ferrall (1997) structurally estimates a DCDP model of job search, concentrating on the transition from school to work, that integrates all of the major features of the Canadian UI system. In Canada, as in the United States, the period of search for one's first job after leaving school is usually not covered by the UI system. Although that spell of search unemployment is not insured, there is still the potential for the UI system, given its structure, to affect search behavior. To understand why, consider the structure of the UI system in Canada that prevailed during the time period studied by Ferrall. In that system:

1. An unemployed worker who is eligible for insurance must wait 2 weeks after becoming unemployed before collecting benefits.[27]

2. The benefit level depends on the previous wage through a fixed replacement rate (0.60 at the time). The insurable weekly wage is bounded from below by $106 and from above by $530. Thus benefits are $0 if the wage on the previously held job was less that $106, 0.6 times the wage if the wage is between the bounds, and $318 for wages at or above $530.

3. To be eligible for UI benefits, a person must have worked on insurable jobs a certain number of weeks in the 52 weeks prior to becoming unemployed. The number of weeks depends on the regional unemployment rate and the person's previous employment and UI history.

4. The number of weeks of benefits depends on the number of weeks worked on the previous job and on whether the individual is eligible for extended benefits but is capped at 52.

There are two elements of the UI system that would affect search during an uninsured spell. First, because benefits are paid during insured spells, there is an incentive for individuals in an uninsured spell to become employed to be eligible for benefits during future unemployment spells. Thus, the UI system reduces the reservation wage in an uninsured spell; further, the reservation wage will be lower the higher are the benefits (Mortensen, 1977). On the other hand, because the level of benefits increases with the wage on the prior job, there will be an incentive for someone in an uninsured spell to wait for a higher wage offer and thus to have a higher reservation wage. This incentive, however, only applies to individuals whose reservation wage would otherwise be below the maximum insurable wage. Moreover, the magnitude of these incentive effects depends on the probability that an individual will be laid off from future jobs.

The model estimated by Ferrall, aside from the explicit incorporation of UI rules, differs from the standard single-spell search model in a number of ways. The model allows for a search period during school, an initial uninsured spell after leaving school, the first job spell, and a subsequent insured unemployment spell if a layoff occurs. The individual maximizes the expected present value of the log of consumption, where consumption equals the wage while working and the sum of UI benefits net of the cost of search plus the value of home production. In each period of unemployment, the individual receives a job offer with some positive probability. However, a job offer comes not only with a wage offer but also with a layoff rate. The wage offer function is Pareto, and the layoff rate can take on a fixed number of

values, randomly drawn.[28] Individuals differ, according to their unobserved type, in their market skill level and in their value of home
production.

The solution method is by backward recursion, where the value
function for the infinite horizon search problem when UI benefits are
exhausted after a layoff occurs serves as the terminal value function
for the insured unemployment spell at the time of benefit exhaustion.
The model is solved backward from there as a finite horizon problem
until the beginning of the search period while in school. The estimation
is by maximum likelihood. Ferrall provides evidence of model fit.

Ferrall performs a number of counterfactual experiments that vary
the parameters of the UI system. The most extreme is the elimination
of the UI system. Recall from the earlier discussion that there was no
unambiguous prediction of how reservation wages of ineligibles would
be affected by such an experiment. Ferrall finds that for those with at
most a high school education residing outside of the Atlantic region,
reservation wages rise; the expected duration of unemployment after
leaving school (including those who have no unemployment spell) is
estimated to increase by about 50 percent. Similarly, for those with
some college residing outside of the Atlantic region, the increase is 40
percent. However, there is almost no effect on the expected duration
for those residing in the Atlantic region regardless of education.

3.1.2   The Effect of Public Welfare on Female Labor Market and Demographic Outcomes

3.1.2.1   Background

The Aid for Dependent Children (AFDC) program has been among the
most widely studied programs in the social sciences. Introduced in
1935, and since replaced in 1996 by the Temporary Assistance for Needy
Families (TANF), AFDC provided means-tested welfare benefits to
(primarily) single women with children.[29] As a by-product of providing
income assistance, it has been argued that the AFDC program created
a dependent underclass characterized by low levels of schooling, high
fertility, low marriage rates, and low employment rates (Murray, 1984).
Evidence on the effect of AFDC on these demographic and labor market
outcomes has been reviewed by Moffitt (1992, 1998) and Hoynes (1997).
They report two major empirical findings from the literature: (1) AFDC
reduces labor supply by 10 to 50 percent, and (2) AFDC had a negative

effect on marriage and a positive effect on fertility, but there is no consensus on the magnitude.

Much of the modern empirical literature on estimating welfare effects is based on microlevel longitudinal data. Given that program rules for AFDC differ by state and vary over time, both between- and within-state variation can be exploited in estimation. The existence of these two sources of variation has led to a conundrum in the regression-based literature—should state-fixed effects be included, thus exploiting only within-state variation, or should they be omitted? The rationale for including state-fixed effects is to be able to better account for unobservable individual preferences that might differ across states as well as other omitted state-level programs, whose existence and generosity might influence behavior and be related to AFDC program rules. It was often found that regression estimates of welfare effects on demographic outcomes became smaller and statistically insignificant when state-fixed effects were included in the regression. This was interpreted as correcting for the bias from omitted variables (see Hoynes, 1997, for example).

The notion that the two sources of variation yield theoretically different effects was alluded to in a footnote by Moffitt (1997), but it was not seriously considered within an estimation strategy until Rosenzweig (1999) did so. Keane and Wolpin (2002), in a simulation exercise, provided an explicit demonstration of the mechanisms through which between- and within-state variation in welfare benefits can differentially affect behavioral outcomes. The simple insight is that decisions about behaviors that have long-term benefits and/or costs will be less affected by transitory changes in welfare generosity than by permanent changes. For example, a woman will be less likely to be induced to have a child when a change in welfare benefits is perceived to be of a short duration than if perceived to be permanent. Cross-state variation consists of both a permanent and a transitory component. Controlling for permanent differences using state-fixed effects leaves only within-state transitory fluctuations in benefits.

Figure 3.2 presents the time-series plot of the benefit amounts between 1971 and 1990 available to women who have two children and zero earnings in two states, New York and Texas. As seen, both the levels and patterns differ. Although benefits declined in both states over the entire period, the trend was not monotonic in either. Benefits in New York rose from about $850 per month in 1971 to $1,050 in 1976, then fell to $640 and remained constant.[30] In Texas, benefits were less

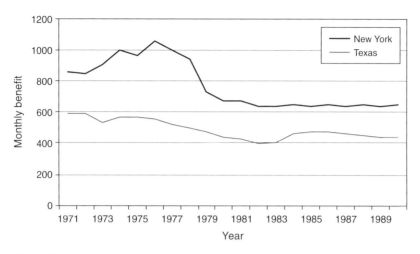

Figure 3.2
Welfare benefit in New York and Texas.

volatile, remaining roughly constant from 1971 to 1976 at around $550, then falling to about $400 in 1982, and then rising and remaining constant at about $450 from 1985.

3.1.2.2 The Regression-Based Approach

Regression specifications have not distinguished between these two types of effects, conventionally taking the form (Hoynes, 1997)

$$y_{its} = \alpha B_{its} + \beta X_{its} + u_{its}, \tag{3.14}$$

where y_{its} is the decision variable for an individual i at time t residing in state s, B_{its} is the level of welfare benefits, X_{its} are other determinants of the decision, and u_{its} are unobserved factors determining the decision. Including state dummies in X implies that only within-state variation in B is used to identify α. A linear regression equation that distinguishes these two effects would include both permanent and transitory components of benefits, B_{is}^P and B_{its}^T, where $B_{its} = B_{is}^P + B_{its}^T$:

$$y_{its} = \alpha_1 B_{its}^P + \alpha_2 B_{its}^T + \beta X_{its} + u_{its}. \tag{3.15}$$

The implicit assumption, given equation 3.14, is that the same parameter governs the effect of both permanent and transitory changes, that is, $\alpha_1 = \alpha_2 = \alpha$. If state-fixed effects are included in equation 3.14, then α_2, the effect of the transitory change, is recovered. Researchers have interpreted the estimate of the transitory effect, α_2, as if it were the permanent effect, α_1. McKinnish (2008) interprets the lower estimate using state-fixed effects as evidence of measurement error and suggests using an IV approach as a remedy. Of course, if what is being estimated is α_2, in the presence of measurement error, IV recovers a consistent estimate only of α_2, not α_1. If state dummies are not included in equation 3.14 and the transitory component of benefits is omitted (even if there are no other omitted variables), then, assuming that $\alpha_1 > \alpha_2$, a downward-biased estimate of the permanent effect, α_1, is estimated.[31]

Rosenzweig's approach is to calculate for different cohorts of women the average benefit in their state of residence over a period of 9 years, from ages 14 to 22. Variation in this average benefit amount arises because different cohorts of women *within* a state span different years over those ages. Thus, unlike the approach described above, this variation in benefits persists in the presence of state-fixed effects. Rosenzweig estimates the impact of that variation in benefits on early nonmarital childbearing and finds larger effects than the previous literature. The idea is that this measure of benefits reflects differences (across cohorts) that are more permanent than reflected in year-to-year variation.

Keane and Wolpin (2002) illustrate the dependence on the benefit stochastic process of the impact of benefits based on within-state variation by specifying and simulating a DCDP model of fertility (contraceptive use) and welfare take-up. To outline the DCDP model, in each period a woman decides whether to contracept and whether or not to receive welfare (if eligible). A woman who chooses to contracept avoids a pregnancy that period with certainty. A woman who chooses not to contracept has a birth one period later with a known probability that depends on the woman's age. The woman receives a utility flow that depends on a composite consumption good, the number of children ever born, on whether or not she contracepts, and on whether she receives welfare (reflecting a potential stigma effect). The "marginal" utility of contraception and welfare receipt are subject to *iid* stochastic shocks. Consumption in any period depends on that period's earnings, which are stochastic and depend on the woman's age and number of children and on the amount of welfare benefits received that period. Current and past welfare benefits are known, but future benefits are not. The woman maximizes the expected present discounted value of lifetime utility.

Keane and Wolpin (2002) specify a more complete picture of the benefit schedule than is adopted in the literature, which relies on a summary statistic such as the level of benefits given to women who have two children and no earned income. Specifically, the welfare benefit available to a woman residing in state s who is age a at calendar time t is approximated by a rule that depends on the number of children residing in her household (n) and on her earnings (y) according to:

$$B_{at}^s = b_{0t}^s + b_{1t}^s n_{at} - b_{2t}^s n_{at} - b_{3t}^s y_{at} \text{ if } B_{at}^s > 0 \text{ and } N_{at} > 0 \qquad (3.16)$$

$$= 0 \text{ otherwise,}$$

where $b_{0t}^s, b_{1t}^s, b_{2t}^s$ are the "guarantee" parameters and b_{3t}^s is the benefit reduction (or tax) rate. An increase in b_{0t}^s augments benefits independent of the number of children, whereas increases in b_{1t}^s (or a reduction in b_{2t}^s) augment the benefit with respect to additional children. B_{at}^s is denoted as the benefit rule and the b's as the benefit rule parameters. Benefit rule parameters are estimated in each year for each of the two states. The mean value of the constant term in equation 3.16 is about twice as large in New York as in Texas, $454 versus $228. In addition, New York has a larger payout for each additional child that increases essentially linearly with each extra child ($\bar{b}_1 = 161, \bar{b}_2 = 0.6$), whereas the payoff in Texas for additional children increases more slowly and at a diminishing rate ($\bar{b}_1 = 134, \bar{b}_2 = 4.9$).

Changes over time in the level of benefits arise from changes in the underlying benefit rule parameters. Benefit rule parameters evolve according to a general vector autoregression (VAR),

$$\mathbf{b}_t^s = \boldsymbol{\lambda}^s + \boldsymbol{\Lambda}^s \mathbf{b}_{t-1}^s + \mathbf{u}_t^s, \qquad (3.17)$$

where $\mathbf{b}_t^s$ is a 4×1 column vector of the benefit rule parameters, $\boldsymbol{\lambda}^s$ is a 4×1 column vector of regression constants, $\boldsymbol{\Lambda}^s$ is a 4×4 matrix of autoregressive parameters, and $\mathbf{u}_t^s$ is a 4×1 column vector of iid mean zero shocks drawn from a stationary distribution with variance-covariance matrix $\boldsymbol{\Omega}^s$. The evolution of the benefit rule parameters also differs across the two states. The differences are highlighted in table 3.1, which shows the impulse response functions for a change in b_0 of $83.33 per month ($1,000 annualized, the period length of the decision model) and in b_1 of $41.67 ($500 annualized). Women are assumed to use equation 3.17 to update their beliefs about future benefits when deciding on contraception and welfare take-up in any period.

In New York, a once and not for all increase in b_0 of $1,000 annualized in any period is followed immediately in the next period by a decline in b_0 of $16 and further declines that peak at $163 six (and

Table 3.1
Impulse Responses to Innovations in the Overall and Per-Child Guarantees

Period	New York		Texas	
	b_0	b_1	b_0	b_1
1	1,000	500	100	500
2	−16	498	1,148	274
3	−127	521	1,142	139
4	−147	559	1,068	56
5	−155	573	955	4
6	−163	569	841	−24
7	−163	547	727	−36
8	−157	517	625	−44
9	−155	474	528	−40
10	−143	429	443	−8
.				
.				
.				
.				
25	11	−49	33	−4

Source: Keane and Wolpin (2002).

seven) periods later until the effect of the initial increase slowly dissipates. The same increase in Texas is followed by additional increases, peaking at $1,148 in the next period and slowly declining. The increase is still $443 in period 10 and falls to $33 25 periods after the initial innovation. The effect of an innovation of $500 (annual) in b_1 is exactly reversed. In New York, the innovation is followed by slightly higher values in the next seven periods (with the exception of period 2), whereas in Texas, the initial innovation is followed by an increase by $274 in period 2, $139 in period 3, and then small positive and negative fluctuations. In addition to having different impulse response functions, the two states differ in the contemporaneous correlation of the innovations to b_0 and b_1. The contemporaneous correlation of the innovations between b_0 and b_1 is positive with a value of 0.5 in New York but is negative and much smaller in Texas, with a value of −0.19.

To best illustrate the different impacts of permanent and transitory changes in welfare benefits, Keane and Wolpin (2002) parameterize the model to deliver large welfare take-up rates. To isolate the impact of the structure of welfare benefit rules, the other parameters of the model

Table 3.2
Effect of Permanent and Transitory Changes in Guarantee Parameters on Number of Pregnancies

	New York		Texas	
	Total Pregnancies by Period 20	Pregnancies in Period 1	Total Pregnancies by Period 20	Pregnancies in Period 1
Permanent				
$\Delta b_0 = 1{,}000$	0.78	-	0.76	-
$\Delta b_1 = 500$	1.37	-	0.39	-
Transitory				
$\Delta b_0 = 1{,}000$	−0.14	−0.03	0.47	0.05
$\Delta b_1 = 500$	1.20	0.25	−0.06	−0.005

(for example, preferences) are assumed to be the same in both states. The decision horizon is 20 periods. Table 3.2 shows the impact of a permanent $1,000 increase in b_0 on the mean number of pregnancies over the decision horizon in the two states. This effect corresponds to α_1 in equation 3.15 or how researchers were aiming to interpret α in equation 3.14. As seen, the effect of the increase in b_0 is to increase pregnancies similarly in both states, by 0.78 in New York and 0.76 in Texas.

A permanent change in b_1 of $1,000, also shown in table 3.2, is equivalent to a $500 change in b_1 for a mother with two children, which, as noted, is often the summary measure of welfare generosity used in the literature. Unlike the effect of increasing b_0, the increase in the per-child increment differs substantially between the two states, increasing pregnancies by 1.37 in New York and by 0.39 in Texas. Thus, even if the permanent effect could be estimated as was the intention, the effect of welfare benefits on fertility that would be estimated using the summary statistic would depend on the composition of the benefit variation between b_0 and b_1.

Table 3.2 also shows the responsiveness of fertility to transitory changes in b_0 (of $1,000) and b_1 (of $500). Two cases are considered, one in which the change occurs in only one period (the first) and one in which the change occurs in each period of the 20-year horizon, an extremely unlikely event given the *iid* nature of the innovations. Keane and Wolpin (2002) consider the latter case to determine the extent to which a change in the actual mean level of benefits generated from transitory changes would mimic the effect of the permanent change already discussed. This is one interpretation of the effect estimated by Rosenzweig (1999), albeit an extreme version. Alternatively, if women had perfect foresight (or if they believed, incorrectly, that all innovations were permanent), these changes would be viewed as permanent, and Rosenzweig's estimate would correspond to the permanent effect, subject to the caveat associated with using the summary measure of benefits.

The effect of a transitory change in b_0 in the first decision period is essentially zero in both states, trivially reducing pregnancies in New York and increasing pregnancies in Texas. Repeated innovations of the same amount in each of the twenty periods induces larger effects, a fall in pregnancies of 0.14 in New York and an increase of 0.47 in Texas. Recall that the estimate of the permanent effect was to increase mean pregnancies by about three-fourths in both states. The results, as is consistent with the impulse responses, are reversed for a transitory increase in the per-child benefit. The effect of that increase is negligible in Texas regardless of whether the increase occurs only in the first period or in all twenty periods. In New York, the innovation in only the first period increases pregnancies by 0.25, whereas increases in all twenty periods increase pregnancies by 1.20. Relative to the permanent increase, the persistent innovation is close for New York but not for Texas. Thus, if women have imperfect foresight and use updating rules consistent with the actual evolution of benefits over time, the effect on fertility of once and not for all transitory increases in benefits is considerably smaller than the effect of a permanent change in benefits. Innovations lack the persistence necessary to mimic permanent effects. Thus, in this case, state-fixed effect estimates that estimate transitory effects will differ from permanent effects that use cross-state variation in benefit rules.

Keane and Wolpin (2002) demonstrate that the results from the regression-based literature carry over to the data simulated from the model. In particular, in a logit specification of the contraceptive (fertility) decision, the benefit effect (based on the summary measure) is reduced by two-thirds with the inclusion of state-fixed effects. Further, if the benefit is disaggregated into the overall guarantee parameter (b_0) and the per-child guarantee parameter (b_1), the per-child parameter is twice as large, and eight times as large with state-fixed effects. Thus, the prediction of how increasing the benefit to a woman with two children would affect the number of pregnancies depends on how the increase is structured; there would be a many times larger impact if the increase came from a change in the per-child guarantee than from the overall guarantee.

There are a number of lessons to be drawn from these simulations for interpreting the regression-based literature. First, estimates based on cross-section variation confound the impact of permanent and transitory changes in welfare benefits. Second, estimates based on year-to-year fluctuations in benefits within states, which estimate the effect of transitory changes in benefits, may differ greatly, even in sign, from the effect of permanent changes. Third, in a dynamic setting, it matters how expectations are formed about future benefits. Fourth, estimates based on summary measures of welfare generosity confound the effect of different components of welfare rules, for example, the effect of changes in the overall level of benefits and changes in the benefits accruing to having additional children. Fifth, because states have different benefit rules, and they evolve differently over time, the effect of changes in welfare generosity is heterogeneous across states and across cohorts. Thus, the effect that is estimated depends on the composition of the sample in those dimensions. These issues can all be dealt with within a structural estimation approach, to which I now turn.

3.1.2.3 Structural Approach

There are a number of papers that have adopted the DCDP paradigm in estimating the impact of the AFDC program. Sanders (1993) and Miller and Sanders (1997) consider work and welfare participation, and Swann (2005) also includes marriage and welfare participation decisions. Fang and Silverman (2009) also consider work and welfare participation but allow for time-inconsistent agents. Keane and Wolpin (2007, 2010) allow for choices over work, welfare participation, marriage, fertility, and schooling.

As was the theme of chapter 2, consider the possibility of performing an *ex ante* policy evaluation of the AFDC program. Is it possible to do so nonparametrically as was the case in the *ex ante* evaluation of the wage tax or school attendance subsidy program? Ignore some of the complexity of the actual AFDC program and assume that there is a welfare benefit schedule, $b(n, y)$, offered to unmarried women with children, that depends on the number of children, n, and on the woman's non-earned income, y. In that case, assuming no saving or borrowing, the woman's budget constraint is

$$C = y + w(1-l) + b(n,y)l, \tag{3.18}$$

where C is consumption, $l = \{0, 1\}$ indicates nonemployment, and w is the wage offer. In the absence of a welfare program, $b = 0$. Assume that program eligibility depends only on unearned income not exceeding some limit. Notice that equation 3.18 can be written as

$$C = (y + b(n, y)) + (w - b(n, y))(1 - l)$$
$$= \tilde{y} + \tilde{w}(1 - l),$$

which takes the same form as the budget constraint without welfare, $C = y + w(1 - l)$.

The welfare program is identical in terms of the budget constraint to the school attendance subsidy program analyzed previously with multiple children, where the subsidy was in that case $\tau = bn$. As in that case, variation in wage offers (for female as opposed to child labor) and in non-earned income can be sufficient to identify the impact of introducing a (new) welfare program on labor supply; benefit variation is unnecessary. The same limitations of the nonparametric approach apply; for example, there can be no direct utility effect on welfare participation, and fertility cannot be endogenous.

The discussion of the parametric approach to *ex ante* evaluation of the school subsidy program also directly applies. Keane and Wolpin (2007, 2010) provide the most complete behavioral model. Let me touch on some of the major features (ignoring some of the details of the actual specification).

1. Welfare rules: The modeling of the welfare benefit rule, although still an approximation to the actual rules, accounts for more complexities than are seen in equation 3.16. In particular, the benefit rule is a five-parameter function that varies by state (s) and calendar time (t) given by

$$B_t^s(n_{at}^{18}, y_{at}^o, y_{at}^z) = b_{0t}^s + b_{1t}^s n_{at}^{18} - b_{3t}^s \beta y_{at}^z z_{at} \quad \text{for } y_{at}^o < y_{at}^{s1}(n_{at}^{18}) \qquad (3.19)$$

$$= b_{2t}^s + b_{4t}^s n_{at}^{18} - b_{3t}^s [(y_{at}^o - y_{at}^{s1}) + \beta y_{at}^z z_{at}] \quad \text{for } y_{at}^{s1}(n_{at}^{18}) \le y_{at}^o < y_{at}^{s2}(n_{at}^{18})$$

$$= 0 \text{ otherwise.}$$

In the first line segment in equation 3.19, the grant is seen to increase linearly in the number of minor children n_{at}^{18}, and if a woman coresides with parents, $z_{at} = 1$, a part, $\beta < 1$, of parents' income, y_{at}^z, is taxed at rate b_{3t}^s. In general, benefits are taxed away if the woman has positive earnings, y_{at}^o. However, due to work expense deductions and child care allowances, the tax is not assessed until earnings exceed a (state- and time-specific) "disregard" level, denoted by $y_{at}^{s1}(n_{at}^{18})$. The amount of benefits, once earnings exceed this level, is given by the second line segment in equation 3.19. The benefit tax rate or "benefit reduction" rate is taken to be the same as the tax on parents' earnings, b_{3t}^{s}. Finally, $y_{at}^{s2}(n_{at}^{18})$ is the level of earnings at which all benefits are taxed away. Keane and Wolpin (2007, 2010) assume that the stochastic process generating the evolution of the benefit rule parameters within each state follows a VAR as in Keane and Wolpin (2002).

2. Choice set: A woman makes joint decisions at each age of her life about the following set of discrete alternatives: whether or not to attend school, work part-time, or work full-time in the labor market (if an offer is received), be married (if an offer is received), become pregnant (if she is of a fecund age), and receive government welfare (if she is eligible). Thus, a woman chooses from as many as 36 mutually exclusive alternatives at each age during her fecund life cycle stage and 18 during her infecund stage. The fecund stage is assumed to begin at age 14 and to end at age 45; the decision period extends to age 62. Decisions are made at discrete 6-month intervals up to age 45, that is, semiannually, and then annually up to age 62. A woman who becomes pregnant in any period has a birth in the subsequent period. Consumption is determined by the alternative chosen and the woman's state variables.

3. Preferences: The woman receives a utility flow at each age that depends on her consumption and her five choices: (1) work, (2) school, (3) marriage, (4) pregnancy, and (5) welfare participation. Utility also depends on past choices (as there is state dependence in preferences), for example, on the number of children already born, their current ages (which affect child-rearing time costs), and their current level of completed schooling (which affects the utility from attending school). Marriage and children shift the marginal utility of consumption. Preferences are assumed to evolve with age and to differ among individuals by birth cohort, race, and state of residence.

There is also a vector of five permanent unobservables, determined by a woman's latent "type," that shift her tastes for leisure, school, marriage, pregnancy, and welfare participation. In addition, there are age-varying preference shocks to the disutility of nonleisure time (i.e., the sum of time spent working, attending school, child rearing, or collecting welfare), as well as direct utilities or disutilities from school, pregnancy, and welfare participation (unrelated to the time cost) and a fixed cost of marriage.

4. Budget constraint: The budget constraint is assumed to be satisfied each period. Resources available to the woman depend on her marriage and parental coresidence status. In addition to the welfare benefits for which a woman is eligible (as in equation 3.19), a woman who (1) is neither married nor living with her parents receives her labor earnings, (2) is married (and by assumption not also residing with parents) receives a share of the combined household earnings, or (3) is living with her parents receives her own earnings and a share of her parents' income. The shares in the latter two conditions are estimated parameters of the model. A woman who attends college or graduate school pays a tuition cost.

Her husband's earnings depend on his human capital stock. Conditional on receiving a marriage offer, the husband's human capital is drawn from a distribution that depends on the woman's characteristics, some of which, like her schooling, depend on the woman's choices. In addition, there is an *iid* random component to the draw of the husband's human capital that reflects a permanent characteristic of the husband unknown to the woman prior to meeting (which induces marriage market search on the part of the woman). Husband's earnings evolve with a fixed (quadratic) trend subject to a serially independent random shock. Parents' income depends on education and race.

In each period a woman receives full-time and/or part-time job offers with given probabilities. Each offer rate depends on the woman's previous-period work status. If an offer is received and accepted, the woman's earnings are the product of the offered hourly wage rate and the number of hours worked (either part-time hours or full-time hours). As in the Ben-Porath (1967)-Griliches (1977) formulation, the hourly wage rate is the product of the woman's human capital stock and its per-unit rental price, which may differ between part- and full-time jobs. Her human capital stock is a function of completed schooling , work experience, and her skill "endowment" (at age 14).

5. Residence status: In each period a single woman draws an offer to marry with some probability that depends on a subset of her characteristics. If the woman is currently married, then, with some probability she receives an offer to continue the marriage that depends on the duration of marriage and her age. If she declines to continue the marriage, the woman must be single for one period before receiving a new marriage offer. A single woman lives with her parents at any age according to a draw from an exogenous probability rule.

6. Endowment heterogeneity: Both permanent preferences and skill endowments differ for black, Hispanic, and white women, by state of residence, and by a woman's unobserved type. Note that with state of residence controlled, only within-state variation in welfare benefits contribute to identification. However, identification is not dependent on the particular source of benefit variation, and, as shown above, the existence of benefit variation is not needed for identification in some circumstances. All random shocks to preferences and the human capital stock are mutually serially independent and jointly normal.

A woman maximizes the expected present discounted value of remaining lifetime utility at any age conditional on her state space, which depends on her initial (age-14) preferences and skill endowments, her history of prior choices, and the previous period's benefit rule parameters (equation 3.19). The solution procedure, as has been described previously, uses the approximation method developed by Keane and Wolpin (1994). The estimation method is based on Keane and Wolpin (2001), which uses an unconditional simulation of choices to form the likelihood function.[32] The model is estimated using data from the 1979 cohort of the National Longitudinal Surveys (1979) on women who have resided since age 14 in one of five states: California, Michigan, New York, North Carolina, and Ohio. The goal of the estimation is twofold: (1) as is usual, to assess the impact of alternative policies, and (2) specific to this enquiry, to perform counterfactuals that will shed light on the extent to which the observed large racial disparities in demographic and labor market outcomes is the consequence of differences in marital prospects, in labor market opportunities, or in preferences.

Before discussing those issues, it is interesting to contrast the importance of unobserved heterogeneity in this case to the findings about men in Keane and Wolpin (1997) and Sullivan (2010), which are discussed in a later section. For women as well as men, unobserved heterogeneity plays an important role in explaining differences in behavioral outcomes. In the case of women, six latent types were sufficient for the model to provide a reasonable fit to all of the key features of the data. Estimates of several of the structural parameters suggest that types differ greatly and manifest significantly different behavioral outcomes. For example, comparing the behaviors of the two extreme types, types 1 and 6, black women of type 6 have spent 7 more years on welfare by age 30 than have those of type 1, have worked about 8 fewer years, have about 4½ years less education, and have two more children. Differences in welfare receipt between types are smaller for Hispanic and white women but still substantial (i.e., about 5 and 3 years, respectively), and differences in work experience, schooling, and fertility are about as large as for blacks. Type 6 women are a larger group than type 1 women by 10, 6, and 1 percentage points for black, Hispanic, and white women, respectively. Indeed, type 6 women are the largest group for all races.

Keane and Wolpin (2010) find that unobserved heterogeneity is the most important of the initial conditions in accounting for the variance in behaviors. Unobserved type alone accounts for 65 percent of the variation in completed schooling (by age 30). Whatever the process by which these unmeasured preferences and endowments are formed by age 14, they are critical in determining completed schooling levels. In contrast, race/ethnicity accounts for only 2 percent of the variance, state of residence 4 percent, and parental schooling (which affects both type and parental income) 11 percent. Together, initial conditions account for 70 percent of the variance in completed schooling at age 30, with the other 30 percent due to idiosyncratic shocks. However, welfare participation is more volatile. At age 30, only 33 percent of the variance in the total number of (6-month) periods on welfare is explained by type. At age 40 the comparable figure is 36 percent. Being black, Hispanic, or white explains 7 and 9 percent of variance at those two ages, respectively, and parental schooling explains 6 and 5 percent. Although the percentage of variance explained by the different initial conditions varies across different outcomes, in all cases except for years of marriage, type explains the largest percentage.

In general, initial conditions explain a larger percentage of the variation in human capital outcomes, namely schooling, work experience, and wages, than in demographic outcomes, namely children ever born, marriage duration, and the income of potential husbands. Finally, unobserved type, although by far the most important single factor, explains only 32 percent of the variance in utility for white women, 9 percent for blacks, and 17 percent for Hispanics, considerably smaller than for men. In contrast, both Keane and Wolpin (1997) and Sullivan (2010) considered only labor market outcomes. A closer comparison would therefore be the explained variance in full-time wage offers, which is about 65 percent for women.[33] The key reason that type explains less of the variance of lifetime utility for women than it did for men is that demographic outcomes such as fertility and marriage are apparently governed by inherently more noisy processes than labor market outcomes.

Accounting for Minority-Majority Differences in Outcomes
To what extent do differences in marriage market opportunities, labor market opportunities, and tastes account for minority-majority differences in life-cycle outcomes? To answer this question, Keane and Wolpin (2010) perform four counterfactual experiments that involve altering sets of parameters related to (1) the marriage market, (2) the labor market, (3) welfare stigma, and (4) parental schooling. Each experiment reveals how close the outcomes for blacks and Hispanics would be to those for whites if each category of parameters, taken one at a time, were set equal to those of white women. I concentrate the discussion on blacks and refer the interested reader to the paper for a parallel discussion for Hispanics.

Table 3.3 reports some of the results. The first two columns show the baseline model predictions. Columns labeled (1)–(4) show the effects of (1) equalizing potential husband's income and women's preferences for marriage, (2) equalizing offer wage functions (i.e., eliminating labor market discrimination), (3) equalizing welfare stigma, and (4) equalizing (the distribution of) types.

Adopting the marriage market parameters of white women has a large impact on behavior of black women, for whom both the change in preferences and the improved husband's income distribution increase the incentive to marry. For blacks, marriage rates increase almost to parity with whites (for example, from 28.5 percent to 55.7 percent at ages 26–29.5, compared to 65.4 percent for whites). As marriage increases, welfare participation falls, reducing the gap with white women by over a quarter at ages 22–25.5 and by over a third at ages 26–29.5. The gap between white and black women in the percentage of women with an out-of-wedlock pregnancy falls by about one-third at ages 18–21.5 and by almost one-half at ages 22–25.5. A higher probability of marriage reduces the return to human capital investment by lowering the probability of employment. As a result, black women's employment rates fall along with the rise in their marriage rate, doubling the gap with white women. Also reflecting the forward-looking nature of the model, mean schooling falls by a third of a year. Black-white differences in wage offers can result from either or both different skill endowments (at age 14) and differing skill rental prices due to racial discrimination. Providing black women with the same wage offer

Table 3.3
Accounting for Racial Differences in Choices

	Baseline		Counterfactual			
	White	Black	1	2	3	4
Pct. on Welfare						
Age						
15–17.5	1.3	5.1	5.4	4.1	4.1	4.2
18–21.5	4.7	16.8	15.1	12.5	14.0	14.3
22–25.5	7.1	26.5	20.9	17.9	22.8	23.3
26–29.5	7.1	29.7	21.4	19.6	26.4	26.1
Pct. in School						
Age						
15–17.5	85.3	84.4	80.7	87.7	84.2	85.2
18–21.5	29.8	29.6	25.0	30.6	29.8	33.1
22–25.5	8.3	8.1	6.0	9.0	8.1	9.0
26–29.5	3.4	3.5	2.6	3.7	3.5	3.9
Pct. Working						
Age						
15–17.5	28.3	16.9	15.5	31.0	17.0	16.3
18–21.5	63.8	51.9	42.4	68.5	52.8	53.0
22–25.5	70.3	57.4	44.7	71.2	59.1	61.6
26–29.5	69.8	55.7	42.3	70.2	57.3	60.5
Pct. Married						
Age						
15–17.5	5.0	1.1	3.6	1.7	1.1	1.0
18–21.5	28.2	9.6	24.6	12.7	10.0	8.7
22–25.5	52.3	21.7	45.1	27.3	22.5	20.6
26–29.5	65.4	28.5	55.7	36.5	29.4	27.6
Pct. Out-of-Wedlock Pregnancy						
Age						
15–17.5	1.8	3.0	3.0	2.5	2.9	2.8
18–21.5	3.1	5.9	4.9	5.0	5.8	5.7
22–25.5	2.4	5.8	4.2	4.9	5.7	5.7
26–29.5	1.6	4.9	3.1	4.0	4.7	4.7

1. Black women face the same marriage market as white women.
2. Black women have the same wage offer as white women.
3. Black women have the same welfare stigma as white women.
4. Black women have the same type proportions as white women.
Source: Keane and Wolpin (2010).

function, that is, with the same skill endowment and skill rental price, as whites reduces welfare participation more than does equalizing marriage market parameters, closing 44 percent of the black-white gap at ages 22–25.5, while the employment rate for black women reaches parity with that of whites. Marriage rates increase, and out-of-wedlock pregnancies fall, by about 40 percent among women below age 18 and by 25 percent at ages 22–25.5. The effect on welfare participation of replacing the level of welfare stigma of black women with that of white women is relatively small, as is the effect on other outcomes as well. Thus, differences in preferences for welfare participation appear to play little role in explaining differences in outcomes. Finally, equalizing type proportions has a small effect on choices, not too dissimilar to the effect of equalizing welfare stigma.

The Incentive Effects of Altering Welfare Rules
Keane and Wolpin (2010) perform counterfactual simulations to assess the impact of various hypothetical changes in welfare rules on behavior. Results are reported for the 25 percent of black women who are of type 6, women whose preferences, endowments, and opportunities induce them to choose welfare much more frequently than other types. Table 3.4 highlights some of the results. Baseline outcomes under the welfare rules actually in effect for the sample are shown in column 1. About 65 percent of the type 6 black women receive welfare between the ages of 22 and 29.5, and only about a fifth are working. At ages 26–29.5, the marriage rate for black women is only 21.8 percent, while fertility rates are high; on average, 1.5 children have been born to these women by age 24. The low marriage rates combined with the high fertility rates imply that, between the ages of 18 and 21.5, out-of-wedlock pregnancies account for almost 90 percent of all pregnancies for black women of this type. The fraction of women who are high school dropouts ranges from 40 to 50. Welfare benefits, on average, comprise over 40 percent of the total income of black women between the ages of 26 and 29.5.

The behavioral outcomes that result from eliminating welfare, the most extreme contrast, are shown in column 2. In columns 3 and 4, time limits are imposed, first a strict 5-year limit and then a 3-year limit, after which benefits are reduced by a third. Column 5 presents an experiment in which benefits are reduced by 20 percent, and column 6 introduces a work requirement: after having been on welfare for 6 months, a woman has to work or engage in "work-related activities"

Table 3.4
The Effect of Welfare on Choices—Black Women (Type 6)

	1	2	3	4	5
Pct. on Welfare					
Age					
15–17.5	13.2	0.0	13.0	13.2	8.0
18–21.5	39.6	0.0	36.4	39.9	27.2
22–25.5	61.2	0.0	35.6	60.5	45.2
26–29.5	68.1	0.0	16.5	66.5	55.1
Pct. Working					
Age					
15–17.5	9.5	10.4	9.6	9.6	11.9
18–21.5	26.9	36.5	27.2	26.7	42.6
22–25.5	20.8	42.7	25.9	21.4	54.1
26–29.5	15.1	43.4	31.2	18.1	62.2
Pct. Married					
Age					
15–17.5	0.4	0.5	0.4	0.4	0.4
18–21.5	7.8	10.6	8.0	7.8	9.0
22–25.5	16.5	25.3	19.0	16.8	18.9
26–29.5	21.8	36.6	28.9	22.6	25.0
Pct. Out-of-Wedlock Pregnancy					
Age					
15–17.5	5.0	4.5	5.2	5.2	4.9
18–21.5	8.5	7.6	8.6	8.6	8.3
22–25.5	8.5	7.1	8.2	8.6	8.2
26–29.5	7.3	5.4	6.6	7.3	6.9
Pct. High School Dropouts	45.4	36.2	44.0	45.2	43.7

1. Baseline.
2. No welfare.
3. Five-year time limit.
4. Three-year time limit followed by one-third reduction in benefits.
5. Twenty-five hours/week work requirement after 6 months on welfare.
Source: Keane and Wolpin (2010).

for 25 hours per week to continue to receive benefits.[34] Eliminating welfare has a substantial impact on employment. The percentage of black women working between the ages of 26 and 29.5 nearly triples, from 15.1 to 43.4 percent. Also, school attendance rates increase, leading to a decline in the high school dropout rate from 45 to 36 percent for blacks. Marriage rates increase substantially, from 22 to 37 percent for blacks at ages 26 to 29.5, and fertility falls modestly from

2.40 to 2.24 births by age 30. There is a nonnegligible decline in out-of-wedlock pregnancies. In the four age categories, the prevalence of an out-of-wedlock pregnancy falls by 10.0, 10.6, 16.4, and 26.0 percent for blacks.

A strict 5-year time limit (column 3) reduces welfare participation negligibly at young ages but by a large amount thereafter as the limit becomes binding. By age 26 through 29.5, participation falls from 68 to 17 percent for blacks. Increases in employment follow the same age pattern but are of smaller magnitude as marriage rates also increase with the imposition of the time limit. There is a negligible change in fertility (overall and out-of-wedlock) and in schooling. The weaker (and more realistic) time limit (column 4), where benefits are only partially reduced when the limit is reached, has very small effects relative to the baseline.[35]

Imposing a "work" requirement of 25 hours per week to maintain eligibility for welfare benefits beyond 6 months, which is modeled as increasing the time cost of welfare receipt, increases employment by 47 percentage points for black women at ages 26–29.5 (from 15 to 62 percent) but reduces welfare receipt by only 13 percentage points (from 68 to 55 percent). Thus, most of the women who start working after the imposition of the work requirement remain eligible for welfare. However, welfare comprises, on average, only 25 percent of total income after the work requirement is introduced as opposed to 43 percent before, and earnings increase by a factor of 3.

There are two major conclusions from this analysis. (1) There is no simple answer to the question of what causes black (or Hispanic)-white differences in employment, schooling, and demographic outcomes. Labor market opportunities, that is, labor market discrimination and/ or skill endowments in place by age 14, and marriage market opportunities, that is, the earnings potential of prospective husbands, as well as the interaction of these differential constraints with the effects of the welfare system, all provide important parts of the explanation. (2) The AFDC program created strong incentives for a significant minority of women, white, black, and Hispanic, that led to lower school attainment, less employment, lower marriage rates, and more out-of-wedlock births.

Validation
It is clear that the structural parametric approach is a powerful tool for *ex ante* policy evaluation. The question remains, as I have discussed

before, as to the credibility of the results from the counterfactuals. Keane and Wolpin (2007) pursued a range of approaches to model validation. As a first step, the within-sample fit of the DCDP model was examined across a number of dimensions and compared to a group of quasi-structural models, specified as four alternative multinomial logits (MNL) estimated on a subset of the choice data. These quasi-structural models are functions of the same set of state variables that enter into the decision rules derived from the DCDP model and thus are consistent with a myopic random utility model or a flexible approximation to a DCDP model. They are differentiated by whether they include state-fixed effects and by the complexity of the specification of welfare rules, one in which the rules are characterized by one parameter and the other by five parameters). Using a RMSE criterion (the number of parameters are similar), there seemed to be no clear winner in this cross-model competition.

The second step involved an external validation using data from a nonrandom holdout sample, specifically data from the state of Texas, which had a very different welfare policy regime from the five states that were used in estimation.[36] This external validation exercise is in the same spirit as the use of the treatment observations in Todd and Wolpin (2006) except that the holdout sample is not a random sample. Indeed, the Texas sample was chosen because the benefit schedule differed considerably from those of the other states in the same way as the treatment households in PROGRESA differed in that they were offered the school attendance subsidy and the estimation sample (controls) were not.

In terms of the same RMSE criterion, the model without state-fixed effects with the five-parameter welfare benefit rule produced predictions for Texas that were highly inaccurate. Further, the two models with state-fixed effects fit the data from Texas better than either the DCDP model or the remaining logit, although there was no clear ranking of the two better-fitting models. However, as was made clear in the discussion of Keane and Wolpin (2002) above, the state-fixed effect specification identifies the behavioral effects of only transitory changes in welfare benefits. Given the results from the simulations in Keane and Wolpin (2002), which was based on a similar VAR representation of the benefit rule parameters, those specifications should not have provided a better prediction of the effect of Texas's permanently different welfare rules. This result led to a third method of validation, which was to predict the effect of a policy intervention that has no analogue in the historical data, namely to give the five estimation states the same welfare rules as Texas.

Given Texas's considerably less generous benefits, welfare participation should have fallen. However, in the specifications with state-fixed effects, welfare participation actually increased. The only reason that the state-fixed effects specification had performed better in the external validation was that, in that exercise, Texas state dummies had been included in the estimation. Moreover, the one logit model without state-fixed effects that performed about equally well as the DCDP model in the external validation also produced unexpected results, forecasting that the decline in welfare participation would be considerably less than the increase in employment. On the basis of these results, Keane and Wolpin (2007) concluded that, in contrast to the DCDP model, all four MNL models were unreliable for policy prediction.

As a final observation, Keane and Wolpin (2007) conjectured that most economists would have professed a greater a priori faith in the ability of the MNL models to forecast behavior than in the DP model. That is, they would be concerned that, because the many assumptions invoked in setting up the DP model could all be questioned, it is unlikely such a model could forecast accurately. In contrast, they would view the MNL models, which simply model the value of each alternative as a flexible function of the state variables, as being much less restrictive. The evidence presented in the paper would seem to contradict that view.

3.2 The Role of Theory in Inference Based on Instrumental Variables—Estimating the Effect of School Attainment on Earnings

3.2.1 Background

The initial applications operationalizing the concept of human capital as an investment in embodied skills focused on estimating the internal rate of return (or marginal efficiency of investment) to schooling. The first empirical calculations of rates of return were based on comparisons of earnings profiles of synthetic cohorts with different levels of schooling (Carnoy, 1967; Hanoch, 1967; Hansen, 1963). The magnitudes of these estimated internal rates of return provided evidence of the credibility of the investment view of education.

A major innovation was the development of a shorthand way of estimating the internal rate of return based on a regression of earnings on school attainment (Becker and Chiswick, 1966; Mincer, 1974). What has come to be called the "Mincer earnings function" is perhaps the single most estimated relationship in economics. However, as discussed in detail by Heckman, Lochner, and Todd (2008), the interpretation of the schooling coefficient in an earnings or wage regression as an internal rate of return is fragile, depending on a special set of assumptions (for example, no direct costs of schooling, perfect foresight). Yet, it is commonplace to motivate the earnings function as Mincerian even in settings in which the assumptions do not obviously hold.

In hindsight, this tradition is surprising given an alternative interpretation of the wage function that is, in fact, more closely tied to the original notion of human capital as an investment good and to economic theory. Ben-Porath (1967), following the foundational work of Becker (1962, 1964, 1967) and Mincer (1958, 1962), provided a formalization of the acquisition of human capital within an explicit optimization framework. The essential idea was that human capital is produced according to a technology that combines an individual's time and market goods. In Ben-Porath's formulation, the amount of human capital produced over some time period depended on the beginning-of-period stock of human capital, the amount of time (the fraction of the total available time) an individual devoted to producing new human capital, the amount of purchased inputs (for example, books, equipment), and the individual's innate ability.[37] The cost of producing human capital is the forgone earnings associated with the time withdrawn from market work and the direct cost of the purchased inputs. An individual's market wage is the product of a competitively determined rental price per unit of human capital times the amount of human capital employed in the labor market (the stock of human capital times the fraction of time not devoted to producing new human capital).

A basic result from this model is that there would be a beginning period of specialization, when the human capital stock is low, in which individuals would spend all of their time in the production of human capital, and that after that period the production of human capital would decline (due to the finite horizon). Mincer (1974) used the on-the-job training accounting framework developed in Becker and Chiswick (1966) together with the result from Ben-Porath that human capital production would decline over the life cycle to derive the quadratic relationship between (potential) work experience and earnings. Mincer combined the schooling model, based on equating the present value of income streams across schooling levels, with the accounting model to obtain the familiar logarithmic form of the earnings function.

Griliches (1977) used the production function concept and competitive labor market assumption of Ben-Porath to formulate a wage-schooling function with a very different interpretation than that in Mincer. Specifically, letting w be the wage, r the human capital rental price, H the stock of human capital, and S years of schooling, the wage function is derived as follows:

$$w = rH, \tag{3.20}$$

$$H = e^{\beta_0 + \beta_1 S} e^v, \tag{3.21}$$

where v are other determinants of human capital including ability. Substituting equation 3.21 into equation 3.20 and taking logs yields the semilog form

$$\log w = \log r + \beta_0 + \beta_1 S + v. \tag{3.22}$$

The interpretation of the schooling coefficient in equation 3.22 is not as an internal rate of return but rather as a production function parameter. It thus reflects the combined productivity of school inputs and student time in producing marketable human capital or skills. Note that the constant term is the sum of the log of the skill rental price and a skill endowment (β_0). A learning-by-doing model of on-the-job skill accumulation leads to an augmented wage function in schooling and actual work experience that mimics the Mincer formulation, namely

$$\log w = \log r + \beta_0 + \beta_1 S + \alpha_1 X - \alpha_2 X^2 + v, \tag{3.23}$$

where, with positive and declining marginal product, $\alpha_1, \alpha_2 > 0$.

It was recognized quite early that the estimation of equation 3.23 was problematic because unmeasured ability, contained in v, would likely be correlated with years of schooling. Hanoch (1967) explicitly noted that his estimates of the internal rate of return would be biased if more able individuals obtained more schooling. Proposed solutions to the problem included using test scores as (imperfect) measures of ability (e.g., Griliches and Mason, 1972; Hause, 1972) and using siblings to control for family-level unobservables (Chamberlain, 1977). Scores of papers were written trying to assess the extent of the bias based on the specification in equation 3.23.

Hause (1972) argued that the proper specification of the wage function would include an interaction between schooling and ability. Letting A be ability, he proposed (and estimated with a measure of ability) the wage function

$$\log w = \log r + \beta_1 S + \beta_2 A + \beta_3 S \cdot A + Z\gamma + u \tag{3.24}$$

where Z included family background variables. The rationale for the interaction effect was that ability was factor augmenting, enhancing the productivity of schooling inputs, implying that β_3 should be positive.[38]

More recent attempts to estimate the effect of schooling on wages free of ability bias have used instrumental variable approaches that rely on natural experiments or quasi-experiments.[39] The IV approach to the identification of the "causal effect" of schooling on earnings has been studied by Card (1995, 1999), Heckman and Vytlacil (1998), and Heckman, Lochner, and Todd (2006) in the situation exemplified by equation 3.24, which can be rewritten in the form of a regression model with random coefficients, namely

$$\log w_i = \beta_{0i} + \beta_{1i}S + Z\gamma + u_i. \tag{3.25}$$

In equation 3.25, $\beta_{0i} = \log r + \beta_2 A_i$ and $\beta_{1i} = \beta_1 + \beta_3 A_i$. These papers show the sources of bias associated with the OLS estimator that ignores unmeasured ability and the conditions under which an IV estimator can identify the mean schooling effect, $\beta_1 + \beta_3 \bar{A}$.

In general, IV estimators do not recover mean effects when effects are heterogeneous (Heckman, 1997; Imbens and Angrist, 1994). It follows then that alternative instruments estimate different effects. It is precisely in this circumstance that theory is of value. Yet, it is an aspect of the IV literature that theory is usually eschewed. Without a theory incorporating the role of the instrument, it is not possible to interpret the estimates or to tell what assumptions are implicit in any given interpretation.

3.2.2 Instrumental Variables Estimators of the "Causal" Effect of Schooling on Earnings

Angrist and Krueger (1991)[40] present a prominent application of the natural experiment approach. They provide a stark example of the value of using (even quite simple) received theory to interpret empirical work.

Consider a standard model of schooling choice incorporating ability heterogeneity. Assume that the (annual) wage at any age a, w_a, depends on three factors—the level of school attainment, S, the amount of work experience at age a, X_a, and ability, μ, according to

$$w_a = f(S, \mu) + g(X_a, \mu), \tag{3.26}$$

where f and g are monotonically increasing in their arguments.[41] All individuals are assumed to work full time after completing schooling. To conform to the natural experiment in the Angrist and Krueger (1991) paper described below, the model explicitly incorporates a mandated school entry age a_e and a mandated minimum school-leaving age a_l. Thus, school attainment at age a_l, "initial schooling," is $S_0 = a_l - a_e$.

It is convenient for what follows to limit the decision horizon by assuming that the individual decides on whether to attend school only for one period beyond the school-leaving age. School attendance in the period following a_l, period 1, is denoted by $s_1 = 1$ and nonattendance by $s_1 = 0$; completed schooling, at the end of period 1, S_1, is therefore either $S_0 + 1$ or S_0. An individual who decides not to attend school in period 1 works that period and all subsequent periods; that is, the individual works from period $a = 1$ to the end of working life $a = A$, whereas an individual who attends school does not work in that period but works in all subsequent periods, that is, from $a = 2$ to $a = A + 1$. There is a direct cost of attending school denoted by c. The assumption that school attendance precludes working implies that school attendance entails an opportunity cost in terms of the earnings that are forgone.

The individual is assumed to make the choice of whether or not to attend school according to which option maximizes the present discounted value of lifetime earnings. Denoting the discount factor as δ ($= 1/[1 + r]$), the present discounted value of lifetime earnings (the annual wage) under the two schooling alternatives, $V(s = 1 \mid S_0)$ and $V(s = 0 \mid S_0)$, are

$$V(s_1 = 1 \mid S_0) = \exp[f(S_0 + 1, \mu] \sum_{x=0}^{X} \delta^{x+1} \exp[g(x, \mu)] - c$$

$$V(s_1 = 0 \mid S_0) = \exp[f(S_0, \mu] \sum_{x=0}^{X} \delta^{x} \exp[g(x, \mu)].$$

The decision rule is to attend school if $V(s_1 = 1 \mid S_0) \geq V(s_1 = 0 \mid S_0)$, which reduces, after some manipulation, to[42]

$$s_1 = 1 \text{ if } f(S_0 + 1, \mu) - f(S_0, \mu) \geq r + \frac{c}{V(s_1 = 0 \mid S_0)} \qquad (3.27)$$

$= 0$ otherwise.

Thus, the individual attends school if the percentage increase in earnings from attending school for the additional period is sufficiently greater than the interest rate.

If the increase in wages with additional schooling is greater for the more able, $\dfrac{\partial(f(S_0+1,\mu)-f(S_0,\mu))}{\partial\mu}>0$, then there exists a cutoff value of ability, μ^*, such that individuals with ability at or above that cutoff attend school and those below it do not. Thus, the difference in earnings among the two school completion groups will reflect, in part, these induced ability differences. Although ability is distributed randomly in the population, optimizing behavior creates a positive correlation between ability and completed schooling, which implies that the average schooling effect calculated from (log) earnings differences between the two schooling groups (for example, from an OLS regression earning on schooling) overstates the schooling effect averaged over the ability distribution, that is,

$$E_\mu[f(S_0+1,\mu\mid\mu\geq\mu^*)]-E_\mu[f(S_0,\mu\mid\mu<\mu^*)]>E_\mu[f(S_0+1,\mu)-f(S_0,\mu)].$$
(3.28)

The challenge has been to obtain an estimate of $E_\mu[f(S_0+1,\mu)-f(S_0,\mu)]$, the right hand side of equation 3.28. Whether the value of meeting that challenge is a worthwhile goal is an issue that will be discussed below. First, however, I consider whether the approach suggested by Angrist and Krueger (1991) achieves the goal.

Angrist and Krueger (1991) use natural variation in dates of birth, in conjunction with the existence of a birth date cutoff for school entry and a minimum compulsory school-leaving age, as an "instrument" for completed schooling to identify the mean schooling effect. To illustrate, consider a particular locality defined by a school entry age and a minimum school-leaving age in which a child must attain the age of 6 as of September 1 in order to enter the first grade and cannot leave school prior to attaining the age of 16. Thus, in the previous notation, $a_e = 6$ and $a_l = 16$. Then, a child whose birthday falls on September 1 will have 10 years of schooling at the minimum school-leaving age ($S_0 = 10$). However, a child born in the same calendar year but a day later, on September 2, will enter the first grade one year later and will have completed only 9 years of schooling on reaching age 16 ($S_0 = 9$). Thus, if children in the two (day of birth) cohorts are otherwise identical and at least some of them prefer nine or fewer years of schooling, average completed schooling of the two cohorts will differ because some of the children in the September 1 cohort will have been forced to obtain an additional year of schooling.

An additional simplification of the model illuminates how the Angrist and Krueger (1991) instrumental variable estimator works. Assume that there are just two ability types, denoted as μ_1 and μ_2, with the first type of higher ability ($\mu_1 > \mu_2$). Type 1's comprise π_1 proportion of the population, and type 2's $\pi_2 = 1 - \pi_1$. The insight of Angrist and Krueger (1991) is that, given laws governing the ages at which children can enter and leave school, completed schooling will vary with birth date for some part of the population. Date of birth is assumed to be a random variable uncorrelated with ability (as transmitted intergenerationally). Because the instrument relies only on within-state variation in dates of birth, laws governing school-entering and school-leaving ages, set by each state, can be correlated with other state-specific unobservables that influence earnings without inducing bias. Thus, variation in state schooling laws are not treated as natural experiments, can be endogenously determined, and do not contribute to identification.[43] It is variation in date of birth within states that serves to identify schooling effects. Having information on multiple states with differing laws merely adds precision to the estimates.

Angrist and Krueger (1991) present Wald estimates of the schooling effect on earnings based on comparing (log) weekly earnings and school completion levels for two cohorts of men aged 41–50 who differed in their quarter of birth, specifically comparing those born in the first quarter of a calendar year to those born in the other three quarters (of the previous calendar year).[44] In terms of the model, it is easy to show what their Wald estimator identifies. Suppose, according to equation 3.27, that the optimal level of schooling for type 1's, the high-ability type, is $S_0 + 1$ and that for type 2's is exactly S_0, given the school entry age (a_e) and the minimum school-leaving age (a_l). In that case, type 1's obtain $S_0 + 1$ years of schooling and have mean earnings of $f(S_0 + 1, \mu_1)$ regardless of date of birth. Type 2's, however, obtain different levels of schooling depending on when they were born. Older type 2's, those who make the deadline (born on September 1 in the example), obtain $S_0 + 1$ years of schooling and have mean earnings of $f(S_0 + 1, \mu_2)$, whereas younger type 2's who miss the deadline (those born on September 2 in the example) obtain only S_0 years of schooling and have mean earnings of $f(S_0, \mu_2)$. Thus, the mean earnings of younger children is

$$\pi_1 f(S_0 + 1, \mu_1) + (1 - \pi_1) f(S_0 + 1, \mu_2),$$

that of older children

$$\pi_1 f(S_0 + 1, \mu_1) + (1 - \pi_1) f(S_0, \mu_2),$$

and the difference in mean earnings between the younger and older children

$$\Delta E w = (1 - \pi_1)[f(S_0 + 1, \mu_2) - f(S_0, \mu_2)]. \tag{3.29}$$

Similarly, the difference in mean level of schooling in the population is

$$\Delta ES = \pi_1(0) + (1 - \pi_1) \cdot 1 = (1 - \pi_1). \tag{3.30}$$

Thus, the Wald estimator, the ratio of equation 3.29 to equation 3.30 is

$$\frac{\Delta E w}{\Delta ES} = f(S_0 + 1, \mu_2) - f(S_0, \mu_2),$$

which is the marginal effect of schooling on earnings for the less-able children, those induced to change their schooling by the instrument.

Under the maintained assumption that ability augments the effect of schooling on human capital (and thus wages), the Wald estimator is thus less than the population average effect $E_\mu[f(S_0 + 1, \mu) - f(S_0, \mu)]$. The two would coincide only if schooling and ability did not interact in the human capital production function, that is, if $f(S_0 + 1, \mu) = f_1(S) + f_2(\mu)$. Notice that if this latter condition held, there would be no need for the instrument, as the model would predict that the schooling decision is unrelated to ability (as long as the rate of interest and the direct cost of schooling did not vary with ability).

Angrist and Krueger (1991) found that for the group of men aged 41–50 in 1970 (1980), those born in the first quarter of a calendar year obtained 0.1256 (0.1088) fewer years of schooling on average than those born in the other quarters. Presumably, those men born in the first quarter of a calendar year were more likely to have had to delay school entry than those born in the previous three quarters. Dividing those differences by the corresponding differences in (ln) weekly wages implied a return to schooling of 0.0715 in 1970 and of 0.1020 in 1980. In contrast, the OLS estimate was larger in 1970, 0.0801, and smaller in 1980, 0.0709.

Butcher and Case (1994) suggest that natural variation in the sex of siblings, in particular whether a girl has any sisters, can be used to obtain an estimate of the average schooling effect on earnings (of women) that is free of ability bias. They discuss several reasons for the gender of siblings to affect parental human capital investments in a given child. In particular, the gender of siblings may affect the cost of investing in a child's human capital through the existence of borrowing constraints if there are exogenous gender differences in the return to human capital. According to Butcher and Case (1994), in the presence of borrowing constraints and assuming that boys receive a higher return to each level of schooling, "we should expect to see not only that boys receive more education but also that the presence of sons reduces the educational attainment of daughters." Also, independent of preferences, there may be exogenous differences in the cost of raising girls relative to boys, thus affecting the household's overall budget constraint. In addition, they argue that the gender of one's siblings may affect a child's preferences for schooling investments, with girls who have brothers perhaps adopting "masculine" traits and vice versa. Finally, parents may simply prefer to invest differentially in girls and boys depending on the overall gender composition of their children.[45]

To illustrate the Wald estimator of the return to schooling based on the gender of the first birth instrumental variable, in the context of the model used to elucidate the AC (1991) experiment, assume, as is consistent with the Butcher and Case (1994) argument, that the cost of schooling to a secondborn girl is higher if the firstborn is a boy as opposed to a girl, specifically c_b and c_g, respectively, with $c_b > c_g$. Ability is assumed independent of sex. Suppose that given these costs, it is optimal for the girl with a firstborn brother not to attend school regardless of her ability type, so that she completes only the minimum, S_0, years of schooling. On the other hand, suppose that among girls with a firstborn sister, who face a lower cost of schooling, type 1's optimally choose to attend school, thus completing $S_0 + 1$ years, whereas the type 2's still do not attend and complete only S_0 years. In this case, mean schooling of those girls with firstborn brothers is $\pi_1 f(S_0, \mu_1) + (1 - \pi_1)f(S_0, \mu_2)$ and for those with firstborn sisters, $\pi_1 f(S_0 + 1, \mu_1) + (1 - \pi_1)f(S_0, \mu_2)$. Thus, the difference in mean earnings of girls with firstborn sisters and firstborn brothers is $\pi_1[f(S_0 + 1, \mu_1) - f(S_0, \mu_1)]$, and the difference in mean schooling levels is π_1. Therefore, the Wald estimator is

$$\frac{\Delta E w}{\Delta E S} = f(S_0 + 1, \mu_1) - f(S_0, \mu_1),$$

the effect of the additional schooling on earnings for the more able group. Thus, opposite to the Angrist and Krueger (1991) instrument, the variation in completed schooling that arises from the sex of the firstborn sibling overstates the mean schooling effect. The reason that the Butcher and Case (1994) instrument leads to an overstatement of the mean schooling effect, in contrast to the understatement using the Angrist and Krueger (1991) instrument, is due not to the Butcher and Case instrument reflecting variation in the cost of schooling but rather to the relationship of ability to the schooling decision as the instrument varies.

Card (1995), for example, uses variation in the proximity of a 4-year college when growing up as an instrument for school attainment that, like the Butcher and Case instrument, is naturally interpreted as reflecting variation in the cost of schooling, c. Clearly, as seen from equation 3.27, conditional on ability, those who grew up in proximity to a college and thus faced a lower schooling cost would be likely to obtain more schooling than those who were not in close proximity. Maintaining the simplification of only two ability types, we then assume that the more able type, μ_1, would attend college, that is, choose $S_0 + 1$ years of schooling regardless of whether they grew up near a college, whereas the low-ability type, μ_2, would obtain $S_0 + 1$ years of schooling if they grew up near a college and S_0 years if they did not. In that case, mean earnings of those who grew up near a college would be $\pi_1 f(S_0 + 1, \mu_1) + (1 - \pi_1) f(S_0 + 1, \mu_2)$, and mean earnings of those who did not $\pi_1 f(S_0 + 1, \mu_1) + (1 - \pi_1) f(S_0 + 1, \mu_2)$. This is exactly the situation that arises in the Angrist and Krueger (1991) case and, as in that case, leads to a Wald estimator reflecting the effect of schooling on earnings for the less able.

Both the Angrist and Krueger (1991) and Butcher and Case (1994) instrumental variables should yield the same estimate if there is no interaction between schooling and ability. However, as Rosenzweig and Wolpin (2000) discuss, even in that case, the interpretation of the IV estimator is still dependent on specification. Both specifications of the earnings function control for age rather than, as suggested by Mincer (1974), (potential) work experience. Rosenzweig and Wolpin (2000) show that this seemingly innocuous specification choice leads to bias in both the Angrist and Krueger (1991) and Butcher and Case (1994) estimates and that the biases are of opposite sign. The existence of a theoretically valid natural instrument thus does not mean that the specification of the equation of interest does not matter for identification. That is, bias can still arise due to misspecification.[46]

3.2.3   Why Estimate the Causal Effect of Schooling on Wages?

The mark of a mature literature is when the rationale for a new study relies solely on reference to past studies. Identifying the effect of schooling on wages is by that definition very ripe indeed; the preoccupation of labor economists over the last 40 years with the estimation of β_1 in equation 3.22 has become sufficient justification for attaching great value to the development of new methods whose sole purpose is to provide a better estimate. As noted, an important rationale for the early literature on estimating the internal rate of return to schooling was to validate the notion of schooling as an investment. The identification of that parameter as a measure of the internal rate of return perhaps accounts for that preoccupation. However, knowledge of that parameter, when viewed in the context of richer behavioral models, is of considerably less value.

To illustrate this last proposition, consider a simplified version of the DCDP model of schooling, work, and occupational choice in Keane and Wolpin (1997). In that model, individuals choose at each age ($a =$ 16 to 65) whether to work in any of three occupations (white collar, blue collar, or the military), to attend school, or to neither attend school nor work (the home option). These alternatives are mutually exclusive and exhaustive. Per-period utility flows are linear in consumption (C) and nonpecuniary values attached to each option (denoted below by α's). Specifically, letting $d_{ms} = 1$ if alternative m is chosen and equal to zero otherwise, where $m = 1$ indicates working in a white-collar occupation, $m = 2$ working in a blue-collar occupation, $m = 3$ working in the military, $m = 4$ attending school, and $m = 5$ staying home, flow utility at age a is

$$U(C_a, \mathbf{d}_a) = C_a + \sum_{m=1}^{5} \alpha_m d_{ma} + \alpha_6 d_{4a}(1 - d_{4,a-1}), \qquad (3.31)$$

where $\mathbf{d}_a$ is the vector of alternatives d_{ma}. The utility flow from school attendance includes a potential psychic cost of returning to school (α_6).[47]

Consumption is the occupation-specific wage, w_{ma}, if the individual works plus any (alternative-specific) monetary transfers if the individual does not work, γ_4 and γ_5, minus the cost of attending college, t_1, given that alternative is chosen, namely

$$C_a = \sum_{m=1}^{3} w_{ma} d_{ma} + \sum_{m=4}^{5} \gamma_m d_{ma} - t_1 I(12 \le S_a < 15) d_{4a} \qquad (3.32)$$

where S_a is the grade attained by age a. The Ben-Porath/Griliches wage offer function in each occupation is the product of a competitively determined skill rental price (assumed to be constant over time) and the amount of embodied occupation-specific skill. The number of occupation-specific skill units possessed by an individual at age a depends on the years of schooling completed by that age and on the number of years of work experience in each occupation at that age. If we let e_{ma} be the number of skill units, x_{ma} the number of years of work experience, $e_{16,m}$ the endowment of skill units at age 16, and ε_{ma} a shock, the production functions for skill units is given by

$$e_{ma} = \exp(e_{16,m} + \beta_{m1}S_a + \sum_{m=1}^{3} \beta_{m2}x_{ma} - \beta_{m3}x_{ma}^2 + \varepsilon_{ma}) \text{ for } m = 1,2,3.$$

This specification leads to a log wage function of a standard form,

$$\log w_{ma} = \log r_m + e_{16,m} + \beta_{m1}S_a + \sum_{m=1}^{3} \beta_{m2}x_{ma} - \beta_{m3}x_{ma}^2 + \varepsilon_{ma}. \tag{3.33}$$

Note that the constant term is the sum of the (log) skill rental price, r_m, and the individual's skill endowment at age 16. The utility flows to work are stochastic because wage offers are stochastic. Utility flows to school and home (the α's) are also assumed stochastic, that is, $\alpha_{4a} = \overline{\alpha}_4 + \varepsilon_{4a}$ and $\alpha_{5a} = \overline{\alpha}_5 + \varepsilon_{5a}$. These parameters may be thought of as reflecting productivity differences in school attainment (an effort cost) and in home production (leisure). The vector of shocks, $\varepsilon_a = [\varepsilon_{1a}, \varepsilon_{2a}, \varepsilon_{3a}, \varepsilon_{4a}, \varepsilon_{5a}]$ is assumed to be jointly serially independent and distributed joint normal.

Individuals begin the decision process at age 16 with a set of permanent endowments consisting of their occupation-specific skills, $e_{16,m}$ ($m = 1, 2, 3$). and their preferences over attending school, $\overline{\alpha}_4$, and of remaining at home, $\overline{\alpha}_5$. Endowment heterogeneity is captured by assuming there to be K discrete types, with each type distinguished by a vector of endowments, $\mathbf{e}_{16}^k = [e_{16,1}^k, e_{16,2}^k, e_{16,3}^k, \overline{\alpha}_4^k, \overline{\alpha}_5^k]$. Thus, individuals may have comparative advantages among the different alternatives, including in acquiring schooling and in home production, that are known to them. Each person also starts with S_{16} years of schooling and zero work experience ($x_{16} = 0$). Unobserved endowments reflecting premarket skills (including innate abilities) enter the occupation-specific wage functions in the same way as ability does in the "causal effects" literature.

At any age a, the individual's objective is to maximize the expected present discounted value of remaining lifetime utility. Define $V_a^k(\Omega_a^k)$, the value function, as the maximal expected present value of remaining lifetime utility of an individual of type k, where Ω_a^k is the state space, that is, the history relevant for determining remaining expected lifetime utility. On substituting the wage function (equation 3.33) into the budget constraint (equation 3.32) and the resulting budget constraint into equation 3.31, the flow utility at age a for an individual of type k can be written as a function of the state variables $\Omega_a^k = [e_{16}^k, S_a^k, x_a^k, d_{4,a-1}^k, \varepsilon_a]$. Thus,

$$V_a^k(\Omega_a^k) = \max_{\{d_a\}} E \sum_{t=a}^{65} \delta^{t-1} \sum_{m=1}^{5} U_{ma}(\Omega_a^k) d_{ma}. \tag{3.34}$$

The maximization in equation 3.34 is achieved by choosing the optimal sequence of control variables, d_a, for $a = 16$ to 65.

As previously discussed, one can rewrite the value function as the maximum over alternative-specific value functions,

$$V_a^k(\Omega_a^k) = \max_m \{V_{ma}^k(\Omega_a^k)\},$$

where

$$V_{ma}^k(\Omega_a^k) = U_{ma}(\Omega_a^k) + \delta E[V_{a+1}^k(\Omega_{a+1}^k) \mid \Omega_a^k, d_{ma} = 1] \text{ for } a < 65, \tag{3.35}$$

$$= U_{m,65}(\Omega_{65}^k).$$

The expectation in equation 3.35 is taken over the distribution of the random elements in Ω_{a+1}^k conditional on Ω_a^k, that is, over the unconditional distribution of ε_{a+1}, given that $f(\varepsilon_{a+1} \mid \varepsilon_a) = f(\varepsilon_{a+1})$. Schooling at $a + 1$ is given by $S_{a+1} = S_a + d_{4a}$ and occupation-specific work experience at $a + 1$ by $x_{m,a+1} = x_{ma} + d_{ma}$ for $m = 1, 2, 3$.

The solution of the optimization problem serves as the input into estimating the parameters of the model given data on choices and wage offers for workers. Although the solution is deterministic for the individual, it is probabilistic from the researcher's view because contemporaneous shocks are not observed. Consider having data on a sample of N individuals from the same birth cohort who are assumed to be solving the model described above and for whom choices are observed over at least a part of their lifetimes. In addition, assume, as is the case, that wages are observed only in the periods in which market work is chosen and only for the occupation that is chosen. Thus, for each individual, n, the data consist of the outcomes $\{d_{nma}, w_{nma}d_{nma} : m = 1, 2, 3\}$

and $\{d_{nma}: m = 4, 5\}$ for all ages within the age range $\{16, \bar{a}_n\}$.[48] Let c_a denote the outcome data at age a and let $\Omega_a^{k(-)}$ denote the components of the state space observed by the researcher, that is Ω_a^k net of the shocks. The probability of any sequence of outcomes for an individual n given the individual is of type k and has initial schooling $S_{n,16}$ provides the likelihood contribution, L_{nk},

$$L_{nk} = \Pr(c_{n,16}, \dots, c_{n,\bar{a}_n} \mid S_{n,16}, type = k).$$

Because the researcher does not observe an individual's type, the likelihood function is a mixture of these type-specific likelihoods,

$$\prod_{n=1}^{N} \sum_{k=1}^{K} L_{nk} \Pr(type = k, S_{n,16}).$$

It is unlikely that initial schooling (at age 16) is exogenous, in which case conditioning the likelihood on it as though it were nonstochastic is problematic. One remedy would be to specify the optimization problem back to the age at which initial schooling was zero for everyone (say, age 3) and solve for the correct probability distribution of attained schooling at age 16 (conditional on age 3 endowments). However, such a model would have to focus on parental decision making with respect to investments in children (including fertility decisions) and would be very demanding in many dimensions (modeling, computation, and data).[49] The alternative Keane and Wolpin (1997) follow is to assume that initial schooling is exogenous conditional on the age 16 endowment vector. Given this assumption, the likelihood function can be conditioned on initial schooling as follows:

$$\prod_{n=1}^{N} \sum_{k=1}^{K} L_{nk} \Pr(type = k \mid S_{n,16}),$$

where $\Pr(type = k \mid S_{n,16})$ is estimated nonparametrically.[50] Identification in this model is achieved by a combination of exclusion restrictions and functional form and distributional assumptions.[51] The model is estimated using data from the 1979 cohort of the National Longitudinal Surveys of Labor Market Experience (NLSY79).

The first thing to note about this model relative to the "causal effect of schooling" literature is that there is no single causal effect. An increase in schooling affects wage offers in all three occupations. If wage offers were observed and a pooled wage regression estimated, given that occupation is a choice, the effect of additional schooling on wages would depend on the distribution of endowment types across occupations and would not convey anything of interest. The second thing to note is that these causal effects, the β's, are only three of the structural parameters of a rich model of behavior.[52] By themselves, these schooling parameters reveal little, if anything, that is of direct substantive interest.

In contrast, the point and strength of the structural approach are that the estimates of the model enable researchers to address important issues of consequence, issues that cannot be addressed in the causal effects literature. Before we consider some examples, it is useful to summarize some of the results of the estimation in order to better understand the mechanisms at work. Keane and Wolpin (1997) allow for four endowment types and for two levels of initial schooling (at age 16). A principal finding is that endowments differ and matter (a lot). Compared to type 1's, wage offers (at the same levels of schooling and experience) in the white-collar occupations are 8.7 percent lower for type 2's, 60.9 percent lower for type 3's, and 52.0 percent lower for type 4's. Although type 1's are endowed (at age 16) with the most white-collar skill, type 2's have the largest blue-collar skill endowment. Relative to type 1's, type 2's wage offer in that occupation is 30.5 percent higher, type 3's is 21.1 percent lower, and type 4's 5.5 percent lower. In addition, there is considerable heterogeneity in the (net) nonpecuniary values attached to attending school and staying at home. Type 1's value a year of schooling at $11,031 and a year at home at $20,242. The comparable figures are $5,667 and $18,107 for type 2's, $2,131 and $5,564 for type 3's, and $9,562 and $17,330 for type 4's.[53] Keane and Wolpin (1997) calculate that 90 percent of the total variation in expected lifetime utility is the result of between-type variation, with the rest a consequence of within-type idiosyncratic shocks (the sequence of ε_a's).

These endowment differences translate into different behaviors and welfare. Table 3.5 shows the levels of completed schooling and choice probabilities at age 24 and the expected present discounted value of lifetime utility (in 1987 thousands of dollars) for each initial schooling and type. Sample proportions are given in the last row. As shown, of the four distinct types that are identified in the estimation, type 1's, comprising 17 percent of the sample, complete about 4 more years of schooling than any of the others, over 16 years on average, and specialize in white-collar employment. Based on the estimated white-collar wage function, those additional four years of schooling would translate

Table 3.5
Selected Characteristics at Age 24 and EPDV of Lifetime Utility by Type and Initial Schooling

	Initial Schooling ≤ 9				Initial Schooling ≥ 10			
	Type 1	Type 2	Type 3	Type 4	Type 1	Type 2	Type 3	Type 4
Mean Schooling	15.6	10.6	10.9	11.0	16.4	12.5	12.4	13.0
Proportion in: White-Collar	0.509	0.123	0.176	0.060	0.673	0.236	0.284	0.155
Blue-Collar	0.076	0.775	0.574	0.388	0.039	0.687	0.516	0.441
Military	0.000	0.000	0.151	0.010	0.000	0.000	0.116	0.005
School	0.416	0.008	0.013	0.038	0.239	0.024	0.025	0.074
Home	0.000	0.095	0.086	0.505	0.050	0.053	0.059	0.325
Expected Present Value of Lifetime Utility[1]	387	374	214	286	416	396	229	291
Sample Proportion	0.010	0.051	0.103	0.090	0.157	0.177	0.289	0.123

1. Thousands of 1987 dollars.
Source: Keane and Wolpin (1997), Tables 11, 12, and 13.

into a wage offer that is 28 percent higher for type 1's than that for the other types. Although that represents a large differential, recall that the difference in wage offers based on white-collar skill endowments was twice as large as for type 3's and type 4's. Type 2's, comprising another 23 percent of the sample, complete, on average, 12 years of schooling and specialize in blue-collar employment. Interestingly, the expected present value of lifetime utility is about the same for the two types.[54] The third type, 39 percent of the sample, is the only type to enter the military; about 13 percent are in the military at age 24. They also complete about 12 years of schooling and, other than military service, specialize in blue-collar employment. However, as compared to the second type, who have much the same schooling and employment patterns, because type 3's have considerably lower age-16 levels of premarket skills, their expected lifetime utility is only about three-fifths as great. The last type, the remaining 21 percent, also completes about 12 years of schooling on average, but about 40 percent choose to be at home at age 24, about five times as much as any other group.

Initial schooling also significantly affects choices. The difference in school attainment that has already emerged by age 16, a difference of about 1.4 years, that is due to exogenous events unrelated to endowments, for example, illnesses that occurred in the past or date of birth that affects age at entry given the minimum school entry age (as in Angrist and Krueger, 1991), is magnified over time for two of the four types. Although the initial difference is reduced to about 0.8 years for type 1 individuals and is essentially unchanged for type 3 individuals, the completed schooling difference increases to about 2 years for types 2 and 4. However, initial schooling differences have only a small impact on expected lifetime utilities (ranging over types from about 1 to 8 percent higher for the highest initial schooling group).

Under the assumption that the four types capture all unobserved differences in premarket endowments, it is possible to determine the extent to which conventional measures of family background are able to account for differences in lifetime utilities that arise from age-16 endowments. In the baseline, the difference in expected lifetime utility between the first type (the highest) and the third type (the lowest) is estimated to be $188,000 (1987 dollars). In comparison, the difference for individuals whose mothers were college graduates relative to those whose mothers were high school dropouts is estimated to be $53,000, the difference for those who lived with both parents at age 14 relative to those who lived in a single parent home is $15,000, and the difference between those whose parental income was more than twice the median relative to those less than one-half the median $66,000. Although the association of expected lifetime utility with family income and mother's schooling appears to be strong, a regression of expected lifetime utility on those family background characteristics is reported to explain only 10 percent of the variation. Coupled with the fact that 90 percent of the total variation in expected lifetime utility is determined to be due to between-type variation, these family background characteristics are in actuality only imperfect proxies for premarket skills.

3.2.3.1   Ex Ante *Policy Evaluation*

Continuing with the theme of the chapter 2, I consider several applications of the Keane and Wolpin (1997) model to *ex ante* policy analysis. Keane and Wolpin (2000) applied the Keane and Wolpin (1997) model to analyze race differences in educational and labor market outcomes. The disparity in educational attainment between white and black males is substantial. For example, Keane and Wolpin (2000) report that for a subset of males in the 1979 youth cohort of the NLSY79 who were 13–16 years old by October 1977 (people born in the early 1960s), mean highest grade completed at age 23 (at which point education is mostly completed) was 12.7 for whites compared to 11.9 for blacks. In addition, 21.3 percent of whites had completed college, compared to only 6.8 percent of blacks and 35.9 percent of blacks were high school dropouts, compared to 24 percent of the whites. In terms of (accepted) wages, for that same cohort, at age 26 blacks working in a white-collar occupation earned only 61 percent as much as whites, and those working in a blue-collar occupation 75 percent as much.

To understand these differences, Keane and Wolpin (2000) estimated a restricted version of the model in which all parameters for blacks and whites were constrained to be equal except for (1) the type proportions and (2) the intercepts in the earnings functions. The type proportions capture race differences in age-16 skill endowments and preferences through a shift in type-specific population weights. The intercepts capture both race differences in skill rental prices due to discrimination and differences in the level of the skill endowments of each type. Strikingly, compared to a model in which all parameters were allowed to differ by race, this severe restriction on the model was not rejected. Keane and Wolpin (2000) find that the constant terms in the wage offer equations are 7.9 percent lower for blacks in the white-collar occupation and 4.7 percent lower in the blue-collar occupation. The differences in type proportions are even more pronounced: only 17.4 percent of blacks are types 1 or 2 (the high-wage types) compared to 43.2 percent of whites. Conversely, 41.6 percent of blacks are type 4's (which accounts for most high school dropouts) compared to only 20.3 percent of whites.

Keane and Wolpin (2000) examine the extent to which policies that provide financial incentives for school attendance can reduce racial differences in school attainment and wages. Based on the model estimates, they calculate that providing blacks with a bonus of $6,250 for finishing high school and an additional $15,000 for finishing college (both in 1987 dollars) would essentially equalize the distribution of completed education for whites and blacks.[55] They calculate that implementation of such a scheme would cost about $2 billion per year (in 1987 dollars).

One might expect that the equalization of schooling would go a long way to equalizing lifetime earnings, both because schooling directly increases earnings in all occupations and because those with higher schooling work in high-wage (white-collar) occupations. However, Keane and Wolpin (2000) find that the large increase in education induced by this scheme has very little impact on the mean present value of lifetime earnings for blacks. Under the baseline, Keane and Wolpin simulate that the present value of lifetime earnings is $285,000 for whites and $210,000 for blacks, so lifetime earnings for blacks is only 73.7 percent that of whites. The school attendance bonus scheme increases lifetime earnings for blacks only up to $214,000, which is 75.1 percent of that for whites. Thus, the bonus scheme eliminates only about 5 percent of the gap.

The result that reasonably modest attendance bonuses would substantially increase college attendance of blacks is consistent with a large literature that finds a rather elastic response of college attendance to college costs (see, e.g., Leslie and Brinkman, 1987, or Keane and Wolpin, 2001, for reviews). However, raising college attendance per se does nothing to alter the age-16 endowments or to reduce wage discrimination, the factors that account for the earnings differential between blacks and whites. The importance of these factors can be seen through the following two hypothetical experiments. Equalizing type proportions (that is, giving blacks the same type proportions as whites) would raise the present value of lifetime earnings for blacks to $254,000, whereas eliminating racial discrimination and/or equalizing type-specific skill endowments would raise it to $239,000. Thus, these hypothetical experiments would eliminate 52 percent and 39 percent of the earnings gap, respectively. These are large effects, particularly relative to the effects of equalizing school attainment.

The main conclusion that Keane and Wolpin (2000) draw from these results is that policies such as college financial aid and school attendance bonuses can only be effective ways to reduce lifetime earnings inequality between blacks and whites if they also act to change age-16 endowments. These endowments may be determined by many inter-related factors, such as parental education and income, parental investments in children, pre- and postnatal care, the quality of child care, preschools, primary schools and secondary schools, neighborhood effects, and others. The extent to which the kind of educational policies considered above induce behaviors that affect endowments is unknown. The development of effective policy requires opening the black box of what determines age-16 skill endowments. There is now a growing research agenda that is focusing attention on the formation of both cognitive and noncognitive skills during childhood. I turn to this issue below.

A further advantage of the structural approach is that it enables the researcher to address a number of policy issues within the same model. Keane and Wolpin (2000) also examine whether wage subsidies for low-wage workers would be effective as a means to reduce earnings inequality. Wage subsidy policies have been suggested, and sometimes pursued, as a means of reducing joblessness and providing income support for low-wage workers (see Katz, 1996). Keane and Wolpin (2000) implement a wage subsidy policy akin to that suggested by Phelps (1997). In that policy an individual's wage is augmented by 33 percent of the difference between $12 an hour and the accepted wage; for example, an individual who accepted a wage of $9 would actually receive 10 dollars per hour. The result of the policy is to increase the present value of earnings of whites by 6.4 percent and that of blacks by 16 percent. This is the intended result. However, the policy also has the unintended effect of inducing earlier withdrawal from school. The proportion of high school dropouts increases from 26.2 percent to 35.8 percent for whites and from 37.9 to 41.2 for blacks.[56]

Sullivan (2010) developed a DCDP model that combines a model of job market search (as in Wolpin, 1992, and Rendon, 2006) with a human capital model of schooling and occupational choice (as in Keane and Wolpin, 1997). The previous literature considered job search as a separate phenomenon from schooling and occupational choice, although the choices are clearly related. In Sullivan's (2010 model), workers decide in each period whether to attend school and/or work in one of five occupations or neither work nor attend school. An employed individual may stay at the current job or switch jobs either within the same occupation or with a change in occupation. Human capital accumulated through work experience is both firm- and occupation-specific. Individuals have heterogeneous skill endowments and preferences for employment in different occupations. Wage offers depend on an individual's unobserved occupation-specific skill endowment (modeled as in Keane and Wolpin, 1997), on a firm-worker match-specific component, and on an *iid* time-varying shock. The match-specific component introduces serial correlation into the wage offer process, as it is carried over from period to period in the current job, which is what makes job search valuable. Model parameters are estimated by simulated maximum likelihood using data from the NLSY79 on detailed job histories.

Sullivan (2010) finds that occupational and job mobility are critical determinants of life cycle wage growth, quantitatively more important than the accumulation of occupation-specific human capital. As in previous research, the results also indicate the importance of comparative advantage in understanding schooling and occupational choices. There are large differences in occupation-specific skill endowments at age 16; for example, type 1 individuals receive wage offers in the professional and managerial occupation that are 40 to 70 percent larger than the other (three) types. However, a significant part of the variation in wages is due to difference in match-specific draws, variation that in Keane and Wolpin (1997) would have been accounted for in endowment heterogeneity. Sullivan (2010) finds that endowment heterogeneity accounts for a relatively smaller, although still substantial, component of the variance in expected lifetime utility than found by Keane and Wolpin (1997), 56 percent as opposed to 90 percent.

Ex ante policy evaluation should be conducted within an equilibrium framework. Policies that are of consequence and that impact significant parts of the population can be expected to alter market prices that affect the behavior not only of those targeted by the policy but also of agents in the same market who were not targeted. It is thus necessary to have developed methods and models that account for equilibrium effects. There are few examples of *ex ante* policy evaluations carried out in an equilibrium framework. One example that illustrates again the importance of developing model selection criteria is the assessment of the effect of college tuition subsidies on educational attainment.

In contrast to a graduation bonus scheme, which rewards individuals for achieving a threshold number of years of schooling, tuition subsidies are based only on attendance. Leslie and Brinkman (1987), in a survey of twenty-five empirical studies based on cross-state or time-series variation in college costs, report the modal estimate of the response to a $100 tuition increase (in 1982–1983 dollars) to be a 1.8 percent decline in the enrollment rate of 18- to 24-year-olds. Other estimates range from a low of 0.8 percent for 18- to 24-year-old whites to a high of 2.2 percent for 18- to 24-year-old blacks (Kane, 1994). In Keane and Wolpin (1997), the comparable effect is a decline of 1.2 percent.

These policy effects assume that general equilibrium feedbacks are negligible. However, policies that serve to increase schooling levels and thus the aggregate skill level will reduce the skill rental price in equilibrium. Partial equilibrium estimates of the impact of those policies on schooling would, therefore, overstate the general equilibrium impact. The Keane and Wolpin (1997) framework is amenable to a labor market equilibrium setting. More concretely and for simplicity, assume that there is only a single occupation and that production is Cobb-Douglas, that is, $Y = AS^{\alpha}K^{1-\alpha}$. Aggregate skill is given by the sum of the skill levels over individuals, namely $S = \sum_a \sum_{j=1}^{N_a} S_{ja}$, where N_a is the number of individuals of age a in the population. As noted, it is not possible to separately identify, from data on choices and wages, both the skill rental price and the level of premarket skills. Moreover, given the non-observability of skill, the technology shifter, A, also cannot be identified. A baseline case can be established by normalizing either A or the rental price. With the assumption that $A = 1$, a baseline equilibrium rental price can be established that induces a level of aggregate skill that equates the marginal product of skill to that rental price. The general equilibrium impact of a tuition subsidy on schooling is determined by resolving jointly for the equilibrium rental price and optimal choices.

Donghoon Lee (2005) has implemented this procedure in the multi-skill setting, allowing as well for nonstationarity in population size, that is, for changing cohort size. Lee adopts an overlapping generations version of the occupational and schooling choice model of Keane and Wolpin (1997), assuming that individuals have perfect foresight about equilibrium outcomes but imperfect foresight about their idiosyncratic shocks to preferences and skills. Each cohort therefore faces a known, but different, sequence of occupation-specific skill rental prices. Individuals are assumed to face exogenous cohort and age-specific fertility rates and a constant college tuition cost. Aggregate production at any calendar time depends on the aggregate level of white-collar skill, the aggregate level of blue-collar skill, and capital. Capital grows exogenously at a known rate. The production function is Cobb-Douglas with time-varying factor shares (technology parameters), about which individuals also have perfect foresight.

Lee estimates the model by using aggregate data from the 1968–1993 Current Population Surveys (CPS). The model is fit to the empirical moments of school enrollment rates, occupation-specific employment rates, and educational attainment by age, year, and sex and to wage moments by age, year, sex, and educational attainment. The partial equilibrium effects are in line with those of other studies. Similar to Keane and Wolpin (1997), Lee finds that a $100 tuition increase reduces college enrollment rates by 1.12 percent for 18- to 19-year-old males and by 1.34 percent for 18- to 24-year-old males. General equilibrium effects on completed schooling for the 50 percent subsidy range from 92 to 95 percent of partial equilibrium effects on college enrollment rates for the $100 tuition increase.

In an earlier series of papers, Heckman, Lochner, and Taber (1998, 1999) performed a similar comparison based on a general equilibrium model with different characteristics. The data and estimation methods they adopted also differ significantly from those of Lee. As with Lee, I only briefly describe the essential features of their paper: (1) skill classes are defined by educational attainment; (2) in addition to making an initial discrete schooling decision, in each postschooling period individuals explicitly decide on their human capital investment time on the job as in Ben-Porath; (3) individuals make savings decisions in each period; and (4) labor is inelastically supplied in each period. As they noted, accounting in estimation for the restrictions that general equilibrium imposes given the structure of their model is not feasible with available data. In particular, estimation is hindered by the lack of microdata on consumption and on investment time on the job. For that reason the procedure adopted for recovering the parameters of the model involves a combination of calibration based on results from existing studies and new estimation using both aggregate CPS data (over the period from 1963 to 1993) and longitudinal data from the

NLSY. The partial equilibrium effect of a $100 increase in college tuition costs is 1.6 percent, well within the range of other studies and not much different from that of Lee (2005) or Keane and Wolpin (1997). However, the general equilibrium effect is reduced by an order of magnitude, to 0.16 percent.

Clearly, the bound established by Heckman et al. and Lee is extreme. Accounting for the divergence in their results in any quantitative manner is problematic because of the major differences in their models. Yet, in determining the efficacy of tuition subsidies as a means for increasing school attainment, it clearly matters which result one adopts or how the results are weighted. This example again illustrates the importance of establishing some criteria for model validation and model selection.

Although the early human capital literature recognized the importance of understanding skill formation in children (Leibowitz, 1974), the human capital literature became focused, overly so in my view, on estimating the impact of years of school attainment on wages. The recent revival of interest in early childhood skill acquisition is an important development discussed below.

3.3   The Role of Theory in Drawing Inferences to External Populations

3.3.1   Project STAR

Views about the effectiveness of reducing class size on school performance were significantly affected by the results of the Tennessee Student/Teacher Achievement Ratio experiment, more conventionally known as Project STAR. That experiment was mandated by the Tennessee state legislature in 1985 and initiated in the 1985–1986 academic year. All elementary schools were invited to participate. A little more than one-third of the school districts, including about 180 schools, responded positively. Given the class-size requirements of the experiment and other factors, eventually 79 elementary schools located in 42 of the 141 districts were incorporated into the program. The experiment randomly assigned both students and teachers to three kindergarten classes: a small class, ranging from 13 to 17 students, and two regular size classes, with and without a teacher aid, ranging from 22 to 26 students. The experiment was conducted through the third grade, after which random assignment of students and teachers was discontinued.

There were initial studies encompassing the 4 years of the project and later studies that followed students into high school and beyond.

Krueger (1999) and Nye, Hedges, and Konstantopoulos (2000) provide two of the most rigorous studies of the initial 4 years of the program. Both of these studies conclude that class size has a statistically significant and quantitatively large effect on student performance as based on test scores. Krueger (1999) contrasts the experimental results to those obtained from nonexperimental studies as follows: "One well-designed experimental study should trump a phalanx of poorly controlled, imprecise observational studies based on uncertain statistical specifications."[57] Concerning the value of the experiment and its place in the literature, Nye, Hedges, and Konstantopoulos (2000) conclude that "The STAR study provides an important (and perhaps the strongest) piece of the converging evidence about the effectiveness of small class sizes in promoting achievement."[58]

In this section, I address a number of issues concerning these studies, and social experiments more generally, that relate to the role of theory in the development, analysis, and interpretation of social experiments. To fix ideas, let A_{ig} be a continuous measure of achievement for student i at the end of grade g, and S_{ig} be the class size assignment of that student, equal to 1 if the child is assigned to a small class and equal to 0 otherwise. As in the STAR experiment, the class size assignment is made at the beginning of the school year, and the achievement assessment is done at the end of the school year. Given randomization, the (demeaned) regression

$$A_{ig} = \alpha S_{ig} + u_{ig} \tag{3.36}$$

would provide an estimate of α, the average difference in achievement between students in small and large classes. The question is how to interpret α.

3.3.2 Is α a Production Function Parameter?

The title of Krueger's (1999) paper is "Experimental Estimates of Education Production Functions," and one of his stated goals is to "use the experimental results to interpret estimates from the literature based on observational data," where the literature being referenced is the education production function literature. Nye, Hedges, and Konstantopoulos (2000) also compare their estimates to those that come from the estimation of education production functions using observational data. They find that meta-analyses of nonexperimental estimates are similar to those obtained from the experiment. If one is to take comfort in that observation, it is important that the two sources of estimates are measuring the same effect.

To address this issue, consider the following stylized formulation of the process of knowledge accumulation (achievement) as presented in Todd and Wolpin (2003). Define $t = 0$ as the time interval from conception to first attending school, $t = 1$ as the first year of school (kindergarten in the STAR experiment), and $t = 2$ as the second year of school. Let I_0 be the set of family-provided inputs to the child during period $t = 0$ that affect the child's accumulation of knowledge (including, for example, the mother's diet during the pregnancy, the degree of mental stimulation during infancy and early childhood, and others), and μ the child's endowed mental capacity determined at conception. Note that I_0 is meant to be inclusive of all of the determinants of the child's knowledge by the start of school, A_0. Thus, the achievement production function during period $t = 0$ is

$$A_0 = g_0(I_0, \mu).$$

The family is assumed to make (utility-maximizing) preschool input decisions based on their "permanent" resources, W, on the child's endowment and on the family's preference over the child's achievement, ε; that is, $I_0 = g_0(W, \mu, \varepsilon)$.

In addition to family inputs, the household also makes a decision about the potential school inputs the child will be exposed to through a location choice, which, like family inputs, depends on W, μ, and ε. However, at the time of the location decision, parents have incomplete information about the actual level of inputs applied to their child, S_1, for example, the quality of the assigned teacher, which may vary within the school. To simplify notation, the potential school input is given by a single summary statistic, $\bar{S}_1$.

Achievement at the end of the first school year, A_1, depends on family inputs during the preschool period and during the first period of school, I_0 and I_1, and on actual school inputs, S_1, as well as on the child's endowment, namely

$$A_1 = g_1(I_0, I_1, S_1, \mu).$$

Along with the technology for combining inputs to create achievement outcomes, there is a decision rule for both parents and schools that determines the levels of inputs. The family decision rules concerning direct family inputs and potential school inputs associated with their location decision are given by

$$I_1 = \phi_I(A_0, W, S_1 - \bar{S}_1, \mu, \varepsilon) \tag{3.37}$$

$$\bar{S}_1 = \phi_S(A_0, W, \mu, \varepsilon), \tag{3.38}$$

where it is important to note that family input decisions are assumed to be made subsequent to the actual realization of the school inputs applied to their children.[59]

Todd and Wolpin (2003) assume that the school chooses input levels for a particular child purposefully, taking into account the child's achievement level and the endowment, that is,

$$S_1 - \bar{S}_1 = \psi(A_0, \mu).$$

For example, a child who enters first grade able to read may receive different school inputs than a child who is not able to read. Thus, a simple comparison of student achievement based on differences in realized school inputs, $S_1 - \bar{S}_1$, would be contaminated by differences among students in A_0 and μ because of the sorting decision by schools. Of course, a comparison of student achievement across schools would similarly be contaminated because of the parental location decision as embodied in equation 3.38.

Within this simple framework, it is possible to consider different kinds of parameters of interest in empirical research. To focus on class size, one question of interest is the following:

1. How would an exogenous change in class size, holding all other inputs constant, affect achievement?

Knowledge of the production technology would suffice to answer this question. The goal of most observational studies has, in fact, been to uncover features of the production technology, given above by g_0 and g_1.

An alternative question of interest is the non–ceteris-paribus effect of changing school inputs, namely

2. What would be the total effect of an exogenous change in class size on achievement, that is, not holding other inputs constant?

Suppose first that the change in class size is unanticipated by parents, as in the Project STAR experiment. The total effect of this unanticipated change includes both the effect holding other inputs constant as well as any indirect effects that operate through changes in the levels of other inputs. In the simple model with only one school input, the total effect of an exogenous change in the school input (class size) in the first year, S_1, on achievement at the end of the year, A_1, is given by

$$\frac{dA_1}{dS_1} = \frac{\partial g_1}{\partial S_1} + \frac{\partial g_1}{\partial I_1} \frac{\partial I_1}{\partial (S_1 - \bar{S}_1)}. \qquad [60] \qquad (3.39)$$

Knowledge of the technology is not sufficient to answer this question because the production function provides $\dfrac{\partial g_1}{\partial S_1}$ and $\dfrac{\partial g_1}{\partial I_1}$, but not $\dfrac{\partial I_1}{\partial (S_1 - \bar{S}_1)}$. To get the last term requires knowledge of the family input decision rule (equation 3.37), which could in principle be estimated from nonexperimental data. The Project STAR experiment provides an answer to the second question but not the first. Thus, α in equatiion 3.36 corresponds to the expected value of $\dfrac{dA_1}{dS_1}$ in equation 3.39 and is not a production function parameter. It is the "policy effect" of an *unanticipated* change in class size taking into account adaptations in inputs that arise because of the differences in class size, namely

$$E\left(\frac{dA_1}{dS_1}\right) = \int \left[\frac{\partial g_1}{\partial S_1} + \frac{\partial g_1}{\partial I_1} \frac{\partial I_1}{\partial (S_1 - \bar{S}_1)}\right] f(W, \mu, \varepsilon) \qquad (3.40)$$

where $f(W, \mu, \varepsilon)$ is the joint density of W, μ, and ε.[61] Thus, the Project STAR experiment provides the answer to a question that may be of direct policy interest.

This average policy effect defined above can be either larger or smaller than the ceteris paribus effect. For example, families in Project STAR whose children were assigned to small classes may have spent less time teaching their children at home, that is, if school and family inputs are substitutes in producing achievement. In that case, the average policy effect measured by the experiment would be less than the ceteris paribus effect. Alternatively, the effects could reinforce each other, for example, if families were encouraged to apply more family inputs by their child's greater learning at school, that is, if school and family inputs are complements. Only under the assumption that families do not take into account changes in school inputs in choosing family input levels would the experimental estimate correspond to a production function parameter, and it is only in that case that a comparison of estimates obtained in these two ways is warranted.[62]

The model assumes that parents choose among locations that differ in the (permanent) level of school inputs provided, $\bar{S}_1$. The Project STAR experiment was interpreted in this analysis as an unanticipated change in school inputs from $\bar{S}_1$ to $S_1 = \bar{S}_1 + (S_1 - \bar{S}_1)$. The family then may have adapted its own inputs, I_1, to that change. Suppose, however, that all school districts permanently changed their level of school inputs and that, for simplicity, such a change did not alter the location decisions of parents. In this new regime, parents with newborn children face a level of school inputs, $\bar{S}_1$, that differs from the one that parents of newborn children faced under the old regime. In that case, parents in the new regime may be expected to choose a different level of their own inputs in the preschool years, I_0, as well as in the school years. The average policy effect of the change to the new regime would be

$$E\left(\frac{dA_1}{dS_1}\right) = \int \left[\frac{\partial g_1}{\partial S_1} + \frac{\partial g_1}{\partial I_0} \frac{\partial I_0}{\partial \bar{S}_1} + \frac{\partial g_1}{\partial I_1} \left(\frac{\partial I_1}{\partial \bar{S}_1} + \frac{\partial I_1}{\partial (S_1 - \bar{S}_1)} \right) \right] f(W, \mu, \varepsilon).$$

The Project STAR experiment does not provide evidence on this policy change. In addition, if the policy change occurred in only one district, parents would sort differently across school districts leading to a change in the joint density, $f(W, \mu, \varepsilon)$, and thus to a change in the policy effect. Presumably, the actual policy that would be implemented is a permanent reduction in class size. The Project STAR experiment only identifies a subset of the elements that comprise this policy effect.

3.3.3   External Validity

There are two forms of external validity, extrapolating experimental results to different populations and extrapolating results to treatments not considered in the experiment. With respect to the first, as is apparent in equation 3.40, the results of the experiment can generally not be applied to a population that differs from the experimental sample in endowment distribution, $f(W, \mu, \varepsilon)$. Both production function parameters, $\dfrac{\partial g_1}{\partial S_1}$ and $\dfrac{\partial g_1}{\partial I_1}$, depend on μ, and $\dfrac{\partial I_1}{\partial (S_1 - \bar{S}_1)}$ depends on W, μ, and ε. Remaining within the experimental paradigm requires direct experimentation on other populations. Similarly, extrapolation of the experimental results to other treatments, such as a permanent change in class size as discussed above, is also not possible without additional experimentation.

Alternatively, one could design the experiment to include a broader data collection effort, as was done in the PROGRESA program, which would enable the estimation of a structure allowing both types of extrapolations. Such an endeavor requires at least a broad outline of a theory, perhaps like the one above, to guide data collection.

3.3.4 The Estimation of the Achievement Production Function Using Observational Data

These considerations make me much less sanguine than the authors cited above about the singular importance of the Project STAR experiment as a guide to policy. Unfortunately, however, the interpretation of the results from observational research, like that from the experiment, also suffers from a lack of a theoretical underpinning. Todd and Wolpin (2003) provide a detailed discussion of the foundations and assumptions of alternative specifications of the achievement production function commonly employed in the literature.

Todd and Wolpin (2003) distinguish between two parallel literatures. The early childhood development (ECD) branch seeks to understand the role of parental inputs in producing cognitive, and more recently noncognitive, skills. The education production function (EPF) branch seeks to determine the role of school inputs in the determination of cognitive skills. These literatures are directly relevant to the finding that unobserved endowments at young adult ages are critical for the determination of schooling and career choices

In both the ECD and EPF literatures, there is a remarkable lack of consensus about which inputs increase skill acquisition and to what extent (Hanushek, 2003; Hedges, Laine, and Greenwald, 1994; Krueger, 2003). Empirical studies employ a wide variety of estimating equations. Hanushek (1996, 2003) summarizes in several meta-analyses the findings of EPF studies and concludes that although some papers find statistically significant effects, the overall pattern suggests that none of the measured schooling quality inputs is reliably associated with achievement. Krueger (2003) argues that Hanushek's sample of estimates is biased toward his conclusion. Although they disagree about the conclusions that may be drawn from meta-analytic studies, they do agree on the importance of taking into account model specification in combining evidence across studies. As they note, estimating equations are often adopted with little theoretical justification, making it difficult to assess their coherency.

Todd and Wolpin (2003) develop a coherent conceptual framework for interpreting the different estimating equations found in the literature based on the notion of a human capital production function (Ben-Porath, 1967). Skills (cognitive or noncognitive) are acquired through a production process that depends on the levels of current and past individual, family, and school inputs in combination with an individual's genetic endowment (determined at conception). The inputs are determined within a choice-theoretic decision model. These two tenets, that the production process is cumulative and that inputs are choices, have critical implications for the interpretation and estimation of the specifications observed in the ECD and EPF literatures.

Following the formalization in Todd and Wolpin (2003), let T_{ija} be a measure of skills, for example, a test score, for child i residing in household j at age a. Denote the vector of parent-supplied inputs at a given age as I_{ija}, school-supplied inputs as S_{ija}, and the vectors of their respective input histories up to age a as $I_{ij}(a)$ and $S_{ij}(a)$. Further, let a child's endowment be denoted as μ_{ij0}. With allowance for measurement error in test scores (for example, random fluctuation in test performance), denoted by ε_{ija}, the skill production function is given by

$$T_{ija} = T_a(I_{ij}(a), S_{ij}(a), \mu_{ij0}, \varepsilon_{ija}), \tag{3.41}$$

where the notation implies that the production function itself may depend on the age of the child.

The empirical implementation of the model described by equation 3.41 has foundered on two main problems: (1) the genetic endowment of mental capacity is not observed; and (2) data sets on inputs are incomplete—in particular, they have incomplete input histories and/or missing inputs. Todd and Wolpin (2003) clarify the different assumptions required for consistent estimation for the common specifications found in the literature.

3.3.4.1 The Contemporaneous Specification

The contemporaneous specification includes only contemporaneous school and family inputs. To justify that specification requires that either (1) only contemporaneous inputs matter to the production of current achievement or (2) inputs are time invariant, so that current inputs capture the entire history of inputs. In addition, contemporaneous inputs must be independent of the unobserved endowment. The contemporaneous specification can be written as

$$T_{ija} = T_a(I_{ija}, S_{ija}) + \varepsilon'_{ija},$$ (3.42)

with ε'_{ija} an additive measurement error. Neither of the sets of assumptions given above is very plausible.[63] Many inputs of potential importance in the development of cognitive skills vary temporally and may vary for systematic reasons with the child's age (for example, maternal employment) or be specific to particular ages (for example, maternal alcohol use during pregnancy). Estimating the contemporaneous specification when the true technology is that given in equation 3.41 requires that the omitted past inputs and endowed ability are uncorrelated with contemporaneous inputs. Such assumptions are inconsistent with economic models of optimizing behavior. For example, economic models in which parents care about a child's development imply that the amount of resources allocated to the child will be responsive to the parent's perception of a child's ability (for example, Becker and Tomes, 1976). Thus, although the contemporaneous specification can be implemented with only limited data, strong assumptions are required to justify its application.

3.3.4.2 Value-Added Specifications

The lack of data on input histories and on endowments led researchers to adopt a value-added approach to estimating achievement production functions. In its most common form, this specification relates achievement to contemporaneous school and family input measures and lagged (baseline) achievement. Thus, it differs from the contemporaneous specification only in the inclusion of the baseline achievement measure, which is taken to be a sufficient statistic for unobserved input histories as well as the unobserved endowment. Evidence based on the value-added specification has generally been regarded as more convincing than that based on a contemporaneous specification (see, for example, Hanushek, 1996 and 2003, and Krueger, 2000). However, the value-added formulation also imposes strong assumptions on the underlying production technology and strong restrictions for consistent estimation.

To simplify the notation, let X denote the vector of family and school inputs and $X(a)$ their input histories up to age a; the value-added specification assumes that equation 3.41 can be written as

$$T_{ija} = T_a(X_{ija}, T_{a-1}(X_{ij}(a-1), \mu_{ij0}, \varepsilon_{ija}), \eta_{ija}),$$ (3.43)

where it is assumed the baseline achievement measure was administered at $a - 1$. Value-added regression specifications usually treat the arguments in equation 3.43 as additively separable and the parameters as non–age-varying, which leads to the estimating equation:

$$T_{ija} = X_{ija}\alpha + \gamma T_{ij,a-1} + \eta_{ija}. \tag{3.44}$$

A more restrictive specification sometimes adopted in the literature sets the parameter on the lagged achievement test score to 1 ($\gamma = 1$) and rewrites equation 3.44 as

$$T_{ija} - T_{ij,a-1} = X_{ija}\alpha + \eta_{ija}, \tag{3.45}$$

which expresses the test score gain solely as a function of contemporaneous inputs.

To understand the restrictions the value-added formulation implies for the true technology function, consider the linear regression analogue of the true technology (equation 3.41), namely

$$T_{ija} = X_{ija}\alpha_1 + X_{ija-1}\alpha_2 + \ldots + X_{ij1}\alpha_a + \beta\mu_{ij0} + \varepsilon_{ija}. \tag{3.46}$$

This specification imposes the assumption that the production technology, as in equation 3.44, is non–age-varying at least over the ages used in implementing the model. Note that α_1 refers to the effect of the contemporaneous inputs, α_2 to the effect of the inputs one period lagged, and so on.

Subtracting $\gamma T_{ij,a-1}$ from both sides of equation 3.46 and collecting terms gives

$$T_{ija} = X_{ija}\alpha_1 + X_{ija-1}(\alpha_2 - \gamma\alpha_1) + \ldots + X_{ij1}(\alpha_a - \gamma\alpha_{a-1}) + \gamma T_{ij,a-1} \tag{3.47}$$

$$+ (\beta_a - \gamma\beta_{a-1})\mu_{ij0} + \varepsilon_{ija} - \gamma\varepsilon_{ij,a-1}.$$

Two conditions must be met for equation 3.47 to reduce to equation 3.44: (1) input coefficients must be geometrically (presumably) declining with distance, as measured by age, from the achievement measurement, and the rate of decline must be the same for each input ($\alpha_k = \gamma\alpha_{k-1}$ for all k); and (2) the impact of the endowment must be geometrically declining at the same rate as input effects ($\beta_a = \gamma\beta_{a-1}$). For the value-added specification based on the gain in achievement (equation 3.45) to be appropriate, it is required, in lieu of (1) and (2), that (1′) the effect of each input must be independent of the age at which achievement was measured ($\alpha_k = \alpha_{k-1}$ for all k), and (2′) the effect of the endowment must likewise be independent of the achievement age ($\beta_a = \beta_{a-1}$).

With respect to estimation, if the restrictions that lead to the gain specification (equation 3.45) are valid, OLS estimation would provide consistent estimates of input effects. With $\gamma \neq 1$, as in equation 3.44, however, in order that OLS estimation be consistent, the measurement error in test scores must be serially correlated, and the degree of serial correlation must exactly match the rate of decay of input effects (that is, $\eta_{ija} = \varepsilon_{ija} - \gamma\varepsilon_{ij,a-1}$ is an *iid* shock). In the conventionally assumed case that measurement error (ε_{ija}) is *iid*, the estimate of γ will be downward biased given the necessarily positive correlation between the lagged test score measure, $T_{ij,a-1}$, and its measurement error, $\varepsilon_{ij,a-1}$.

If we drop the assumption that the impact of the endowment declines at the same rate as the decay in input effects, then the error in equation 3.44 would include the endowment, that is, assuming that $\beta_a - \gamma\beta_{a-1} = \beta'$ is a constant independent of age, which yields

$$T_{ija} = X_{ija}\alpha + \gamma T_{ij,a-1} + \beta'\mu_{ij0} + \eta_{ija}, \tag{3.48}$$

instead of equation 3.44. Estimation of equation 3.48 by OLS is problematic. As with the contemporaneous specification, one requirement for OLS to be consistent is that contemporaneous inputs and the unobserved endowment be orthogonal. However, even if that orthogonality condition were not violated, an OLS estimation of equation 3.48 would still be biased because baseline achievement must be correlated with the endowment. If the endogeneity is not taken into account, then the resulting bias will not only affect the estimate of γ but may be transmitted to the estimates of all the contemporaneous input effects.

In an optimizing behavioral model, we would expect family and school input choices to be affected by baseline achievement, particularly if, as in equation 3.48, baseline achievement has persistent effects on achievement in future time periods. It is possible to estimate equation 3.48 consistently if there exists a third (earlier) observation on achievement, along with the data on the input set $X_{ij,a-1}$, using a simple differencing procedure.

So far, it has been assumed that there are no missing contemporaneous inputs. However, suppose that ε_{ija} contains unmeasured contemporaneous inputs. And, to make the argument most strongly, suppose that the missing inputs are orthogonal to the included inputs. In this case, neither OLS estimation of equation 3.44 nor applying OLS to a differenced form of equation 3.48 will provide consistent estimates of input effects. Recall that the residual in equation 3.44 or 3.48 is a composite of the underlying current and baseline period residuals, $\eta_{ija} = \varepsilon_{ija}$

$- \gamma \varepsilon_{ij,a-1}$. When ε_{ija} contains omitted inputs, baseline achievement, $T_{ij,a-1}$, will likely be correlated with the composite residual for two reasons. First, baseline achievement, $T_{ij,a-1}$, must be correlated with its own contemporaneous omitted inputs contained in $\varepsilon_{ij,a-1}$. Second, to the extent that omitted inputs are subject to choice, optimizing behavior will create a correlation between the contemporaneous omitted inputs and baseline achievement. For example, parents may respond to realized poor achievement by increasing family inputs (such as parental time or providing tutors).

In the form most commonly adopted, the data requirements of a value-added specification are only slightly more demanding than those of the contemporaneous specification. One additional variable—a baseline test score—is all that is required. As noted, evidence based on value-added specifications is generally regarded as being superior to that based on contemporaneous specifications; however, the benefits of a value-added approach seem less clear when the potential for omitted data on inputs and endowments is taken into account.

3.3.4.3 The Cumulative Specification

Direct estimation of the cumulative specification given by equation 3.46 requires data on both contemporaneous and historical family and school inputs. There are several different approaches to directly estimating the cumulative specification, assuming that we have data on current and past inputs but do not observe endowments. Under the assumption that any omitted inputs and measurement errors in test scores are uncorrelated with included inputs, the remaining estimation problem is that observable inputs will generally be correlated with the unobserved child endowment. A number of methods have been employed in the literature to deal with endowment heterogeneity, although few studies have incorporated contemporaneous and past inputs. One method makes use of observations on multiple children within the same household or family (siblings or cousins), and the other makes use of multiple measurements for the same child at different ages.

In describing these methods and the properties of estimators based on them, we take the following version of equation 3.46 as the baseline specification:

$$T_{ija} = X_{ija}\alpha_1^a + X_{ija-1}\alpha_2^a + \ldots + X_{ij1}\alpha_a^a + \beta_a\mu_{ij0} + \varepsilon_{ij}(a), \tag{3.49}$$

in which input effects vary not only with the distance between the application of inputs and the achievement measure (as indicated by the parameter subscripts) but also with age itself (as indicated by the parameter superscripts). As the notation indicates, the residual includes all current and past unmeasured inputs.

A class of estimators used to account for permanent unobservable factors makes use of variation across observations within which the unobservable factor is assumed to be fixed. Two such "fixed effect" estimators that are prominent in this literature use variation that occurs either within families (across siblings) or within children (at different ages). It is useful in what follows to rewrite equation 3.49 for two different ages, age a and a':

$$T_{ija} = X_{ija}\alpha_1^a + X_{ij,a-1}\alpha_2^a + \ldots + X_{ij,a'+1}\alpha_{a-a'}^a \qquad (3.50)$$

$$+ X_{ij,a'}\alpha_{a-a'+1}^a + X_{ij,a'-1}\alpha_{a-a'+2}^a + \ldots + X_{ij2}\alpha_{a-1}^a + X_{ij1}\alpha_a^a + \beta_a\mu_{ij0} + \varepsilon_{ij}(a)$$

$$T_{ija'} = X_{ija'}\alpha_1^{a'} + X_{ij,a'-1}\alpha_2^{a'} + \ldots + X_{ij2}\alpha_{a'-1}^{a'} + X_{ij1}\alpha_{a'}^{a'} + \beta_{a'}\mu_{ij0} + \varepsilon_{ij}(a'),$$

where the parameter α_x^a indicates the effect of an input on an achievement measure taken at age a that is $x - 1$ periods removed from age a. Note that contemporaneous inputs are, as a matter of convention, zero periods removed from the age of the measurement, although they may be thought of as being applied between a and $a - 1$.

As an example, suppose we are looking at a child's achievement at age $a = 6$. In equation 3.50, the effect of reading to a child at age 3 on the child's achievement at age 6 may differ from the effect of reading to the child at age 2 ($\alpha_4^6 \neq \alpha_5^6$) because the inputs differ in their distance from the achievement measure. In addition, the effect of reading to the child at age 3 on achievement at age 5 may differ from its effects at age 6 ($\alpha_3^5 \neq \alpha_4^6$), again because it is more distant from the achievement measure, and also may differ from the effect of reading to the child at age 4 on reading achievement at age 6 ($\alpha_3^5 \neq \alpha_3^6$) because the efficacy of reading to a child on subsequent performance may depend on the child's age.

3.3.4.4 Within-Family Estimators

Within-family estimators exploit the fact that children of the same parents (or grandparents) have a common heritable component. In particular, assume that the child's endowment can be decomposed into a family-specific component and an orthogonal child-specific component, denoted as μ_0^f and μ_0^c. Thus, siblings have in common the family component but have their own individual-specific child components. Rewriting equation 3.49 to accommodate this modification yields

$$T_{ija} = X_{ija}^a \alpha_1 + X_{ija-1}^a \alpha_2 + \dots + X_{ij1}^a \alpha_a + \beta_a \mu_{ij0}^f + \beta_a \mu_{ij0}^c + \varepsilon_{ija}. \tag{3.51}$$

Now, suppose that longitudinal household data on achievement test scores and on current and past inputs are available on multiple siblings, and consider two types of data. In the first, data are available on siblings at the same age. Notice that unless the siblings are twins, the calendar time at which achievement measures are obtained must differ. In the second, data are available on siblings in the same calendar year, which generally means that they will differ in age.

Data Collected on Siblings at the Same Age
The within-family estimator is based on sibling differences, which eliminates the family-specific component of the endowment but not the child-specific component. Consider the estimator in the case of two siblings, denoted by i and i', observed at the same age a. Differencing equation 3.51 yields

$$T_{ija} - T_{i'ja} = (X_{ija} - X_{i'ja})\alpha_1^a + \dots + (X_{ij1} - X_{i'j1})\alpha_a^a + [\beta_a(\mu_{ij0}^c - \mu_{i'j0}^c) + \varepsilon_{ij}(a) - \varepsilon_{i'j}(a)]. \tag{3.52}$$

In estimation, the residual term will include all the terms within the square brackets. Consistent estimation of input effects, therefore, requires that inputs associated with any child not respond either to own or to sibling child-specific endowment components.

Furthermore, given that achievement is measured for each sibling at the same age, the older child's achievement observation (say child i) will have occurred at a calendar time prior to the younger sibling's observation. Thus, the older sibling's achievement outcome was known at the time input decisions for the younger child were made, at the ages of the younger child between the older and younger child's achievement observations. Thus, consistent estimation by OLS requires that input choices be unresponsive to prior own and sibling outcomes; otherwise, the realizations of $\varepsilon_{ij}(a)$ will affect some of the inputs to sibling i'.

In essence, intrahousehold allocation decisions must be made ignoring child-specific endowments and prior outcomes of all the children in the household. The within-child estimator considered below relaxes this assumption.

Data Collected on Siblings at the Same Calendar Time
The within-family estimator based on siblings of different ages can be viewed as a special case of the within-child estimator based on test scores of the same child measured at different ages.

3.3.4.5 Within-Child Estimators
Within-child estimators are feasible when there are multiple observations on achievement outcomes and on inputs for a given child at different ages. Consider differencing the achievement technology at the two ages shown in equation 3.50. This procedure, after grouping inputs applied at the same age, yields

$$T_{ija} - T_{ija'} = X_{ija}\alpha_1^a + X_{ija-1}\alpha_2^a + ...X_{ij,a'+1}\alpha_{a-a'}^a + X_{ij,a'}[\alpha_{a-a'+1}^a - \alpha_1^{a'}] \tag{3.53}$$

$$+X_{ij,a'-1}[\alpha_{a-a'+2}^a - \alpha_2^{a'}]+...+ X_{ij2}[\alpha_{a-1}^a - \alpha_{a'-1}^{a'}]$$

$$+X_{ij1}[\alpha_a^a - \alpha_{a'}^{a'}]+[\beta_a - \beta_{a'}]\mu_{ij0} + \varepsilon_{ij}(a) - \varepsilon_{ij}(a').$$

Without any restrictions on the relationship among parameters, the within-child estimator recovers (1) age-specific input effects for the inputs that are applied between the two age observations and (2) differences in parameters that depend on both age and time from the achievement measure for inputs applied contemporaneously or prior to the earlier achievement observation.

The parameters of equation 3.53 can be consistently estimated under the following assumptions. (1) The impact of the endowment on achievement must be independent of age ($\beta_a = \beta_{a'}$), in which case the differencing eliminates the endowment. In that case, orthogonality between input choices and endowments need not be assumed. Second, similar to the within-family estimator based on sibling observations at the same age, because any prior achievement outcome is known when later input decisions are made, it is necessary to assume that (2) later input choices are invariant to prior own achievement outcomes.

The difference between the within-child estimator and the within-family estimator based on observations for siblings that differ in age is that in the latter only the family component of the endowment disappears from equation 3.53. Thus, consistency of that estimator requires the same behavioral assumption with respect to intrafamily allocations as did the within-family estimator based on sibling observations at the same age.

Suppose, however, that the researcher is willing to impose the restriction that input effects are age invariant; that is, $\alpha_x^a = \alpha_x^{a'}$ as is often assumed in the application of fixed-effects estimators. Then, equation 3.53 can be rewritten as

$$T_{ija} - T_{ija'} = [X_{ija} - X_{ija'}]\alpha_1 + ... + [X_{ija'} - X_{ij1}]\alpha_{a'} \tag{3.54}$$

$$+X_{ij,a-a'-1}\alpha_{a'+1} + ... + X_{ij1}\alpha_a + \varepsilon_{ij}(a) - \varepsilon_{ij}(a')$$

that would identify all of the parameters of the production function.

3.3.4.6 Instrumental Variables Within-Child Estimators
It is possible to relax the assumption that input choices do not respond to previous realizations of achievement. If the residuals in equation 3.54 consist only of unforeseen factors (for example, randomly being ill or randomly drawing a bad teacher), and if the impact of these factors on achievement has limited persistence, then input levels prior to the earliest achievement observation (a') can serve as instrumental variables in estimating equation 3.53 or 3.54. For example, if the achievement tests are taken at ages 8 and 5, then perhaps the set of inputs at ages earlier than age 3 might satisfy this requirement. However, even if that were the case, there are more parameters in equation 3.54 than instruments—at least as many as the number of measured inputs—so identification cannot be achieved with these orthogonality conditions alone. However, it is also the case that inputs associated with the child's siblings applied at a time sufficiently prior to the earliest observation used to implement the within-child estimator could also be used as instrumental variables. Thus, we can still possibly estimate equation 3.53 or 3.54 consistently using own prior and sibling inputs as instrumental variables.

Some researchers have used cross-sectional variation in prices and other location-specific characteristics as instrumental variables to estimate human capital production functions (Rosenzweig and Schultz, 1983). One potential problem with that approach if applied directly to the baseline specification (equation 3.49) is that state-level variation in the endowments of its residents will plausibly be correlated with the demand for different market or politically supplied services and products, for example, school inputs. If applied to the within-sibling specification given by equation 3.52, those instruments will be valid to the extent that location decisions are independent of child-specific (though not necessarily family-specific) endowments and are also independent of the actual achievement realizations of the siblings. Applying the same approach to within-child specification (equation 3.53 or 3.54), given that the sample includes children who have lived in different locations, avoids the biases from omitting child-specific endowments but would still be subject to the potential problem that families may change locations to find more suitable schools for their children based on their prior achievement.

Finally, none of the IV approaches are valid if omitted inputs are not orthogonal to the included ones. Omitted inputs that reflect choices are as likely to be correlated with an instrumental variable as are included inputs. Thus, any instrument that has power will also not be valid. It is therefore important to have data that contain a large set of inputs spanning both family and school domains.

3.3.4.7   Choosing a Specification

As noted, a possible reason for the range of findings in the ECD and EPF literatures is the diversity of specifications of the production function. This diversity is partly the result of data limitations, partly the result of a lack of a theoretical foundation and also partly the result of a lack of consensus on the best approach to model selection. With respect to the latter, in a recent paper, Todd and Wolpin (2007) explore the use of cross-validation criteria for the purpose of model selection.[64] Cross-validation methods choose the best-performing specification according to an out-of-sample forecasting criterion. They provide a useful alternative to specification testing when specifications are nonnested. The data set used by Todd and Wolpin (2007), the children born to the women in the NLSY79 (NLSY79-CS), contains an extensive history of family inputs starting from birth and cognitive achievement tests starting from early childhood, thus permitting the estimation of the achievement production function under a number of alternative assumptions as described above. In addition to home inputs, the NLSY79-CS also contains a measure of maternal "ability," the AFQT test.

Todd and Wolpin (2007) consider the following set of alternative specifications: (1) contemporaneous; (2) cumulative; (3) within-family fixed effect (siblings at same age); (4) within-child fixed effect; (5) value added; and (6) value added with lagged inputs.[65] They find strong support for the notion that skills are acquired through a cumulative process; indeed, the value-added with lagged inputs specification does best in the cross-validation exercise.

3.3.5   The Dynamic Factor-Model Approach

Cunha and Heckman (2008) begin from the observation that the most comprehensive data sets used in the study of early childhood development tend to have multiple measures of home inputs. The NLSY79-CS, for example, administers a battery of questions about the home environment, the Home Observation Measurement of the Environment—Short Form (HOME-SF). The HOME-SF consists of four instruments that depend on the child's age: ages 0–2, 3–5, 6–9, and 10 and above. Responses to the individual items and a scale based on a summation of responses that form a total raw score are available to researchers. There are about twenty items in any age group. To maintain estimation precision, researchers either must choose a (small) subset of the items, use the existing scale, or create their own scale. Cunha and Heckman (2008) suggest that a natural way to use these data that avoids an arbitrary choice of items or scales is to place the estimation problem within a dynamic factor-model framework.

In addition to the estimation approach, Cunha and Heckman (2008) depart from the ECD literature by considering the joint development of cognitive (C) and noncognitive skills (N) in early childhood. In contrast to the assumptions made in the conventional approach to identification as described above, their factor-model approach achieves identification through the use of covariance restrictions. The production functions of those skills take the form of value-added specifications of the form:

$$A_a^C = \gamma_0^C + \gamma_1^C A_{a-1}^C + \gamma_2^C A_{a-1}^N + \gamma_3^C X_a^C + \eta_a^C, \qquad (3.55)$$

$$A_a^N = \gamma_0^N + \gamma_1^N A_{a-1}^N + \gamma_2^N A_{a-1}^C + \gamma_3^N X_a^N + \eta_a^N.$$

Note that the production function of each skill depends on the previous level of both skills and on skill-specific inputs (which may be the same).[66] Skills are latent factors and are unobservable. Test scores provide measurements of skills with error. Similarly, inputs are considered as latent factors and are also unobservable. Individual items on the HOME-SF would be measures, with error, of the lower-dimensional latent inputs.

As Cunha and Heckman (2008) show, identification is achieved through covariance restrictions on the measurement error equations (and sometimes also depending on assumptions with instruments). Given longitudinal data, it is not necessary to restrict the measurement errors to be serially uncorrelated. Distributional assumptions are also not necessary for identification. It is also shown that the assumption of orthogonality between observed (latent) and unobserved (latent) inputs can be relaxed in the case that unobserved inputs do not vary over time. An additional measurement equation relating adult outcomes (earnings and schooling) to the level of skills achieved on reaching adulthood gives substantive content to input productivities and test scores.[67]

Estimation is carried out using data from the NLSY-CS. The results of the analysis are provocative and important. They find that (1) both cognitive and noncognitive skills exhibit strong persistence at all child ages (measured in standardized test score units, γ_1^C is generally about 0.95 and γ_1^N about 0.90); (2) cognitive skills 2 years prior affect noncognitive skill formation, although the effect is small ($\gamma_2^N = .03$ in standardized test score units), but prior noncognitive skills do not have a statistically significant effect on cognitive skill formation; (3) parental inputs affect both cognitive and noncognitive skill formation; (4) the effect of parental inputs are greater at younger child ages in the case of cognitive skill formation but greater at older child ages in the case of noncognitive skill formation; (5) estimates of input effects are sensitive to correcting for measurement error; and (6) the HOME scale, which weights responses equally, would not be a good representation of the latent HOME input.

There is much to recommend the factor-model approach. Given historical data on both inputs and outcomes, as in the NLSY79-CS, it would be desirable to estimate a cumulative specification using information back to conception. The NLSY79-CS includes data on child motor and social development and personality development outcomes starting from birth and data on inputs starting from conception (for example, smoking during pregnancy). The most significant shortcoming is the lack of information on school inputs. Todd and Wolpin (2007) merge school input data at the county and state level with the NLSY79-CS data, but that is clearly a gross proxy for the child-specific school inputs. The Early Childhood Longitudinal Studies (ECLS-B and ECLS-K) are both representative samples that could be combined within a dynamic factor model to study child cognitive and noncognitive skill formation from birth through the eighth grade.

3.3.6 Limitation of the Production Function Literature

We have now come full circle. Unlike the goal of the Project STAR experiment, the estimation of the cognitive (or noncognitive) achievement production function cannot tell us what the effect would be of any particular policy initiative to foster the development of skills during childhood. To do that requires estimating a model of the behavior that governs the choice of inputs. Developing an estimable model of family investments in skill acquisition, including schooling quality, within a dynamic setting and incorporating multiple children (and perhaps the choice of fertility), is an ambitious undertaking. To date, there have been only a few such attempts to incorporate the estimation of the achievement production function in a household dynamic optimization problem. I choose two examples to illustrate.

Bernal (2008) develops and structurally estimates a DCDP model of a woman's employment and child care decisions that directly affect a child's cognitive achievement.[68] Bernal adopts a cumulative specification for the cognitive achievement production function that includes an unobserved child endowment. Women have heterogeneous labor market skills.[69] The model is estimated by maximum likelihood using data from the NLSY79-CS. Bernal predicts the effects of policy interventions that include child care subsidies and maternity leave entitlements, which she finds, on average, have adverse affects on pre-school-age children's cognitive outcomes.

Tartari (2007) developed and structurally estimated a DCDP model of a married couple's decision about the investments they make in their children's "quality" and the decision of whether to divorce.[70] Child quality is a public good in the household and is produced by parental time and goods inputs and by the degree of conflict within the marriage, the latter also being a choice. The achievement production function is modeled as an extended value-added specification that includes a family-specific unobserved permanent component. Divorce is an endogenous outcome of the decision model, along with fertility, the wife's labor supply, and the level of child support if the couple divorces (and has children). Divorce does not directly enter into the child quality production function; instead, divorce indirectly affects child quality by reducing the amount of joint time the parents can spend with the child and, presumably, expenditures on the child. On the other hand, divorce shields children from the potentially negative consequences of exposure to parental conflict within the home. Tartari estimates the model by indirect inference with data from the NLSY79-CS. The model estimates are used to perform several counterfactual exercises. In one, the divorce option is removed, which addresses the question of whether children of divorced parents would be better or worse off had the marriage continued. Tartari finds that the cognitive achievement of children is increased because the positive effect of the increase in parental investment time and investment goods exceeds the negative effect of exposure to conflict.

An implicit assumption in these models is that the skill acquisition technology is known to parents. Clearly, that assumption is false; it cannot be the case that researchers are attempting to determine what everyone else already knows. The question, of course, is how the assumption of perfect knowledge affects estimates of policy effects. The problem in introducing imperfect knowledge is that a model in which parents differ in their beliefs about the productivity of child investment inputs is observationally equivalent to one in which there is variation across parents in the marginal product of inputs and/or in which parents have direct preferences over inputs that vary in the population. To distinguish among these alternatives as explanations for the variation in input choices of parents and the achievement outcomes of children would require collecting information on beliefs or preferences (or both).

Recently, there has been (renewed) interest in the collection of data on subjective beliefs (Manski, 1990, 2004). Data have been collected on expectations about choices, such as school attainment and retirement age, and expectations about future states of the world, such as realizations of future income. Recently, Cunha (2012) has taken a first serious step   towards designing and administering questions about the productivities of alternative inputs in producing cognitive or noncognitive skills in children. Given the early nature of this work, whether subjective beliefs in this domain can be elicited in a meaningful way is unclear; however, the payoff is potentially large.

The power of combining data on subjective beliefs with structural estimation is nicely illustrated by Delavande (2008). Delavande (2008) designed and administered a survey that elicited subjective beliefs about the efficacy of alternative contraceptive methods in preventing pregnancies, beliefs about their side effects, their ability to prevent sexually transmitted diseases, the propensity of partners to disapprove, their expected monetary cost, and their mode of administration. Combining the subjective data with actual contraceptive choices, Delavande estimates a static random utility model from which she recovers underlying preferences for alternative contraceptive methods. She shows that assuming instead homogeneous beliefs, based on contraceptive failure rates computed from national statistics, would yield very different estimates for preferences.

4 A Brief Conclusion

The proper role of economic theory in empirical research has been and remains a controversial issue. In these two lectures, I have tried to illustrate the value for inference of connecting data and theory. In the first lecture (chapter 2), I showed how theory can be used to perform *ex ante* policy evaluation in the most challenging circumstance in which there is no direct policy variation. Theory was shown to be critical in providing a structure within which existing variation that provides an analogue to direct policy variation can be exploited. In the case of a wage tax, wage variation was the analogue to introducing a tax; and in the school attendance subsidy program, less obviously, joint variation in the child wage and parental income was the analogue to introducing a subsidy. In both cases, I considered assumptions under which nonparametric estimation was feasible. I showed how parametric assumptions permit the use of richer behavioral models in performing *ex ante* policy evaluation and concomitantly expand the types of policies that can be considered.

The main aim of the second lecture (chapter 3) was to show how the quality of inference in existing literatures could be improved by explicitly connecting theory and data analysis. Two of the examples, one on estimating the impact of unemployment benefits on unemployment duration and the other on estimating the impact of welfare benefits on the labor market and demographic choices of women, showed the importance of that connection in developing econometric specifications, for example, with respect to what variables should or—just as importantly—should not be included. The third example, using natural experiments to recover the relationship between school attainment and wages, illustrated how theory clarifies assumptions under which an interpretation is valid and also enables disparate results to be reconciled. The last example, the use of a field experiment to estimate the impact of class size on student learning, showed how theory can shed light on the generalizability of experimental effects to other populations. Although each of the examples was used to focus on a specific methodological issue, all of them are relevant for understanding the role of theory in interpretation, specification, and external validity.

What I hope my lectures have accomplished is to convince empirical researchers (and journal editors and referees) that sharper inferences do indeed result from drawing explicit connections to coherent and relevant theory. The empirical approach, be it structural, quasi-structural, quasi-experimental, or experimental, is of secondary importance. Theory provides the only way to fully appreciate the behavioral assumptions that underlie inference from data.

Notes

Chapter 1

1. Tjalling C. Koopmans (1947), p. 172. Italics added.

2. I am obviously not referring to the large set of experiments, those conducted both in the laboratory and in the field, the goal of which has been to test the validity of predictions obtained from theory. Those experiments require a strict adherence to theory in their design and implementation.

3. This is the view taken by Angrist and Krueger (1999).

4. Actually, there was one exception in which a behavioral model was relegated to the appendix. The issue contained papers based on quasi-experimental and experimental (randomized controlled trial) approaches.

5. Jacob Marschak (1953), p. 26.

Chapter 2

1. I address this issue in the next chapter. There is also the additional assumption that the variation induced by the "experiment" is independent of unobserved determinants of the outome—the question of "what's in the error." The distinction between randomness and exogeneity is drawn in Rosenzweig and Wolpin (2000).

2. See, however, Bourgignon and Spadaro (2006) for a discussion of microsimulation methods for *ex ante* evaluation.

3. This section draws from and extends the arguments in Todd and Wolpin (2008).

4. In contrast to a parametric approach (see Heckman, 1974), no assumption is made about the way unobserved preferences affect the marginal rate of substitution. Usually, a monotonicity assumption is made in order to obtain a unique cutoff value of ε, given observables, that determines the choice of zero versus positive hours. No such assumption is made here in part because, as shown below, the goal of *ex ante* policy evaluation does not require the estimation of the utility function or even the full estimation of the hours of work function.

5. The analysis applies equally well to a wage subsidy, which is a negative tax ($\tau < 0$).

6. When viewed as a function of the tax rate, τ, as described by the η function, the hours of work function would not be considered structural with respect to the tax policy as

it is not invariant to changes in the tax rate. However, viewed as a function of the net wage, $(1 - \tau)w$, as described by the φ function, the hours of work function would be considered structural as it affects the value of a variable in the function and not the function itself.

7. In terms of notation, throughout this chapter, when it is clarifying, the optimal level of a choice variable, h in the current example, in the absence of the policy is denoted with an asterisk (as in equation 2.3). The same choice variable at its optimum in the presence of the policy is denoted with a double asterisk (as in equation 2.5). Choice functions that are invariant to the policy (and can thus be given a structural interpretation) are denoted by $\varphi(\cdot)$, and those that are not invariant (and thus cannot be given a structural interpretation) are denoted by $\eta(\cdot)$.

8. Note, however, that the effect of y or X on expected hours of work cannot be obtained from equation 2.6 without the additional independence assumption that $f(\varepsilon \mid y, X) = f(\varepsilon)$.

9. Ichimura and Taber (2000) also draw an analogy between their proposed method of nonparametrically recovering policy impacts and matching.

10. This observation is just a more general statement of what Heckman (2000) calls Marschak's maxim, namely, that *ex ante* policy evaluation may not require recovery of the entire structure, in this case the φ function.

11. See Todd and Wolpin (2008) for a discussion of the relationship of matching in this context to the more conventional matching estimator (e.g., Rosenbaum and Rubin, 1983).

12. Analogous to the use of nonparametric estimation of the conditional mean hours function, if the support of w and the support of $\tilde{w}$ do not overlap, the average impact based on the matched samples may differ from the population impact. See Ichimura and Taber (2000) for more discussion on this point.

13. See, for example, Haerdle and Linton (1994) and Heckman, Ichimura, and Todd (1997).

14. For the same reason, it would also not be possible to estimate the effect of introducing the tax on the participation rate.

15. Although our interest is only in recovering the wage offer function, estimation of the hours function would be problematic with only a wage error (that is, without the preference unobservable). Conditional on the wage, which is observed for participants, hours of work would be deterministic. Thus, for any given set of parameters, the likelihood contribution for at least one participant, that is, the joint density of hours and the wage, would almost surely be zero. To avoid degeneracy in the likelihood function would require an additional error, for example, measurement error in reported hours of work or in the reported wage.

16. The problem that arises from including the preference unobservable, ε, is that the marginal rate of substitution is now a function also of ε, that is, given by $M(y; X, \varepsilon)$. In that case, after integrating over ε as in equation 2.12, H is no longer a function of the participation probability.

17. It is also assumed that ξ is distributed independently of y and X.

18. One can also obtain an estimate of the measurement error variance given a distributional assumption, for example, if the measurement error in equation 2.10 is additive and normal.

19. Note that because the hours function depends parametrically on the fixed cost (assuming there are no available measures), the hours of work function would not be considered structural, that is, policy invariant, in the presence of a policy that provides a subsidy for the fixed cost.

20. See also Blomquist, Eklof, and Newey (2001).

21. The β would have to be bounded from above in order that the tax is not turned into a subsidy along any segment.

22. This result also holds in the Blomquist and Newey approach. Knowledge of the expected hours function given in equation 2.22 would still not allow a prediction of the effect of changing individual or subsets of the tax rates.

23. Blomquist and Newey (1997, 2002) do not make such extrapolations.

24. Nonconvexities arise, for example, in public welfare programs such as AFDC or the EITC (see Blundell and MaCurdy, 1999).

25. Note that the school attendance function could also be written, less revealingly, as a function of $y + \tau$ and $y + w$.

26. I return to this point in the later discussion of parametric models.

27. For convenience, I rule out the case that there are multiple children in the household eligible to attend a given grade.

28. If subsidy levels also depend on other child characteristics such as gender, then the configuration of children in the household would also condition on those characteristics.

29. Without the additional unobservable preference shifter, the number of choices will be more than the number of errors.

30. If family income were proportional to the number of children so that the budget constraint contained the term $(y + \tau)n$ instead of $y + \tau n$, the demand function with and without the subsidy would be the same. However, this restriction would be a rather unusual one to impose on the model.

31. The claim in Todd and Wolpin (2008) to the contrary is incorrect.

32. If, instead, households can freely borrow and lend, the budget constraint (with zero rate of interest) would be

$$\sum_{t=1}^{T} C_t = \sum_{t=1}^{T} y_t + \sum_{t=1}^{T} w_t(1 - s_t) + \sum_{t=1}^{T} \tau_t s_t$$
$$= \sum_{t=1}^{T} (y_t + \tau_t) + \sum_{t=1}^{T} (w_t - \tau_t)(1 - s_t). \tag{2.57}$$

The school attendance demand function would then depend on $\sum_{t=1}^{T} (y_t + \tau_t)$, and matching would be done on that basis rather than the basis of the period-by-period income profile.

33. It is of course necessary to maintain the assumption that ε is orthogonal to income and the child wage in order for the matching estimator to remain valid.

34. If income is serially correlated, that is, if $f(y_2 | y_1) \neq f(y_2)$, then s_1 will also depend on y_1 (as well as $y_1 + \tau$). It is obviously not possible to match on both y_1 and $y_1 + \tau$ simultaneously for given τ.

35. The two unobservable preference shifters, ε_s and ε_l, affect the marginal utility of school attendance and child leisure, respectively.

36. It is also not possible to infer the effect of the program based on the nonparametric estimation of the school attendance demand function, which in this case is not policy invariant, that is, not structural.

37. The parameters α and/or β can be made parametric functions of observable preference shifters, X, without affecting the analysis.

38. Although the distributional assumption is unnecessary in this case (clearly, the matching estimator does not require it), it is useful to establish results with the distributional assumption because it will be necessary when dynamic models are considered.

39. The * and ** notation, indicating optimality without and with the subsidy, is not useful in the parametric case and so is dropped.

40. If the linear consumption term entered the utility function as γC, then either $\gamma = 1$ or $\sigma_\varepsilon = 1$ could serve as a normalization. Because the subsidy is in monetary units, the normalization of the utility function facilitates interpretation.

41. Note that if there is no income effect on school attendance, $\beta = 0$, then the nonparametric matching estimator can be implemented without matching on household income. Moreover, in that case, the effect of an increase in the subsidy amount is identical to the effect of an equal reduction in the child wage.

42. Keane (1992) has shown in Monte Carlo experiments that the model without exclusion restrictions may be difficult to identify in practice. Exclusion restrictions in this model could take the form of variables that appear in α, for example, distance from school, but not in β. An alternative restriction would be to set the covariance of the unobserved preference shifters to zero, that is, $\sigma_{\varepsilon v} = 0$.

43. The additive error (ξ_{it}) is convenient in calculating choice probabilities and is maintained for illustrative purposes. However, the additive structure is fragile. It is lost, for example, if the wage function, as is conventional, takes on the semilog form or if the utility function is nonlinear in consumption (e.g., CRRA or logarithmic).

44. Although I refer to $\Pr(s_{it} = 1, w_{it} \, \Omega_{it}^-)$ as a probability, it is actually a mixed probability for s_{it} and a density for w_{it}. The Jacobian of the transformation from the wage density to the wage error density is 1.

45. If the structure does not yield an additive (composite) error, the latent variable function becomes $v_i^*(\Omega_{it}^-, \eta_{it}, \varepsilon_{it})$. Calculating the joint regions of $\eta_{it}, \varepsilon_{it}$ that determine the probabilities that enter the likelihood function and that are used to calculate the $E \max(\Omega_{it}^-)$ function must, in that case, be done numerically.

46. Although the example assumes that the heterogeneity is in the intercept terms, more general specifications in which slope coefficients are heterogeneous are also possible.

47. The existence of unobserved heterogeneity creates an initial-conditions problem (see Heckman, 1981, and Keane and Wolpin, 1997, for an application to a DCDP model).

48. Heckman and Navarro (2007) develop a semiparametric estimator for a specific application.

49. The program also provided a transfer contingent on visiting a health clinic as well as nutritional supplements for children under the age of 2. The school attendance component of the tranfer amounted to more than 75 percent of the total.

50. A peso at that time was equivalent to about one-tenth of a U.S. dollar.

51. Todd and Wolpin (2008) use a biweight kernel function:

$$K(s) = (15/16)(s^2 - 1)^2 \text{ if } |s| \le 1$$
$$= 0 \text{ else,}$$

which satisfies the standard assumptions $\int K(s)ds = 1$, $\int K(s)sds = 0$, and $\int K(s)s^2ds < \infty$. Asymptotic consistency of this estimator requires that the smoothing parameters satisfy $n\lambda_n^w\lambda_n^y \to \infty$, $\lambda_n^w \to 0$ and $\lambda_n^y \to 0$ as $n \to \infty$.

52. This procedure is similar to that used in Heckman, Ichimura, and Todd (1997).

53. The exact matching estimator, which would have to match households with the same distribution of children by grade and gender, was not feasible given sample sizes.

54. Sample sizes of single ages were too small to be reliable for nonparametric estimation. The bandwidth was set equal to 200.

55. Azevedo, Bouillon, and Yanez-Pagan (2009) report a p-value of 0.604. The percentage of overlapping support was 62.2.

56. Infecundity is assumed to occur at age 45 and to be known with certainty at the beginning of the marriage.

57. To demonstrate how the subsidy effect can be estimated from the control sample ($\tau = 0$), Todd and Wolpin (2006) used an example with $\beta = 0$, which may have led to some confusion as to the necessity of that assumption as well as to whether Todd and Wolpin's (2006) specification actually assumed the absence of an income effect.

58. As with most DCDP models with a large choice set and state space, the Todd and Wolpin (2006) model is solved numerically using an approximation method in which the $E\max(\Omega_{it}^-)$ functions are evaluated at a subset of the state points and interpolation is used to evaluate $E\max(\Omega_{it}^-)$ at other values of the state space. This approach requires that the $E\max(\Omega_{it}^-)$ interpolating functions be specified parametrically, for example, by a regression function in the state space elements. This approach was originally proposed by Bellman, Kalaba, and Kotkin (1963) and extended to models generally of interest to economists by Keane and Wolpin (1994).

59. A nonparametric estimator of the type probabilities would be exact.

60. The parameters of the approximation, although treated in estimation as unrestricted, are actually themselves functions of the structural parameters. The estimation method does not take into account these restrictions and is thus not fully efficient even if the approximation is close to exact.

61. Todd and Wolpin (2006) follow this strategy as opposed to allowing for child-specific wage shocks to avoid having to integrate over all of the child shocks in solving the dynamic programming problem. As they note, the problem of degeneracy exists more generally, namely that with family level preference shocks, some choices may not be generated by the model. However, Todd and Wolpin (2006) placed a number of restrictions on the choice set, for example, assuming that no older child can attend school without a younger child also attending school, which reduces the likelihood of this event but does not eliminate it necessarily. Estimation is feasible when such events occur because the likelihood is smoothed over zero likelihood events. After estimating the model, Todd and Wolpin (2006) verified that simulations of the model could generate all of the outcomes that were observed in the data.

62. There were 1,885 households in the treatment villages, 5,561 children ever born, and 2,694 children aged 6–15.

63. The utility function contained about 90 parameters.

64. This argument is not meant to imply that the model has not been overfit. Indeed, there is some indication of overfitting given that a significant number of the parameters are imprecisely estimated. Overfitting arises in DCDP models when parameters are added that, although intended by the researcher to capture population characteristics, actually capture idiosyncratic characteristics of the sample.

65. I follow Attanasio, Meghir, and Santiago (2011) in not normalizing utility, that is, in not setting $\theta_w = 1$.

66. In the specification given by equation 2.56, some components of Y^w and Y^s would be related directly to preferences and other components to parental income, y, which would be estimable using data on y. α would arise from a constant term in the coefficient vector for X_{it}. The identification of β would require that the family income and utility components of Y^w and Y^s be specified, which is not done by Attanasio, Meghir, and Santiago (2011).

67. Attanasio, Meghir, and Santiago (2011) assert that their specification corresponds to a collective model in which the husband and wife have control over different sources of income. The attendance subsidy, for example, is paid directly to the wife. They do not show that the identification of a collective model, if actually specified, would require using the treatment data.

68. Notice that one can write the school attendance decision (equation 2.56) as:

$s = 1$ iff $\varepsilon \geq -\alpha + \theta_w (w - \tau) - \beta (y + \tau) - \lambda \tau,$
  $= 0$ otherwise.

Thus, if $\lambda > 0$, because τ enters as a separate argument, it is not possible to use the matching estimator based on control villages.

69. To fully characterize equilibrium effects of the PROGRESA program, one would need to account for changes in adult wages and labor supply separately from child wages and labor supply, given that parental income affects the school attendance decision.

70. To explicitly incorporate equilibrium effects using only the control sample (as in Todd and Wolpin, 2006) would require an exogenous village-level shifter of child labor supply. One possibility would be the existence of a secondary school in the village.

71. In calculating the failure rate, it is assumed that all children who did not attend a particular grade level would have failed had they attended. However, their model predicts nonattendance for other reasons, for example, a particular preference shock. Todd and Wolpin estimate the failure probability function jointly with the attendance decision and allow it to depend on household type.

72. The alternative, as followed by Todd and Wolpin (2006), is to estimate the wage offer function and failure probability function jointly with the school attendance decision. In estimating the wage function, the assumption in Attanasio, Meghir, and Santiago (2011) that the schooling choice is governed by a probit is not consistent with the assumptions of the decision model, which would contain a composite logistic and normal error.

73. Under that assumption, the expected wage needed to compute the expected utility of working would be $\exp(\mu_w)$ times the exponential of 0.5 times the variance of the log wage offer error. Alternatively, if it were assumed that the wage error arose only from

measurement error, then no integration is necessary, and one could simply substitute the exponential of the predicted wage offer for the wage in the utility of work and a selectivity correction would be unnecessary. Attanasio, Meghir, and Santiago (2011) do not discuss which of these assumptions is made.

74. This procedure requires an exclusion restriction, a variable that affects accumulated schooling but does not affect the school attendance decision. Attanasio, Meghir, and Santiago (2011) use distance to a secondary school in the period preceding the program for this restriction.

75. These counterfactuals in Todd and Wolpin (2006) pertain to households prior to having children and reflect the "long-run" effect of the program. Predictions of the one-step-ahead effect of the subsidy that takes as given the current household composition reflects the "short-run" effect of an unanticipated policy change.

76. Todd and Wolpin (2006) also find that the proportion of children who complete at least sixth grade actually falls below the nonsubsidy level, suggesting that, in order to earn the bonus, families are substituting more schooling for some children and less for others. In fact, as evidence for this behavior, the within-family coefficient of variation in completed schooling increases by 25 percent with the bonus as compared to the no-subsidy case. Thus, the effect of the bonus would be largely to induce children who were already attending junior secondary school to complete ninth grade.

77. This amount is close to the maximum benefit that families may currently receive under the program in any year and represents about a 50 percent increase in annual family income.

78. Attanasio, Meghir, and Santiago set the distance to newly built schools to 3 kilometers.

79. This figure is an estimate the author made of the effect by averaging over single-age effects reported in Attanasio, Meghir, and Santiago (2011).

80. Todd and Wolpin (2006) assumed the change in the child wage to be the same independent of gender and age.

81. This experiment does not appear in the Attanasio, Meghir, and Santiago (2011) paper. I thank the authors for performing this experiment at my request.

82. A similar pattern exists for girls. The predictions are increases of 2.35 times for the single-child estimator in Todd and Wolpin (2008) and 2.28 times for the estimator in Todd and Wolpin (2006) but only 1.27 times for the multiple-child estimator in Todd and Wolpin (2008). Note that although a naive estimate of doubling the effect would be reasonably close for boys, based on the three similar estimates, that estimate would be considerably worse for girls based on the two similar estimates.

83. This discussion is taken from Keane and Wolpin (2007).

84. The idea is an old one in psychology. Mosier (1951) named the procedure "validity generalization," that is, validation by generalizing beyond the sample. Recently, Busemeyer and Wang (2000) have argued for its more widespread adoption in psychology and provide Monte Carlo evidence on its performance in model selection. The use of models to forecast out-of-sample behavior is also common in the marketing literature, where considerable effort has been devoted to forecasting demand for new products. Few of the papers in that literature, however, compare predictions to subsequent demand after the product is introduced.

85. The models and methods discussed above have been partial equilibrium. Although estimation of the partial equilibrium effects of a policy intervention is clearly a necessary ingredient for performing an *ex ante* policy evaluation, such estimates may be far off the mark if there are important general equilibrium effects. Although that does not seem to be the case for the PROGRESA evaluation of Todd and Wolpin (2006), as discussed below, the development of methods that incorporate general equilbrium effects should be a priority.

Chapter 3

1. The papers by Ehrenberg and Oaxaca (1976) and Burgess and Kingston (1976) were not published in this volume but were presented at the conference.

2. Flinn and Heckman (1982) had previously structurally estimated a stationary search model.

3. Burdett (1978) extended the standard unemployment search model to allow for search on the job.

4. It is a common theme in the structural literature to build on and extend the theoretical literature in developing estimable models. This is the case with Rendon's (2006) paper, which builds on the earlier work of Danforth (1979). Lentz (2009) also structurally estimates a sequential search model with savings. Unlike the standard model, the wage offer distribution is taken to be degenerate, and agents choose their search intensity, which affects the rate at which job offers are received. Lentz uses the model to empirically determine the optimal unemployment insurance scheme.

5. Detailed reviews of this literature can be found in the chapter by Mortensen and Pissarides in the *Handbook of Labor Economics* (Volume 3b, 1999) or the more recent survey by Eckstein and van den Berg (2007).

6. This section draws on Wolpin (1995).

7. The LHS is linearly increasing in V and passes through the origin. The RHS is monotonically decreasing in V until it reaches b and is then constant. There will be a unique intersection, and a unique $V > 0$, as long as $b > -\beta q E \max(W(w), 0)$.

8. In a continuous time model in which the arrival of offers follows a Poisson process with parameter λ, the implicit reservation wage equation is identical except that the instantaneous arrival rate (λ) replaces the offer probability, q.

9. Wolpin (1995) provides a proof.

10. The distribution of accepted wages is the truncated distribution of wage offers, namely, $f(w \mid w \geq w^*) = \dfrac{f(w)}{1 - F(w^*)}$.

11. It has been shown that the latter effect dominates for distributions that are log concave (Burdett and Ondrich, 1985; Flinn and Heckman, 1983).

12. There are statistical issues better handled by specifying the hazard function, such as dealing with incomplete spells and time-varying regressors. See Meyer (1990) for an example of this approach. The issues I raise, however, are easier to demonstrate in a regression framework but hold in the hazard framework as well.

13. The assumption that new unemployment spells are renewal processes rules out any structural connection between spells; for example, it rules out that the benefit level depends on the preunemployment wage. In that case the correlation between the wage offer distribution and the benefit level could arise, for example, if the more generous states were those with higher wages.

14. An alternative would be to assume that once the terminal period is reached, the individual accepts the next offer that arrives, in which case the reservation wage at T (and after) is zero.

15. See Wolpin (1987) for the particular case in which $F(w)$ is either normal or log normal.

16. Meyer also presents a static labor supply model as an alternative to the search model.

17. Whether an individual is eligible for an extension may also depend on an individual's work history, which I ignore.

18. Note that in equation 3.8, the probability that the eligibility horizon will change at $t + 1$ is written as a function of the state of the economy at t. To motivate that formulation, assume that the horizon is changed at $t + 1$ if $Z_{t+1} \geq \underline{Z}$ and that Z_{t+1}, which is unknown at t, follows a first-order autoregressive process. Then $\omega(Z_t) = \Pr(Z_{t+1} \geq \underline{Z} \mid Zt)$.

19. Any variable that belongs in the reservation wage also belongs in the hazard rate.

20. In the more general case where there than can be more than one extension, the probability of an extension may differ for each extension.

21. In order to better fit the spikes observed at typical exhaustion periods, Meyer includes in the hazard rate specification an indicator variable equal to 1 in period t of an individual's employment spell if benefits would have lapsed in that period: $I(t = t_c)$. He ascribes this effect to advanced planning on the part of firms to recall workers when benefits are exhausted and/or to workers postponing the start dates of new jobs. This behavior is not part of either model Meyer references.

22. This section follows the development in Flinn and Heckman (1982) and Wolpin (1995). The identification results here carry over to the richer model with benefit exhaustion.

23. The minimum observed wage is a superconsistent estimator of the reservation wage in that it converges at rate N. This leads to nonstandard asymptotics in the likelihood estimation of the search model (see Flinn and Heckman, 1982, and Christensen and Kiefer, 1991).

24. Setting $w_t^* = w_{t+1}^* = w^*$ and $h_{t+1} = h$ yields the infinite horizon implicit reservation wage function.

25. The implicit reservation wage equation given above would no longer hold in this case. In particular, the integration would also have to be taken over the distribution of the unobserved cost of search, recognizing that the reservation wage would be a function of that cost.

26. In some instances, wage rates that are directly reported in hours or weeks are inaccurate. In other cases, wage rates are derived from a division of earnings reported over a longer period, say annually, and hours worked reported over that period. The inaccuracy arises from a seeming mismatch in the time period between earnings and hours.

27. Actually, this waiting period is only for those who are unemployed through layoff. Those who quit or were fired had a waiting period of 5 weeks. Ferrall assumes the waiting period to be 2 weeks independent of the reason for the unemployment spell.

28. As previously noted, the lower bound of the support for the Pareto distribution cannot be identified. Ferrall fixes that value. Kiefer and Christensen (2009) also use the Pareto distribution and impose, based on the wage-posting model of Burdett and Mortensen (1998), the individual's reservation wage as the lower bound.

29. The TANF program was promoted by the Clinton administration as an end to "welfare as we know it."

30. The amounts are in real 1987 New York dollars.

31. To see that, rewrite equation 3.15 as $y_{its} = \alpha_1 B_{its} + (\alpha_2 - \alpha_1) B_{its}^T + \beta X_{its} + u_{its}$ and note that B_{its} and B_{its}^T are positively correlated.

32. This method avoids the integration problem that arises with missing state variables.

33. Even that figure is not comparable because work experience and schooling, which influence wage offers, are affected by preferences shocks that alter demographics.

34. These last two experiments attempt to provide reasonable approximations to time-limit and work requirement rules adopted by states after TANF was introduced (see Fang and Keane, 2004).

35. This is consistent with the findings in Fang and Keane (2004) that time limits as they have actually been applied under TANF can account for very little of the fall of welfare participation since 1996.

36. Because state dummies were included in the model, in order to simulate the data a model was estimated with the same parameters incorporating the data from Texas and allowing for Texas-specific effects.

37. This value-added specification, in which the previous stock is a sufficient statistic for all prior inputs, is prominent in the literature on estimating cognitive achievement production functions, as discussed in a later section. The inclusion of ability in a value-added specification is not common, although it can be motivated (see below).

38. Hause (1972) did not explicitly associate the constant term in equation 3.24 with the (log) rental price.

39. Card (1999) provides a summary of the results from that more recent literature.

40. This section draws on Rosenzweig and Wolpin (2000) and Wolpin (2003).

41. The additive separability between schooling and experience in equation 3.26 is made for convenience and has no effect on the basic conclusion.

42. The derivation uses the approximation that $\log(1 + x) = x$ for small x, for both $x = r$ and

$$x = \frac{c}{V(s = 0 \mid S_0)}.$$

This latter case will hold if the direct cost of schooling is small relative to the present value of earnings with completed schooling S_0.

43. Rosenzweig and Wolpin (2000) draw a distinction between natural "natural experiments," such as the variation utilized in Angrist and Krueger (1991), and natural experiments that use nonnatural variation such as differences in state laws.

44. The assumption that quarter of birth is random has not gone unchallenged (Bound and Jaeger, 1996). Notice, however, that with enough data, the instrument could be defined by dates of birth that differ by only 1 day (as in the illustration), effectively eliminating the instrument validity issue.

45. Rosenzweig and Wolpin (2000) question the validity of the instrument on the grounds that the existence of a sister is increasing with fertility. If fertility is a choice that is affected by parental ability and ability is heritable, then the existence of a sister will be correlated with ability. They propose that using the gender of the first birth as the instrument for the schooling of subsequent children would circumvent this problem, They provide evidence that the gender of the first birth is random and, thus, would not be correlated with the ability of higher-order children.

46. The interested reader is referred to Rosenzweig and Wolpin (2000) for a discussion of the biases that arise due to the endogeneity of work experience and to discussions of alternative approaches, for example, the use of twins, to the estimation of the schooling effect on wages.

47. The reason for including this psychic cost to returning to school is that the fraction of individuals who do so in the data is very low. Adding such a term illustrates the natural, and quite necessary, interplay between model development and data as discussed in chapter 2.

48. It is not necessary that the age range begin at age 16, nor that there be no gaps in the data. The estimation approach would need to be modified.

49. I discuss some of that literature in the next section.

50. Multiplying this likelihood by $\Pr(S_{n,16})$, which is not dependent on parameters, would not affect any of the parameter estimates. There is no assumption as to the interpretation of the correlation between type and initial schooling. Keane and Wolpin (1997) also allow for normally distributed additive mean zero measurement error in wages to reduce the impact of outlier wages on parameter estimates.

51. As seen from the structure of utility and the budget constraint, $\bar{\alpha}_m$ and γ_m ($m = 4,5$) cannot be separately distinguished; γ_m, for example, can be normalized to zero for all m. In addition, one α_m must be normalized; for example, if α_3 is normalized to zero, all other α_m's will be relative to the nonpecuniary value of the military occupation.

52. In the extended model estimated by Keane and Wolpin, there are over seventy-five parameters.

53. All figures are in 1987 dollars.

54. It is, however, 20 percent higher for the first type as measured from age 26 as lifetime utility from that age becomes dominated by life cycle earnings paths.

55. High school graduation bonuses have been advocated by Robert Reich, former Secretary of Labor in the Clinton administration.

56. As discussed in the previous chapter, the credibility of structural estimation exercises hinges on providing evidence on model validation. Keane and Wolpin (1997) use

data on nearby cohorts from the CPS to assess the ability of the model to forecast occupational choices later in the life cycle. They find that the forecasts of white-collar employment are quite close, whereas those of blue-collar employment are somewhat overstated.

57. Krueger (1999), p. 528.

58. Nye, Hedges, and Konstantopoulos (2000), p. 147.

59. I_1 is also a function of $\bar{S}_1$, so equation 3.37 is based on having substituted in equation 3.38. Notice that one could also eliminate A_0 from both equations 3.37 and 3.38 by substituting the input demand equation for I_0 into equation 3.36 and the resulting equation into equations 3.37 and 3.38. Thus, the input demand equations can be written solely as a function of family endowments, in wealth, the child's endowment, and parental preferences.

60. The change in the school input in the first school year can have effects on achievement not only in the first year but also in later years (see the discussion below). Follow-up studies of the effect of Project STAR on achievement in years subsequent to the termination of the experiment have found long-run effects (e.g., Krueger and Whitmore, 2001; Nye, Hedges, and Konstantopoulos, 2000).

61. Notice that although A_0 enters the demand function for I_1 as written, the population can be fully described solely as a function of the endowment distribution, which determines the distribution of A_0.

62. The comparison does provide evidence on the value of the average indirect effect:

$$\int \frac{\partial g_1}{\partial I_1} \frac{\partial I_1}{\partial \left(S_1 - \bar{S}_1\right)} f\left(A_0, W, \mu, \varepsilon\right).$$

63. Theories of child development posit important links between experiences during infancy and early childhood and later childhood cognitive and noncognitive outcomes.

64. Their main goal is to assess the role of home and school inputs and of maternal "ability" in producing cognitive achievement and in explaining the black-white and Hispanic-white test score gaps This assessment is carried out through the use of out-of-sample forecasts in which the inputs of minorities are replaced by those of whites. The use of cross-validation seems particularly appropriate for this exercise.

65. This specification would arise if the following restrictions in equation 3.47 hold: $\alpha_k - \gamma \alpha_{k-1} \neq 0$; $\beta_a - \gamma \beta_{a-1} = 0$; and $\varepsilon_{ija} - \gamma \varepsilon_{ij,a-1} = \eta_{ija}$ is iid.

66. Recall that Todd and Wolpin (2003) take the cumulative specification as the starting point. With two skills, the corresponding cumulative specifications would presumably be:

$$A_a^C = \varsigma_0^C + \varsigma_1^C X_a^C + \ldots + \varsigma_a^C X_1^C + \delta_1^C \mu_a^C + \delta_2^C \mu_o^N + \varepsilon_a^C,$$

$$A_a^C = \varsigma_0^N + \varsigma_1^N X_a^N + \ldots + \varsigma_a^N X_1^N + \delta_n^N \mu_a^C + \delta_2^N \mu_o^N + \varepsilon_a^C.$$

Although backward substitution in equation 3.55 would reverse engineer a function that looks like the above cumulatives, the coefficients would not have the same skill-specific interpretation.

67. Cunha, Heckman, and Schenach (2010) extend the factor model of Cunha and Heckman (2008) to a nonlinear nonparametric setting.

68. The literature on assessing the impact of maternal employment and child care on child outcomes is extensive. Reviews of that literature can be found in Blau (1999), and Bernal and Keane (2011).

69. Identification of the achievement production function is achieved in part with the exclusion restriction that the local unemployment rate affects maternal employment but not cognitive achievement.

70. Brown and Flinn (2011) also study the relationship between divorce and child quality. I discuss Tartari because of the closer connection of her model to the DCDP approach.

References

Aguirregebaria, Victor, and Pedro Mira. 2010. Dynamic discrete choice structural models: A survey. *Journal of Econometrics* 156 (1): 38–67.

Albrecht, James, and Bo Axell. 1984. An equilibrium model of search employment. *Journal of Political Economy* 92 (5): 824–840.

Angrist, Joshua, and Alan B. Krueger. 1991. Does compulsory school attendance affect schooling and earnings? *Quarterly Journal of Economics* 106 (4): 979–1014.

Angrist, Joshua D., and Alan B. Krueger. 1999. Empirical strategies in labor economics. In *Handbook of Labor Economics, Vol. 3A*, edited by Orley C. Ashenfelter and David Card, pp. 1277–1366. Amsterdam: North-Holland.

Attanasio, Orazio, Costus Meghir, and Ana Santiago. 2011. Education choices in Mexico: Using a structural model and a randomized experiment to evaluate Progresa. *Review of Economic Studies* 79 (1): 37–66.

Azevedo, Viviane M. R., Cesar P. Bouillon, and Patricia Yanez-Pagan. 2009. How much are we willing to pay to send poor adolescents to school? Simulating changes to Mexico's *Oportunidades* in urban areas. IDB Working Paper (June): 566.

Becker, Gary S. 1962. Investment in human capital: A theoretical analysis. *Journal of Political Economy* 70 (Supplement): 9–49.

Becker, Gary S. 1964. *Human capital: A theoretical and empirical analysis, with special reference to education*. New York: National Bureau of Economic Research.

Becker, Gary S. 1967. *Human capital and the personal distribution of income. Woytinsky Lecture*. Ann Arbor: University of Michigan Press.

Becker, Gary S., and Barry R. Chiswick. 1966. Education and the distribution of earnings. *American Economic Review* 56 (1/2): 358–369.

Becker, Gary S., and H. Gregg Lewis. 1973. On the interaction between the quantity and quality of children. *Journal of Political Economy* 81 (2 Part II): S279–S288.

Becker, Gary S., and Nigel Tomes. 1976. Child endowments and the quantity and quality of children. *Journal of Political Economy* 84 (4, Part 2): S143–S162.

Bellman, Richard, Robert Kalaba, and Bella Kotkin. 1963. Polynomial approximation: A new computational technique in dynamic programming allocation processes. *Mathematics of Computation* 1:155–161.

Ben-Porath, Yoram. 1967. The production of human capital and the life-cycle of earnings. *Journal of Political Economy* 75 (4): 352–365.

Bernal, Raquel. 2008. The effect of maternal employment and child care on children's cognitive development. *International Economic Review* 49 (4): 1173–1209.

Bernal, Raquel, and Michael P. Keane. 2011. Child care choices and children's cognitive achievement: The case of single mothers. *Journal of Labor Economics* 29 (3): 459–512.

Blau, David. 1991. Search for nonwage job characteristics: A test of the reservation wage hypothesis. *Journal of Labor Economics* 9 (2): 186–205.

Blau, David M. 1999. The effect of child care characteristics on child development. *Journal of Human Resources* 34 (4): 786–824.

Blomquist, Soren, Matias Eklof, and Whitney Newey. 2001. Tax reform evaluation using non-parametric methods: Sweden 1980–1991. *Journal of Public Economics* 79 (3): 543–568.

Blomquist, Soren, and Whitney Newey. 1997. Nonparametric estimation of labor supply functions generated by piece-wise linear budget constraints. Uppsala University Working Paper 1997: 24. .

Blomquist, Soren, and Whitney Newey. 2002. Nonparametric estimation with nonlinear budget sets. *Econometrica* 70 (6): 2455–2480.

Blundell, Richard, and Thomas MaCurdy. 1999. Labor supply: A review of alternative approaches. In *Handbook of Labor Economics* 3A, edited by Orley C. Ashenfelter and David Card, pp. 1560–1695. Amsterdam: North-Holland.

Bontemps, Christian, Jean-Marc Robin, and Gerard J. van den Berg. 1999. An empirical equilibrium job search model with search on the job and heterogeneous workers and firms. *International Economic Review* 40 (4): 1039–1074.

Bontemps, Christian, Jean-Marc Robin, and Gerard J. van den Berg. 2000. Equilibrium search with continuous productivity dispersion: Theory and nonparametric estimation. *International Economic Review* 41 (2): 305–358.

Bound, John, and David Jaeger. 1996. On the validity of season of birth as an instrument in wage equations: A comment on Angrist and Krueger's "Does compulsory school attendance affect schooling and earnings." National Bureau of Economic Research Working Paper W5835.

Bourguignon, Francois, Francisco H. G. Ferreira, and Phillippe G. Leite. 2003. Conditional cash transfers, schooling, and child labor: Micro-simulating Brazil's Bolsa Escola program. *World Bank Economic Review* 17 (2): 229–254.

Bourguignon, Francois, and Amadeo Spadaro. 2006. Microsimulation as a tool for evaluating redistribution policies. *Journal of Economic Inequality* 4 (1): 77–106.

Bowlus, Audra J., Nicholas M. Kiefer, and George R. Neumann. 2001. Equilibrium search models and the transition from school to work. *International Economic Review* 42 (2): 317–343.

Brown, Meta, and Christoher J. Flinn. 2011. Family law effects on divorce, fertility, and child investment. New York University Working Paper.

Burdett, Kenneth. 1978. A theory of employee job search and quit rates. *American Economic Review* 68 (1): 212–220.

Burdett, Kenneth, and Dale T. Mortensen. 1998. Wage differentials, employer size and unemployment. *International Economic Review* 39 (2): 257–273.

Burdett, Kenneth, and Jan I. Ondrich. 1985. How changes in labor demand affect unemployed workers. *Journal of Labor Economics* 3 (1): 1–10.

Burgess, Paul L., and Jerry L. Kingston. 1976. The impact of unemployment insurance benefits on reemployment success. *Industrial & Labor Relations Review* 30 (1): 25–31.

Burns, Arthur F., and Wesley C. Mitchell. 1946. *Measuring Business Cycles*. New York: National Bureau of Economic Research.

Busemeyer, Jerome R., and Yi-Min Wang. 2000. Model comparisons and model selections based on generalization criterion methodology. *Journal of Mathematical Psychology* 44 (1): 171–189.

Butcher, Kristin F., and Anne Case. 1994. The effect of sibling composition on women's education and earnings. *Quarterly Journal of Economics* 109 (3): 531–563.

Cahuc, P., F. Postel-Vinay, and J.-M. Robin. 2006. Wage bargaining with on the job search: Theory and evidence. *Econometrica* 74 (2): 323–364.

Card, David. 1995. Using geographic variation in college proximity to estimate the return to schooling. In *Aspects of Labor Market Behaviour: Essays in Honor of John Vanderkamp*, edited by Louis N. Christofides, E. Kenneth Grant, and Robert Swidinsky, pp. 201–222. Toronto: University of Toronto Press.

Card, David. 1999. The causal effect of education on earnings. In *Handbook of Labor Economics, Vol. 3A*, edited by Orley C. Ashenfelter and David Card, pp. 1801–1863. Amsterdam: North-Holland.

Carnoy, Martin. 1967. Rates of return to education in Latin America. *Journal of Human Resources* 2 (3): 359–374.

Chamberlain, Gary. 1977. Education, income, and ability revisited. *Journal of Econometrics* 5 (2): 241–257.

Christ, Carl F. 1994. The Cowles Commission's contributions to econometrics at Chicago, 1939–1955. *Journal of Economic Literature* 32 (March): 30–59.

Christensen, Bent J., and Nicholas M. Kiefer. 1991. The exact likelihood function for an empirical job search model. *Econometric Theory* 7 (4): 464–486.

Christensen, Bent J., and Nicholas M. Kiefer. 2009. *Economic Modeling and Inference*. Princeton: Princeton University Press.

Classen, Kathleen P. 1977. The effect of unemployment insurance on the duration of unemployment and subsequent earnings. *Industrial & Labor Relations Review* 30 (4): 438–444.

Cogan, John. 1981. Fixed costs and labor supply. *Econometrica* 49 (4): 945 964.

Cohen-Goldner, Sarit, and Zvi Eckstein. 2010. Estimating the return to training and occupational experience: The case of female immigrants. *Journal of Econometrics* 156: 86–105.

Cunha, Flavio. 2012. Reference points, subjective beliefs about the technology of skill formation, and early investments in children. University of Pennsylvania Working Paper.

Cunha, Flavio, and James J. Heckman. 2008. Formulating, identifying and estimating the technology of cognitive and noncognitive skill formation. *Journal of Human Resources* 43 (4): 738–782.

Cunha, Flavio, James J. Heckman, and Susanne M. Shenach. 2010. Estimating the technology of cognitive and non-cognitive skill formation. *Econometrica* 78 (3): 883–931.

Danforth, John P. 1979. On the role of consumption and decreasing absolute risk aversion on the theory of job search. In *Studies in the economics of search*, edited by Stephen A. Lippman and John J. McCall, 109–131. New York: North-Holland.

Deaton, Angus. 2009. Instruments of development: Randomization in the tropics and the search for the elusive keys to economic development. National Bureau of Economic Research Working Paper 14690.

Delavande, Adeline. 2008. Pill, patch or shot? Subjective expectations and birth control choice. *International Economic Review* 49 (3): 999–1042.

Diamond, Peter A. 1971. A model of price adjustment. *Journal of Economic Theory* 3 (2): 156–168.

Diamond, Peter A., and Eric Maskin. 1979. An equilibrium analysis of search and breach of contracts. I: Steady states. *Bell Journal of Economics* 10 (1): 282–316.

Duflo, Esther, Hanna Rema, and Stephen Ryan. 2012. Monitoring works: Getting teachers to come to school. *American Economic Review* 102 (2): 1241–1278.

Eckstein, Zvi, and Gerard J. van den Berg. 2007. Empirical labor search: A survey. *Journal of Econometrics* 136 (2): 531–564.

Eckstein, Zvi, and Kenneth I. Wolpin. 1990. Estimating a market equilibrium search model from panel data on individuals. *Econometrica* 58 (40): 783–808.

Eckstein, Zvi, and Kenneth I. Wolpin. 1995. Duration to first job and the return to schooling: Estimates from a search-matching model. *Review of Economic Studies* 62 (2): 263–286.

Ehrenberg, Ronald L., and Ronald D. Oaxaca. 1976. Unemployment insurance, duration of unemployment and subsequent wage gain. *American Economic Review* 66 (5): 754–766.

Engberg, John. 1990. The impact of unemployment benefits on job search: Structural unobserved heterogeneity and spurious spikes. Mimeo, Carnegie Mellon University.

Fang, Hanming, and Michael P. Keane. 2004. Assessing the impact of welfare reform on single mothers. *Brookings Papers on Economic Activity* 1: 1–116.

Fang, Hanming, and Daniel Silverman. 2009. Time-inconsistency and welfare program participation: Evidence from the NLSY. *International Economic Review* 50 (4): 1043–1077.

Ferrall, Christopher. 1997. Unemployment insurance eligibility and the school to work transition in Canada and the United States. *Journal of Business & Economic Statistics* 15 (2): 115–129.

Flinn, Christopher J. 2006. Minimum wage effects on labor market outcomes under search, matching and endogenous contact rates. *Econometrica* 74 (4): 1013–1062.

Flinn, Christopher J., and James J. Heckman. 1982. New methods for analyzing structural models of labor force dynamics. *Journal of Econometrics* 18 (1): 114–142.

Flinn, Christopher J., and James J. Heckman. 1983. Are unemployment and out of the labor force behaviorally distinct labor force states? *Journal of Labor Economics* 1 (1): 28–42.

Gemici, Ahu. 2007. Family migration and labor market outcomes. Diss. University of Pennsylvania.

Gotz, Glenn A., and John J. McCall. 1984. A dynamic retention model for air force officers: Theory and estimates. RAND, R-3028-AF.

Griliches, Zvi. 1977. Estimating the returns to schooling: Some econometric problems. *Econometrica* 45 (1): 1–22.

Griliches, Zvi, and William Mason. 1972. Education, income, and ability. *Journal of Political Economy* 80 (3, Part II): S74–S103.

Haerdle, Wilhelm, and Oliver Linton. 1994. Applied nonparametric methods. In *Handbook of Econometrics*, Vol. 4, edited by R. Engel and D. McFadden, pp. 2295–2339. Amsterdam: Elsevier.

Hanoch, Giora. 1967. An economic analysis of earnings and schooling. *Journal of Human Resources* 2 (3): 310–329.

Hansen, W. Lee. 1963. Total and private rates of return to investments in schooling. *Journal of Political Economy* 71 (2): 128–140.

Hanushek, Eric A. 1996. A more complete picture of school resource policy. *Review of Educational Research* 56 (3): 397–409.

Hanushek, Eric A. 2003. The failure of input-based schooling policies. *Economic Journal* 113 (485): F64–F98.

Hause, John. 1972. Earnings profile: Ability and schooling. *Journal of Political Economy* 80 (3): S108–S138.

Heckman, James J. 1974. Shadow prices, market wages and labor supply. *Econometrica* 42 (4): 679–694.

Heckman, James J. 1979. Sample selection bias as a specification error. *Econometrica* 47 (1): 153–162.

Heckman, James J. 1981. The incidental parameters problem and the problem of initial conditions in estimating a discrete time–discrete data stochastic process and some Monte Carlo evidence. In *Structural Analysis of Discrete Data with Econometric Applications*, edited by C. F. Manski and D. McFadden, pp. 179–197. Cambridge, MA: MIT Press.

Heckman, James J. 1997. Instrumental variables. *Journal of Human Resources* 32 (3): 441–462.

Heckman, James J. 2000. Causal parameters and policy analysis in economics: A twentieth century retrospective. *Quarterly Journal of Economics* 115 (1): 45–97.

Heckman, James J., Hide Ichimura, and Petra E. Todd. 1997. Matching as an econometric evaluation estimator: Evidence from evaluating a job training program. *Review of Economic Studies* 64 (4): 605–654.

Heckman, James J., Lance Lochner, and Christopher Taber. 1998. Explaining rising wage inequality: Explorations with a dynamic general equilibrium model of earnings with heterogeneous agents. *Review of Economic Dynamics* 1: 1–58.

Heckman, James J., Lance Lochner, and Christopher Taber. 1999. Human capital formation and general equilibrium treatment effects: A study of tax and tuition policy. *Fiscal
Studies* 20 (1): 25–40.

Heckman, James J., Lance Lochner, and Petra E. Todd. 2006. Earnings functions, rates of
return and treatment effects: The Mincer equation and beyond. In *Handbook of the Economics of Education 1,* edited by Eric A. Hanushek, Stephen Machin, and Ludger Woessmann,
pp. 307–458. Amsterdam: North-Holland.

Heckman, James J., Lance Lochner, and Petra E. Todd. 2008. Earnings functions and rates
of return. *Journal of Human Capital* 2 (1): 1–31.

Heckman, James J., and Thomas MaCurdy. 1982. New methods for estimating labor
supply functions: A survey. National Bureau of Economic Research Working Paper 858.

Heckman, James J., and Salvador Navarro. 2007. Dynamic discrete choice and dynamic
treatment effects. *Journal of Econometrics* 136 (2): 341–396.

Heckman, James J., and Guilherme Sedlacek. 1985. Heterogeneity, aggregation, and
market wage functions: An empirical model of self-selection in the labor market. *Journal
of Political Economy* 93 (4): 1077–1125.

Heckman, James J., and Jeffrey Smith. 1995. Assessing the case for social experiments.
Journal of Economic Perspectives 9 (2): 85–100.

Heckman, James J., Sergio Urzua, and Edward Vytlacil. 2006. Understanding instrumental variables in models with essential heterogeneity. National Bureau of Economic
Research Working Paper 12574.

Heckman, James J., and Edward Vytlacil. 1998. Instrumental variables methods for the
correlated random coefficient model: Estimating the average rate of return to schooling
when the return is correlated with schooling. *Journal of Human Resources* 33 (4):
974–987.

Hedges, Larry V., Richard D. Laine, and Rob Greenwald. 1994. Does money matter? A
meta-analysis of studies of the effects of differential school inputs on student outcomes.
Educational Researcher 23 (3): 5–14.

Holen, Arlene. 1977. Effects of unemployment insurance entitlement on duration and job
search outcome. *Industrial & Labor Relations Review* 30 (3): 445–450.

Hotz, Joseph V., and Robert A. Miller. 1993. Conditional choice probabilities and the
estimation of dynamic models. *Review of Economic Studies* 60: 497–530.

Hoynes, Hilary W. 1997. Does welfare play any role in female headship decisions. *Journal
of Public Economics* 65 (2): 89–117.

Ichimura, Hide, and Christopher Taber. 2000. Direct estimation of policy effects. NBER
Technical Working Paper 254.

Ichimura, Hide, and Christopher Taber. 2000. Semi-parametric reduced form estimation
of tuition subsidies. *American Economic Association, Papers and Proceedings* 92 (2):
286–292.

Imai, Sumai, Neelam Jain, and Andrew Ching. 2009. Bayesian estimation of discrete
choice models. *Econometrica* 77 (6): 1865–1900.

Imbens, Guido W. 2009. Better LATE than nothing: Some comments on Deaton (2009) and
Heckman and Urzua (2009). National Bureau of Economic Research Working Paper 14896.

Imbens, Guido W., and Joshua D. Angrist. 1994. Identification and estimation of local average treatment effects. *Econometrica* 62 (2): 467–475.

Kaboski, Joseph P., and Robert M. Townsend. 2011. A structural evaluation of a large-scale quasi-experimental microfinance initiative. *Econometrica* 79 (5): 1357–1406.

Kane, Thomas J. 1994. College entry for blacks since 1970: The role of college costs, family background, and the returns to education. *Journal of Political Economy* 102 (5):878–911.

Katz, Lawrence F. 1996. Wage subsidies for the disadvantaged. National Bureau of Economic Research Working Paper 5679.

Keane, Michael P. 1992. A note on identification in the multinomial probit model. *Journal of Business & Economic Statistics* 10 (2): 193–200.

Keane, Michael P. 1995. A new idea for welfare reform. *Federal Reserve Bank of Minneapolis Quarterly Review* 19:2–28.

Keane, Michael P., and Robert Moffitt. 1998. A structural model of multiple welfare program participation and labor supply. *International Economic Review* 39 (3): 553–590.

Keane, Michael P., Petra E. Todd, and Kenneth I. Wolpin. 2011. The structural estimation of behavioral models: Discrete choice dynamic programming methods and applications. In *Handbook of Labor Economics*, Vol. 4A, edited by Orley C. Ashenfelter and David Card, pp. 331–462. Amsterdam: North-Holland.

Keane, Michael P., and Kenneth I. Wolpin. 1994. The solution and estimation of discrete choice dynamic programming models by simulation: Monte Carlo evidence. *Review of Economics and Statistics* 76 (4): 648–672.

Keane, Michael P., and Kenneth I. Wolpin. 1997. The career decisions of young men. *Journal of Political Economy* 105 (3): 473–522.

Keane, Michael P., and Kenneth I. Wolpin. 2000. Eliminating race differences in school attainment and labor market success. *Journal of Labor Economics* 18 (4): 614–652.

Keane, Michael P., and Kenneth I. Wolpin. 2001. The effect of parental transfers and borrowing constraints on educational attainment. *International Economic Review* 42 (4): 1051–1103.

Keane, Michael P., and Kenneth I. Wolpin. 2002. Estimating welfare effects consistent with forward looking behavior: An article in two parts. *Journal of Human Resources* 37 (3): 570–622.

Keane, Michael P., and Kenneth I. Wolpin. 2007. Exploring the usefulness of a non-random holdout sample for model validation: Welfare effects on female behavior. *International Economic Review* 48 (4): 1351–1378.

Keane, Michael P., and Kenneth I. Wolpin. 2010. The role of labor and marriage markets, preference heterogeneity, and the welfare system in the life cycle decisions of black, Hispanic and white women. *International Economic Review* 51 (3): 851–892.

Kiefer, Nicholas M., and George R. Neumann. 1993. Wage dispersion and homogeneity: The empirical equilibrium search model. In *Panel Data and Labor Market Dynamics*, edited by H. Bunzel and P. Jensen. Amsterdam: North-Holland.

Koopmans, Tjalling C. 1947. Measurement without theory. *Review of Economics and Statistics* 29 (3): 161–172.

Krueger, Alan B. 1999. Experimental estimates of education production functions. *Quarterly Journal of Economics* 114 (2): 497–532.

Krueger, Alan B. 2000. An economist's view of class size research. Milliken Institute Award for Distinguished Economic Research Paper. Santa Monica, CA: Milliken Institute.

Krueger, Alan B. 2003. Economic considerations and class size. *Economic Journal* 113 (485): F34–F63.

Krueger, Alan B., and Diane M. Whitmore. 2001. The effect of attending a small class in the early grades on college-test taking and middle school test results: Evidence from Project Star. *Economic Journal* 111 (468): 1–28.

Kumar, Anil. 2008. Labor supply, deadweight loss and tax reform act of 1986: A nonparametric evaluation using panel data. *Journal of Public Economics* 92 (1–2): 326–353.

Kydland, Finn, and Edward C. Prescott. 1990. Business cycles: Real facts and monetary myths. *Federal Reserve Bank of Minneapolis Quarterly Review* (Spring): 3–18.

Lee, Donghoon. 2005. An estimable dynamic general equilibrium model of school, work and occupational choice. *International Economic Review* 46 (1): 1–34.

Leibowitz, Arlene. 1974. Home investments in children. *Journal of Political Economy* 82 (2, Part 2): S111–S131.

Lentz, Rasmus. 2009. Optimal unemployment insurance in an estimated job search model with savings. *Review of Economic Dynamics* 12 (1):37–57.

Leslie, Larry L., and Paul T. Brinkman. 1987. Student price response in higher education: The student demand studies. *Journal of Higher Education* 55 (3): 181–204.

Lise, Jeremy, Shannon Seitz, and Jeffrey Smith. 2004. Equilibrium policy experiments and the evaluation of social programs. National Bureau of Economic Research Working Paper 10283.

Lumsdaine, Robin L., James H. Stock, and David A. Wise. 1992. Pension plan provisions and retirement: Men and women, Medicare, and models. In *Studies in the Economics of Aging*, edited by D. A. Wise, pp. 183–220. Chicago: University of Chicago Press.

Manski, Charles F. 1990. The use of intentions data to predict behavior: A best-case analysis. *Journal of the American Statistical Association* 85 (412): 934–940.

Manski, Charles F. 2004. Measuring expectations. *Econometrica* 72 (5): 1329–1376.

Marschak, Jacob. 1953. Economic measurements for policy and prediction. In *Studies in Econometric Method*, edited by William Hood and Tjalling Koopmans, pp. 1–26. New York: John Wiley.

McCall, John J. 1970. Economics of information and job search. *Quarterly Journal of Economics* 84 (1): 113–126.

McFadden, Daniel, A. P. Talvitie, and Associates. 1977. Validation of disaggregate travel demand models: Some tests. In Urban Demand Forecasting Project, Final Report, Vol. V. Institute of Transportation Studies, University of California, Berkeley.

McKinnish, Terra. 2008. Panel data models and transitory fluctuations in the explanatory variable. In *Advances in Econometrics 21*, edited by Tom Fomby, R. Carter Hill, Daniel L. Millimet, Jeffrey A. Smith, Edward J. Vytlacil , pp. 335–358. Bingley, UK: Emerald Group.

Meyer, Bruce. 1990. Unemployment insurance and unemployment spells. *Econometrica* 58 (40): 757–782.

Miller, Robert A. 1984. Job matching and occupational choice. *Journal of Political Economy* 92 (6): 1086–1120.

Miller, Robert A., and Seth G. Sanders. 1997. Human capital development and welfare participation. *Carnegie Rochester Conference Series on Public Policy* 46: 1–43.

Mincer, Jacob. 1958. Investment in human capital and person income distribution. *Journal of Political Economy* 66 (2): 281–302.

Mincer, Jacob. 1962. On-the-job training: Costs, returns and some implications. *Journal of Political Economy* 70 (1): 50–79.

Mincer, Jacob. 1974. *Schooling, Experience, and Earnings*. New York: National Bureau of Economic Research.

Moffitt, Robert A. 1992. Incentive effects of the U.S. welfare system: A review. *Journal of Economic Literature* 30 (1): 1–61.

Moffitt, Robert A. 1997. The effect of welfare on marriage and fertility: What do we know and what do we need to know? Discussion paper 1153–1997, Institute for Research on Poverty, University of Wisconsin.

Moffitt, Robert A. 1998. The effect of welfare on marriage and fertility: What do we know and what do we need to know? In *The Effect of Welfare on the Family and Reproductive Behavior*, edited by R. Moffitt, pp. 50–97. Washington, DC: National Research Council.

Mortensen, Dale T. 1970. A theory of wage and employment dynamics. In *Microeconomic Foundations of Employment and Inflations Theory*, edited by E. S. Phelps, New York: W. W. Norton.

Mortensen, Dale T. 1977. Unemployment insurance and job search decisions. *Industrial & Labor Relations Review* 30 (4): 505–517.

Mortensen, Dale T. 1982. The matching process as a noncooperative game. In *The Economics of Information and Uncertainty*, edited by John J. McCall, pp. 233–258, Chicago: National Bureau of Economic Research, University of Chicago Press.

Mortensen, Dale T. 1986. Job search and labor market analysis. In *Handbook of Labor Economics*, edited by O. Ashenfelter and R. Layard, pp. 849–919. Amsterdam: North-Holland.

Mortensen, Dale T., and Christopher A. Pissarides. 1999. New developments in models of search in the labor market. In *Handbook of Labor Economics, Vol. 3b*, edited by Orley C. Ashenfelter and David Card, pp. 2567–2627. Amsterdam: North-Holland.

Mosier, Charles I. 1951. The need and means of cross-validation. *Educational and Psychological Measurement* 11: 5–11.

Murray, Charles. 1984. *Losing Ground: American Social Policy, 1950–1980*. New York: Basic Books.

Norets, Andriy. 2009. Identification in dynamic discrete choice models with serially correlated unobserved state variables. *Econometrica* 77 (5): 1665–1682.

Nye, Barbara, Larry V. Hedges, and Spyros Konstantopoulos. 2000. The effect of small classes on academic achievement: Results of the Tennessee class size experiment. *American Educational Research Journal* 37 (1): 123–151.

Pakes, Ariel. (1986). Patents as options: Some estimates of the value of holding European patent stocks. *Econometrica* 54 (940): 755–784.

Paserman, M. Daniele. 2008. Job search and hyperbolic discounting: Structural estimation and policy evaluation. *Economic Journal* 118 (531): 1418–1452.

Phelps, Edmund S. 1997. *Rewarding Work: How to Restore Participation and Self-Support to a Fee Enterprise.* Cambridge, MA: Harvard University Press.

Postel-Vinay, Fabien, and Jean-Marc Robin. 2002. Equilibrium wage dispersion and with heterogeneous workers and firms. *Econometrica* 70 (6): 2295–2350.

Rendon, Silvio. 2006. Job search and asset accumulation under borrowing constraints. *International Economic Review* 47 (1): 233–264.

Rosenbaum, Paul, and Donald Rubin. 1983. The central role of the propensity score in observational studies for causal effects. *Biometrika* 70 (1): 41–55.

Rosenzweig, Mark R. 1999. Welfare, marital prospects, and nonmarital childbearing. *Journal of Political Economy* 107 (S6): S3–S32.

Rosenzweig, Mark R., and T. P. Schultz. 1983. Estimating a household production function: Heterogeneity, the demand for health inputs, and their effects on birth weight. *Journal of Political Economy* 91 (5): 723–746.

Rosenzweig, Mark R., and Kenneth I. Wolpin. 1980. Testing the quality-quantity fertility model: The use of twins as a natural experiment. *Econometrica* 48 (1): 227–240.

Rosenzweig, Mark R., and Kenneth I. Wolpin. 2000. Natural "natural experiments" in economics. *Journal of Economic Literature* 38 (4): 827–874.

Rust, John. 1987. Optimal replacement of GMC bus engines: An empirical model of Harold Zurcher. *Econometrica* 55 (5): 999–1034.

Rust, John. 1994. Numerical dynamic programming in economics. In *Handbook of Computational Economics,* edited by Hans. M. Amman, David A. Kendrick, and John Rust. Amsterdam: North-Holland.

Sanders, Seth. 1993. A dynamic model of welfare and work. Mimeo, Carnegie-Mellon University.

Schorfheide, Frank, and Kenneth I. Wolpin. 2011. To hold out or not. Mimeo, University of Pennsylvania.

Skoufias, Emmanuel, and Susan Parker. 2000. *The Impact of PROGRESA on Work, Leisure and Time Allocation.* Washington, DC: International Food Policy Research Institute.

Stern, Steven. 1989. Estimating a simultaneous search model. *Journal of Labor Economics* 7 (3): 348–369.

Sullivan, Paul. 2010. A dynamic analysis of educational attainment, occupational choices and job search. *International Economic Review* 51 (1): 289–317.

Swann, Christopher A. 2005. Welfare reform when recipients are forward-looking. *Journal of Human Resources* 40 (1): 31–56.

Tartari, Melissa. 2007. Divorce and cognitive achievement of children. Mimeo. Yale University.

Todd, Petra E. 2008. Evaluating social programs with endogenous program placement and selection of the treated. In *Handbook of Development Economics 4*, edited by T. Paul Schultz and John A. Strauss, pp. 3847–3894. Amsterdam: North-Holland.

Todd, Petra E., and Kenneth I. Wolpin. 2003. On the specification and estimation of the cognitive achievement production function. *Economic Journal* 113 (485): F3–F33.

Todd, Petra E., and Kenneth I. Wolpin. 2006. Assessing the impact of a school subsidy program in Mexico: Using a social experiment to validate a dynamic behavioral model of child schooling and fertility. *American Economic Review* 96 (5): 1384–1417.

Todd, Petra E., and Kenneth I. Wolpin. 2007. The production of cognitive achievement in children: Home, school and racial test score gaps. *Journal of Human Capital* 1 (1): 91–136.

Todd, Petra E., and Kenneth I. Wolpin. 2008. *Ex-ante* evaluation of social programs. *Annales d'Economie et de Statistique* 91–92: 263–292.

Todd, Petra E., and Kenneth I. Wolpin. 2010. Structural estimation and policy evaluation in developing countries. *Annual Review of Economics* 2: 21–50.

van den Berg, Gerard J. 1990. Nonstationarity in job search theory. *Review of Economic Studies* 57 (2): 255–277.

van den Berg, Gerard J., and Geert Ridder. 1998. An empirical equilibrium search model of the labor market. *Econometrica* 66 (5): 1183–1221.

Welch, Finis. 1977. What have we learned from empirical studies of unemployment insurance? *Industrial and Labor Relations Review* 30 (40): 450–461.

Wise, David. 1985. A behavioral model versus experimentation: The effects of housing subsidies on rent. *Methods of Operations Research* 50: 441–489.

Wolinsky, Asher. 1987. Matching, search and bargaining. *Journal of Economic Theory* 42 (2): 311–333.

Wolpin, Kenneth I. 1984. A dynamic stochastic model of fertility and child mortality. *Journal of Political Economy* 92 (5): 852–874.

Wolpin, Kenneth I. 1987. Estimating a structural search model: The transition from school to work. *Econometrica* 55 (4): 801–817.

Wolpin, Kenneth I. 1992. The determinants of black-white differences in early employment careers: Search, layoffs, quits and endogenous wage growth. *Journal of Political Economy* 100 (3): 535–560.

Wolpin, Kenneth I. 1995. *Empirical Methods for the Study of Labor Force Dynamics*. Luxembourg: Harwood Academic Publishers.

Wolpin, Kenneth I. 2003. Wage equations and education policy. In *Advances in Econometrics and Economics*, Vol. II, edited by M. Drewatripont, L. P. Hansen and S. J. Turnovsky, pp. 41–72. Cambridge: Cambridge University Press.`

Wu, Ximing. 2005. Labor supply and income effects of the earned income tax credit and welfare programs. Mimeo, University of Guelph.

Index